Growing Hardy Perennials

Growing Hardy Perennials

Kenneth A. Beckett

CROOM HELM LONDON

©1981 Kenneth A. Beckett
Croom Helm Ltd, 2-10 St John's Road, London SW11

British Library Cataloguing in Publication Data

Beckett, Kenneth A.
    Hardy perennials.
    1. Perennials
    I. Title
    635.9'32   SB434
    ISBN 0-7099-0621-8

Photographs by Gillian Beckett

Typeset by Columns
Printed in Great Britain by Redwood Burn, Trowbridge
and Bound by Dorstel Press, Templefields

Contents

List of Figures

For all members of the Hardy Plant Society

Preface

What is a hardy perennial? Beginners to gardening are rightly puzzled by this rather vague term. Perennials have persistent roots, and clumps or colonies of stems and buds at or below ground level. Each year, leaves, stems and flowers develop, mature and die away again before the following winter. The true herbaceous perennial is deciduous like many trees and shrubs and has little to offer in winter. There are also a number of perennials that retain their basal leaves at least and which are essentially evergreens. Formerly, the term herbaceous perennial was used to cover both the deciduous and evergreen kinds but because of the anomaly, herbaceous has largely been dropped and hardy perennials is now used to cover both groups.

Although all shrubs are essentially perennials, their persistent stems proclaim them as such. Nevertheless some shrubs can be and are cut back hard annually, e.g. *Spiraea japonica*, *S. bumalda*, *Buddleia davidii*, and then function as herbaceous perennials. Some semi-woody plants (sub-shrubs) are regularly treated as perennials, e.g. *Perowskia*. Technically, bulbous-rooted plants are herbaceous perennials too, but because of their compact, rootless dormant phase as bulbs, corms and tubers, they form a clearly distinct group with a literature and garden use all of their own.

The main confusion is with rock and alpine plants, most of which are condensed, deciduous or evergreen perennials. In this case, height must be the arbiter and in the main only plants normally above 30 cm are included.

Hardy perennials have much to offer the gardener. Chosen with care they can provide colourful or beautiful flowers and fine foliage for much of the year. If the taller, weaker-stemmed subjects are avoided they present a minimum of maintenance problems, as no skilled pruning or staking is required. Planted at the correct distances, even weeding is reduced to almost nothing once they are established. They do need periodic lifting and dividing, but this provides the excuse for discarding or moving those not satisfactorily placed and for adding something new. It also makes moving the entire bed or border to another part of the garden much easier, if this is desired. The shrub-grower enthusiast does not have such a luxury of mobility and ease! Not that there needs to be any conflict between a desire to grow hardy perennials and shrubs. These two plant groups combine well and a very pleasing compromise can be effected in the so-called mixed border or bed with perhaps an occasional garnish of bulbs and annuals. Mixed selections of this sort have long been favoured by some gardeners and steadily gain in popularity.

When talking with fellow enthusiasts of hardy perennials, and as editor of the Hardy Plant Society's Bulletin, I have long been aware of the need for a reference book devoted to these plants. A landmark in the British literature on hardy perennials was seen in 1976 with the publication of *Perennial Garden Plants* (The Modern Florilegium) by Graham Thomas. This book effectively fills the gap and is essential reading for the devoted hardy plantsman. It is however a rather expensive tome for the average gardener and does contain many species not commercially available, plus some tender or half-hardy subjects, and bulbs which are easily referred to elsewhere. When asked to write this book my endeavour was to provide a reasonably priced, working dictionary dealing strictly with the hardy herbaceous and evergreen perennials. For ease of use, every genus has cultivation notes and all species and varieties are, it is hoped, described clearly enough to give an impression of the plant even if it is quite unknown to the reader. In choosing the plants to be included, availability has been my primary arbiter. Although a handful of personal favourites are included for which a commercial source appears not to be available, in general every plant described has been found in a nurseryman's catalogue. If after a reasonable shop-around the user of this book cannot find a source of supply for a coveted plant, I will willingly aid him or her to find one.

Plants that are difficult to get commercially can sometimes be obtained from fellow enthusiasts either as a gift or on a barter system. This and other benefits can result from membership of the Hardy Plant Society. Founded in 1957, this British society publishes a bulletin and several newsletters each year. It also produces a seed list and holds meetings. For further information contact the Secretary, Miss Barbara White, 10 St Barnabas Road, Emmer Green, Reading, RG4 8RA.

Hardiness is very much a relative thing when applied to plants. As used here it refers to those that survive the winter without protection in Britain, or other countries or areas with a similar climate.

Most of the plants described are truly hardy by that definition, but just a few that are not have crept in here and there. The excuse for including them is that I feel the little trouble needed in providing protection is amply rewarded by their enhancement of the garden scene.

History   In the context of the history of gardening in Britain, the development of the beds and borders purely for herbaceous and evergreen perennials is a fairly recent one, not much more than 100 years or so. Nevertheless it is perhaps not too much of a fancy to see the early origins in the beds of herbs and other plants grown by the Romans around their villas 2,000 years ago. The gardens of renaissance England certainly had similar mixtures; culinary and medicinal herbs brightened with ornamental bulbs, annuals and perennials. It is but a short step further to the idea of using perennials purely for the beauty of their flowers and leaves. This was more easily carried to its finest expression with the aid of the many Asian perennials — particularly from China — that poured into this country from the late nineteenth century onwards. Gertrude Jekyll (1843-1932) did much to formulate the now 'old-fashioned' herbaceous borders. They were wonderful tapestries of colour but rather labour intensive with all the necessary staking and seasonal replacements. These borders were straight or curving, traditionally backed by a dark hedge or sometimes a wall. Double-faced borders then developed with paths and lawns on either side.

More recently (in the 1950s) Alan Bloom, nurseryman and author, of Bressingham, Norfolk pioneered island beds — informal beds set in grass. The island-bed concept involved the use of sturdy wind-proof species or cultivars, thus doing away with the chores of staking. Today there is also an increasing interest in the old idea of mixed borders and beds and these can be particularly effective with all the new plants now available.

Hardy Perennials in their Natural Habitat

Throughout the world wherever a cool climate prevails hardy perennials will be found. They are nicely adapted to their environment; dying back to ground level in autumn when temperatures and light values become too low for growth, then surging into life in spring and blooming in high summer. Of course this is a broad generalisation. There are species that flower in spring and make leafy growth later, e.g. hellebores, *Trachystemon* and *Hacquetia* (*Dondia*), but they are in the minority. A not inconsiderable number flower in autumn only weeks before they are ready to die down, as do some of the sunflowers, Michaelmas daisies, *Vernonia* and that extreme example *Saxifraga fortunei*.

By far the greater number of hardy perennials come from the continental countries of the Northern hemisphere where seasonal changes are fairly sharply divided: a brief spring, a warm showery summer, a dryish autumn of cool nights and warm days and a cold, often snowy winter. Where continents abut the sea the climate tends to be milder in winter and cooler in summer. In the mountains the winters are longer and colder and though summer days may be hot, the nights are cool. Strong winds and snow are a more regular feature and the light intensity increases with altitude. Hardy perennials occur in these regions just as freely, but sometimes with minor variations of growth form and lifecycle. In the milder winter areas more plants are evergreen and some make a new flush of growth in autumn that may or may not persist through the winter. Where winters are long or summers tend to be dry, more species with fleshy storage roots, tubers or rhizomes are to be found.

Climate alone does not decide what grows where; soil and situation are also important. Hardy perennials are in fact very adaptable and exploit most of the major habitats: marsh and grassland, heath and moorland, scrub, forest, mountain slopes and cliffs.

Most of the wild plants of Britain are perennials but few of them have true garden worthiness. There are of course some noteworthy exceptions. Where would our beds and borders be without the common columbine, globe flower, purple loosestrife, meadow crane's bill, thrift and spiked speedwell? In gardens, British perennials were soon supplemented by the best from Europe and a surprisingly large number of familiar plants come from there including *Adonis vernalis*, *Anthemis*, *Aster amellus*, *Astrantia*, *Catananche*, *Centaurea montana*, *Chrysanthemum maximum*, *Delphinium elatum*, *Epimedium*, *Eryngium alpinum*, *Gentiana asclepiadea*, *Gypsophila paniculata*, *Hesperis*, *Lamium maculatum*, *Lysimachia ephemerum*, several peonies, all species of *Pulmonaria*, *Pulsatilla vulgaris* and *Veratrum*.

North America was the next continent to contribute to our borders. Some of the plants from the eastern states have now been in British gardens for 300 years or more and are among the hardy planter's indispensables. Some of the more familiar genera are *Aster* (Michaelmas daisies), *Cimicifuga*, *Dodecatheon* (shooting stars), *Echinacea*, *Gillenia*, *Helenium*, *Helianthus*, *Heuchera*, *Monarda didyma*, *Oenothera*, *Phlox paniculata*, *Physostegia*, *Rudbeckia*, *Solidago* (the golden rods) *Tradescantia virginiana*, *Trillium* and *Yucca*. The great plains and prairies yielded different species in the same and other genera, well-known examples being *Agastache*, *Chelone*, *Coreopsis*, *Gaillardia*, *Liatris* and *Monarda fistulosa*. The western states gave us the three fine columbines that, crossed together, created the popular long-spur hybrids. California in particular has provided the progenitors of Russell lupins, several penstemons, *Sidalcea*, *Tellima*, and that fine foliage plant *Peltiphyllum peltatum*.

Explorations into the great Asian land mass have resulted in a wealth of good hardy perennials. Western Asia, particularly the Caucasus region is the home of *Achillea filipendulina*, *Brunnera macrophylla*, *Campanula lactiflora*, *Centaurea dealbata*, several *Eremurus*, *Heracleum mantegazzianum*, *Inula orientalis*, and that queen of species peonies, *P. mlokosewitschii*. Passing over the drier lands of Iran and Afghanistan we come to the Himalayas which form a great mountain highway to the floral riches of China. The Great Himalayan Range is of course a plant paradise in its own right and has given us *Bergenia ciliata*, and *B. purpurascens*, several hardy geraniums, *Euphorbia griffithii* and *E. sikkimensis*, *Incarvillea mairei*, *Inula hookeri*, *Meconopsis grandis*, *M. napaulensis*, *M. regia* and *M. superba*, *Podophyllum hexandrum*, some of the finest species of *Polygonum*, *Thalictrum chelidonii* and others.

Many of the genera mentioned above are also found in China, but others are special to that huge country. Among those that are particularly noteworthy — mostly from the mountainous areas — are species of *Astilbe*, *Chrysanthemum*, *Incarvillea delavayi*, *Ligularia*, *Macleaya*

(*Bocconia*), *Paeonia, Platycodon, Primula, Rheum, Rodgersia* and *Thalictrum*.

Japan, though essentially an island extension of Asia, has many choice plants peculiar to its mountainous terrain. Some of these plants have real quality, among them being most of the 40 known kinds of *Hosta, Kirengeshoma palmata* and some of the best *Filipendula* species, to mention but a few.

The temperate lands of the southern hemisphere are very much lesser in extent than those of the northern hemisphere and generally are less cold in winter. As a result, comparatively few perennials that are hardy in Britain come from them. There are exceptions however, some of which it would be hard to do without. South Africa provides *Agapanthus, Berkheya, Phygelius* and *Schizostylis*, all of which are surprisingly hardy. The southern part of South America, and particularly the slopes of the Andes in that area, can get fairly cold in winter but never severely so. It is the home of the popular pampas grass (*Cortaderia selloana*) and such delightful plants as *Alstroemeria, Francoa, Gunnera tinctoria, Libertia formosa, Mimulus cupreus, Sisyrinchium striatum* and several desirable sorts of *Tropaeolum*. New Zealand is generally too mild for our purposes and its unique flora — largely evergreen and of tropical origins — yields few perennials that are anything approaching hardy. A most striking exception is New Zealand flax (*Phormium*), plus a few species of *Aciphylla, Bulbinella* and *Ourisia*, and the grasses *Chionochloa* and *Cortaderia richardii*.

As some of the above examples show, plant genera are not necessarily confined to a particular country or region. Some are wide ranging indeed. Many have representatives throughout the north temperate zone, for example *Aquilegia, Aruncus, Aster, Delphinium, Erigeron, Eryngium, Iris, Polygonatum, Potentilla, Sedum* and *Thalictrum*. A few even bridge the tropics and appear in the south temperate zone as well; *Caltha, Eryngium* and *Geum* have this wide distribution.

It is interesting to note that these widespread genera sometimes produce more garden-worthy species in one country or region than another. For example, though Europe provides *Aster amellus* and *A. sedifolius*, North America is very much the homeland of the majority of our Michaelmas daisies. Similarly, the best *Eryngium* species are European and the finest sorts of *Thalictrum* and *Polygonum* are Asiatic. All the most decorative border potentillas are native to the Himalayas, while in the closely allied *Geum* — mainly a northern hemisphere genus — the progenitor of the finest cultivers is Chilean.

This brief survey of hardy perennials in their wild homelands gives some idea of their variety and adaptability. Happily all facets of the climates they inhabit combine in the variable annual cycle of British weather, making it one of the most favoured areas in the world for temperate plants. Certainly no other country grows such a wide range of perennials or uses them so effectively.

Using Hardy Perennials

These are strips of land, usually straight but sometimes curving and of a width to suit the situation. Ideally, they need a living background of an evergreen hedge such as yew or holly, but a fence or wall can serve as well particularly if covered with climbing plants. There should always be an access path between wall, fence or hedge. Not only does this facilitate maintenance but it prevents the tall back plants from becoming drawn up and then more likely to blow over in a wind. For a really effective display the border should be 3-4 m wide. This allows the tallest kinds of perennials to be used at the back, grading progressively to smaller plants at the front. Here and there some slightly taller subjects can be used towards the front to break up any monotony of line. The plants must be used in groups of about five, more for the shorter front-of-the-border kinds, less — about three or four — for the largest at the back. An even bolder effect can be created if groups twice the size are used, but this cuts down the potential variety available. Much narrower borders are of course possible, even 1-2 m. The plant material then needs to be scaled down; as a general guide, the height of the tallest plant should not exceed the width of the bed. Alternatively, a few well-spaced groups of tall subjects can be used as specimens with very much smaller plants filled in around their feet.

Traditional Single- and Double-sided Borders

There is much to be said for having a grass path or wider area of lawn fronting the border. To prevent grass from growing into the border or being smothered by bushy or sprawling front-of-the-border plants, a stone edging is advisable. This can be natural stone-set crazy-paving style with the longest edge of each stone butting each other at the end of the border. Alternatively, square or oblong paving can be used. If grass is not possible, a wide gravel, tarmac or flagged path can be almost as effective. A border by the garage drive is a possibility, particularly if it has a sweeping curve.

The double-sided border is essentially the same but wider, with the

5

tallest plants in the middle and grass or paths on either side. In this case, when choosing plants for the centre make sure they do not exceed half the total width of the bed.

Single- and Two-colour Borders

Whether on a large or small scale, a border devoted to plants of one or two colours and their shades can be very effective. The idea is seen to best advantage in the larger garden especially where it can be screened by hedges and appreciated without the clash of nearby plants. Searching for the greatest variety of genera and species with flowers of a similar tint can become an absorbing interest. Single- and two-colour plant collections need not be confined to borders, and in the smaller garden, beds of geometric or informal design can be chosen. Even the island-bed concept can be used.

Island Beds

Formal or informal beds of flowers in a setting of grass is by no means a new idea. Summer or sub-tropical bedding plants have been so displayed for well over a century. It is to Alan Bloom of Bressingham however that we owe the adaptation of this idea to hardy perennials. Seeking for a way of displaying perennial plants to better advantage and hoping to do away with the annual chore of sticking or staking, he put down some experimental beds in 1952. The plants grew sturdily, looked good in the informally shaped beds and were generally a great success. He proselytised the idea and it soon caught on as a simple but so very effective way to trouble-free gardening with perennials. Although islands beds look best in informal curving shapes, more formal outlines can be used. Overall size is a matter of personal taste and available room but the bed should not be so large that the central plants loose their individuality. If a really large bed is required it should be longer rather than wider. Some perennials, e.g. tall hybrid delphiniums, are always prone to wind damage however much sun and free air circulation they receive. If island beds are to be the labour-saving success they undoubtedly can be, then such weak-based plants must be avoided or staking has to be accepted.

Bog, Waterside, Moisture Beds

Some of the finest hardy perennials grow naturally either in areas of high rainfall, by rivers or lakes or in boggy or marshy places. Although most of them will grow in ordinary soil in the garden, they react splendidly to extra moisture, attaining optimum size and effectiveness. The ideal place to grow these plants is on the banks of a natural river, stream, lake or pond, but few gardens have such features to play with. They can be equally good planted close to artificial ponds, but as these are usually made with concrete or a plastic liner, special provision must be made to see that the soil is truly moist. Either the pond must have deep pockets of boggy soil let into its margins, or the water must seep over the edge into the surrounding soil. Alternatively, an overflow point can be made through which water can slowly flow into a sunken area or bogbed. Even where there is no pond, bog or special moisture beds can be created by lining a hole with plastic sheeting and filling it with humus-rich soil.

Covering the ground with attractive foliage and flowers should be the aim of all who garden with ornamentals. If we do not cover the bare ground, weeds soon will. This is particularly relevant where awkward sites are concerned; those steep banks, shady corners and areas under trees which for most plants are often too dry in summer. Hardy perennials of one sort or another can be used in all these instances, giving interest and beauty where none was before.

As Ground Cover

This is really a return to an older practice, but superior in overall effect because of all the different kinds of trees, shrubs and perennials that have come from Asia, North America and other temperate areas of the world during the past 200 years. Basically, the border or bed to be planted is given a backbone of shrubs — small trees also can be used in the large garden — which are background for perennials and bulbs. In seasonal gaps a few suitable annuals, those that have not been over-refined by the plant breeder, can also be used. The *ensemble* must be put together with some care to avoid perennials being swamped by vigorous shrubs and initially even the reverse if slow-growing shrubs are used. Evergreen and a few winter-flowering shrubs are the best to use so that there is something to gladden the eye in winter. The perennials chosen should flower over as great a part of the year as possible and preference should be given to those that are also evergreen or have ornamental leaves. Properly planted, a mixed border can give a maximum amount of satisfaction the year round with a minimum of maintenance.

Mixed Borders

It is an accepted part of garden planning and design that a particularly ornamental tree or shrub is used as a focal point, to obscure a less-than pleasing view or to mask an awkward corner. Many of the larger hardy perennials can be used in just the same way, either singly or in small close groups. The best sorts to use are those with good basal leaves that in the border or bed would be masked from view. Such genera as *Heracleum*, *Macleaya*, *Inula* can look splendid in isolation. Even shorter plants, especially those like *Hosta* and *Bergenia* with imposing leaves can take on a new dimension when grown in groups by themselves. If set in a lawn or occupying an awkward corner where

As Specimen Plants

there are no other distracting plants, the effect can be greatly heightened.

<table>
<tr><td>Propagation</td><td>Propagating one's own plants is one of the joys of gardening. Most hardy perennials are easy to increase by one of the fairly simple propagating methods, i.e. seeds, division or cuttings.</td></tr>
</table>

Propagation   Propagating one's own plants is one of the joys of gardening. Most hardy perennials are easy to increase by one of the fairly simple propagating methods, i.e. seeds, division or cuttings.

Seeds are the most general and natural means by which plants increase their numbers. It is the sexual means of reproduction and involves the sort of genetic variability that is common to animals. The other means of propagation is known as vegetative, involving as it does the severing or cutting up of the whole plant or parts of it and inducing the pieces to root and form new plants, each one identical in make-up to the parent.

Division

This is the most frequently used and easiest method of increasing a great many hardy perennials. It is done when the plant is dormant, in most cases from autumn to the following spring, though certain species respond more surely in early autumn or spring. The plant should be healthy and well established with a broad crown that will split easily into three or four or more pieces. The plant is dug up carefully, the loose soil shaken or prised away and two forks are thrust back to back into the centre. First pushing the fork handles together, then pulling them apart should result in the plant separating into two. Both portions can then be treated in the same way. The quarter sections should be just right for replanting immediately, or they can be pulled into smaller pieces by hand. If Michaelmas daisies are being split they can be separated into single-rooted shoots.

Suckers

Some clump-forming plants produce shoots a little way away from the main clump. If only a few young plants are required, these suckers can be removed and treated as for division. The sucker should be carefully unearthed with a handfork and severed as close to the parent part as possible with a sharp trowel, or better still, a knife.

Cuttings

These are pieces of plant, generally non-flowering leafy shoots, but they can also be pieces of root. Fleshy-leaved plants such as the stonecrops (*Sedum*) can be reproduced by leaf cuttings.

Basal shoots in spring provide the easiest means for a large variety of perennials. A cold frame or even cloches are all that is required in the way of equipment. The soil should be sharply drained and well laced with coarse sand. The ideal is the so-called sand frame; a cold

Figure1 : Propagation by Division

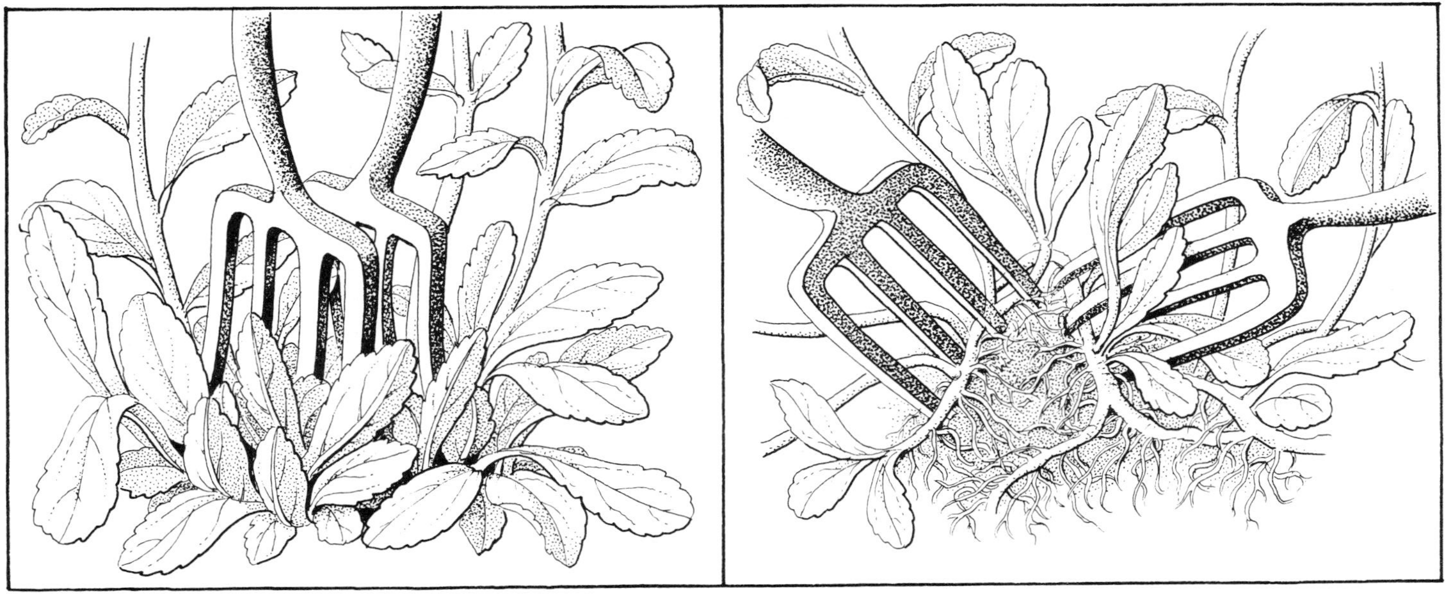

Two Forks Inserted Back to Back

Forks Levered Apart

frame with at least 10 cm of coarse sand in the bottom to take the cuttings. Shoots chosen for cuttings should have several pairs of leaves and a short sturdy stem. Each shoot is severed close to the base of the plant, the basal leaves are removed neatly and the base cut cleanly just below a joint with a sharp knife or razor blade. Although not usually essential it is a good idea to dip the base of each cutting into one of the proprietary hormone rooting powders which are usually combined with a fungicide. The cuttings must now be inserted immediately, with one third to a half of the stem length being buried. A thorough watering with a fine-rosed watering can must be given once the batch of cuttings is in and the cloche or frame top (light) put in place. If direct sunlight can get to the frame, shading with whitewash or a proprietary greenhouse shading liquid must be carried out. Alternatively, light hessian or old cotton sheeting can be used. If cloches are used those with opaque, milky plastic sheeting should be chosen, so extra shading will not be needed. Basal cuttings of this sort usually root rapidly and in four to six weeks from insertion are ready for potting or setting-out in nursery rows. This must be done as soon as the cuttings have a sturdy little root system forming and the growing point starts to elongate. Delay will mean drawn and starved young plants.

Some perennials produce short, non-flowering shoots on the main stems in late summer. These shoots can be carefully severed and treated as for basal cuttings. Potting or lining-out should be delayed until the following spring.

Root Cuttings

A limited number of perennials can be increased by root cuttings, short sections of root being suitably trimmed and inserted either direct into a sand frame or in pots or pans in a cold or cool green-house. Mid-winter to early spring is the best time. If it can be spared, the easiest way is to dig up a whole healthy, preferably not old, plant and wash off the soil in a bucket of water. Root systems vary greatly; some are fibrous with numerous, relatively thin roots, e.g. border phlox; others, like anchusa have long, thick but rather sparse roots. Cuttings of the fibrous sorts should be made from the thickest roots cut in pieces 6-8 cm long. These are inserted horizontally about 1 cm apart. If started in pans or boxes, a proprietary potting compost can be used. John Innes No. 1 is good. The cuttings are placed on the top of the compost then covered with 1 cm of coarse sand. The thick roots of anchusa are treated somewhat differently. These are cut into sections about 5 cm long. The bottom should be sliced obliquely, the top horizontally. This ensures that when inserted they are not placed upside down. The cuttings are then inserted vertically with the top just proud of the surface of the compost. After insertion the tops

Figure 2: Propagation by Stem Cuttings

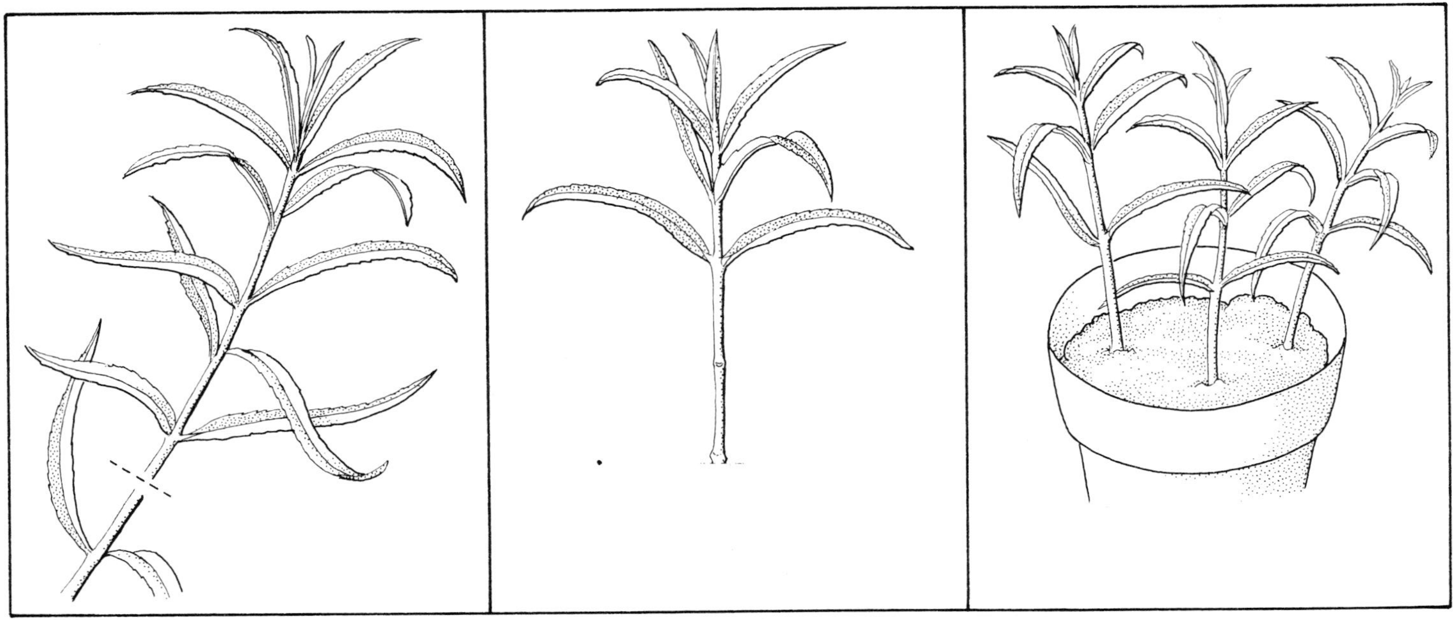

Shoot being Severed

Trimmed to a Node and Leaves Removed

Inserted in Pot

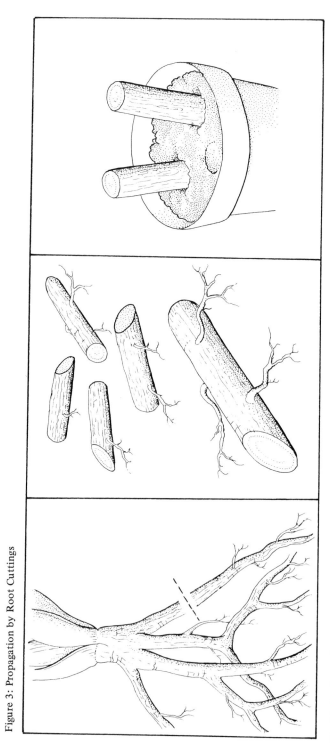

Figure 3: Propagation by Root Cuttings

Root being Severed   Cut into Sections   Inserted

are covered with a 1 cm layer of coarse sand or fine grit. When the root cuttings develop shoots with several leaves and are actively growing they should be potted or planted out in nursery rows. Set into a fertile soil they will grow into plants large enough to place in permanent sites the following autumn or spring.

Natural Vegetative Increase

A few hardy perennials produce plantlets in various ways that can be detached and provide a ready means of increase. Particularly intriguing are those plants that produce tiny replicas of themselves on their leaves. Very well known is the pick-a-back plant, *Tolmiea menziesii*. Often grown in pots as a curiosity, but fully hardy, each leaf bears a plantlet at the junction of the leaf blade and stalk. Well-grown plantlets can be removed and treated as cuttings or the leaves can be pegged down onto the soil or into pots until well rooted. The fern *Polystichum setiferum* 'Acutilobum' produces buds along the leaf midrib, particularly towards the base. These grow into little plants the second year and can be induced to perform more rapidly if mature leaves are severed, pinned to the surface of potting compost in seed trays and covered with a plastic bag to maintain humidity. When the plantlets are nicely rooted the old leaf can be cut into sections and potted. Some primulas produce plantlets at the top of the old flowering stems and these can be treated as for *Tolmiea*. Day-lily (*Hemerocallis*) occasionally does the same thing. These little quirks of plant life can turn up in other genera and species, and if noticed can be made use of to increase a favourite plant.

Grafting

Very few perennials are grafted and only the simple cleft graft is used. Grafting involves the uniting of a rootstock with a scion (shoot) of the desired plant. It is only carried out on plants that are difficult to root from cuttings or are slow growing or weak on their own roots. Double forms of *Gypsophila paniculata* are the primary candidates for grafting. One-year-old plants from seeds of the ordinary single-flowered *G. paniculata* provide the best rootstocks but lateral roots taken from older plants can be used. The scion plant is dug up and potted in late winter and brought into a cool greenhouse to induce early growth. When the shoots have about three pairs of leaves they are severed low down and carefully pared with a sharp knife to make a slim wedge at the base. The seedling rootstocks, which have been stored in moist peat in the same greenhouse, are beheaded below the crown and cut vertically with a sharp knife. The scion is inserted towards the perimeter of the stock and tied in place with raffia or plastic strip. The grafts are then potted and placed in a cool propagating case. When union has taken place and the scions are actively growing they can be hardened off and either grown on in pots or planted out.

Seeds

The vegetative methods of increase described above are reasonably foolproof even for the beginner and provide the easiest means of propagation for hardy perennials. Nevertheless, practically all the plants described in this book can also be raised from seeds and doing so can provide lots of interest. When the plants grown from seeds reach flowering size and prove themselves to be all that was expected, and perhaps even more, then the cup of satisfaction is full indeed. In order to germinate and grow into healthy plants, seeds require an adequate temperature, the right amount of moisture, light and air and a rooting medium containing essential plant foods. High temperatures are not required for the germination of most hardy perennials and they can be sown outside or in a cold frame or greenhouse. Spring is a convenient time but there is much to be said for sowing home-saved seeds as soon as they are ripe. This is nature's way and generally a high percentage germinate. There are many examples of seeds which, if allowed to dry out and then stored in packets over winter, will take at least a year to germinate. Familiar examples are peonies and hellebores. If these are sown direct from the pod they will germinate the following late winter to spring. As with many alpines some perennial seeds germinate more freely if subjected to the low temperatures of winter. These aspects of getting certain hardy perennial seeds to grow reflect built-in dormancy factors. Less commonly occurring are seeds with hard coats which need to rot partially before they will germinate. There are also chemical inhibitors in the seed coat of some plants which need to be leached out by winter rains. All these factors help to ensure that in the wild, seeds germinate when weather conditions and the seasons ahead are favourable for growth and establishment.

If small amounts of seeds are being dealt with, pots or pans are ideal. Larger quantities can be sown in boxes or the open ground. Any of the standard seed composts are suitable but a properly made up John Innes seed or potting compost No. 1 takes some beating. Whatever medium is used it should be free of weed seeds. Weed seedlings not only compete with the sown plant but can also be confused with them in the early stages. All commercially available composts should have been sterilised to kill pests, diseases and weed seeds. A virtually weedfree substitute can be made up of equal parts of moss peat and coarse washed sand or fine grit. Once the seeds are germinated, water with a half strength liquid feed up to the pricking-off stage. Seeds must not be sown too deeply. As a rule-of-thumb guide they should be covered with a layer of compost equal in depth to their own diameters. Very small seeds such as *Verbascum* and *Astilbe* should be sown on the surface with no more than a dusting of compost. Seeds known to need chilling or leaching by rain should be covered with a layer of fine grit or shingle and placed in a sheltered spot outside or in an open cold frame. Most hardy perennials however will benefit from being placed in a cold green-house or closed frame. Except in winter, light shading will be needed until the seedlings appear, to prevent overheating. Fine surface sown or shallowly covered seeds should be covered with glass or plastic sheeting and a layer of newspaper to prevent drying out of the com-post surface during the critical germination period.

Once the seedlings are up and growing well they must be pricked off into an approved potting compost. Allowing them to become congested leads to starvation and further severe checks to growth when they have to be pulled apart to pot or plant out. The ideal stage to prick off is when the seed leaves (cotyledons) are fully ex-panded and the first true or rough leaf is visible. Very small seedlings, e.g. those of *Astilbe* and *Filipendula* are best left until they are larger and thus more easily handled. There is much to be said for pricking-off direct into nursery beds or soil-based frames, but if only small quantities are involved it may be more convenient to prick-off singly into small pots — 6-8 cm sizes are the most useful. If the seedlings are of quick-growing plants they may need potting on when well rooted. Once the plants are big enough they should be set out in their perma-nent sites. Generally speaking, seedlings that appear in the spring are ready for their final positions from late summer onwards.

Siting

Cultivation

Although there are hardy perennials for practically all sites and situa-tions, mixed beds and borders need at least a moderate amount of sun and ideally some shelter from the strongest winds. If the site is windy, then the shorter, windproof species should be chosen. Most soils in Britain are acceptable and there are virtually none that cannot be made suitable. Ideally, they should be of a fertile loam but if this is not available the addition of organic matter and fertiliser will make the soil acceptable to all but the fussiest plants. If it is always very moist or waterlogged land drains can be laid but there are two alterna-tives. The first is to build raised beds, either by mounding up the existing top soil, or buying in extra soil, say from a building site. Alternatively and easiest is to grow only the really moisture-loving bog plants, many of which are extremely handsome.

Soil Preparation

Having marked out the outline of the border or bed — a piece of hose-pipe is most useful for this operation — there are two approaches to preparing the soil. The traditional way is to dig at least one spit deep with a fork or spade. Alternatively the no-digging technique can be applied. In either case it is very important first to eradicate persistent perennial weeds such as ground elder, bindweed and couch grass. If these invade the clumps of perennials they are impossible to eradicate without lifting each plant and pulling it to pieces to get out the weed 'roots'. Hand digging such weeds is very effective if done carefully. Alternatively, one of the weed killers containing MCPA and Dalapon can be used to makers' instructions. Complete eradication can be a lengthy business and at least two to three applications will be necessary. The more expensive and newer herbicide known as Tumbleweed is more efficient. The key to soil fertility is organic matter, e.g. decayed manure, garden compost, leafmould, spent hops and peat. If the soil is to be dug, this can be mixed in as digging proceeds. If no-digging is followed it should be applied as a mulch after planting, with some in the holes as the plants are set out. Apply at least one bucketful to each square metre, but double this on the poorer chalky and sandy soils.

Planting

Hardy perennials can be purchased in containers or so-called bare-root (lifted direct from the nursery soil). Whichever sort is obtained the planting procedure is much the same. A hole is dug out with trowel or spade half again as large as the root ball. Set the plant in position so that its crown is 2-3 cm below the surrounding soil surface. Fill around with soil and firm with fists or feet, depending on plant size. If a no-digging method is followed it is advantageous to mix in organic matter as the hole is filled in. How far apart to plant can be a problem for beginners. As a rule-of-thumb guide, a suitable distance is that equal to half the ultimate height of the plant species concerned. Where two species adjoin in beds or borders, a suitable distance can be arrived at by combining their heights and dividing by four. Bare-root plants are best set out during the dormant season, generally October to March. There are some plants, notably grasses, that are best put out in spring. Less than fully hardy plants are also best in spring or very early autumn. The planting times in the text are for bare-root plants. Container-grown stock can be planted any time providing the soil is not wet and sticky or frozen. Really well-rooted containerised plants may need watering during dry spells especially if set out in full growth. After planting, the application of a light dressing of general fertiliser will be advantageous on all but the most fertile soils.

Supporting and General Maintenance

If the taller or less sturdy perennials are favoured, especially in windy or open sites, some sort of support system must be employed. A favourite method is to use twiggy pea sticks, two to four to each plant depending on size. The height of the sticks above the soil should be equal to about two-thirds of the ultimate plant height. This will ensure adequate support and complete concealment of the sticks when the plants are in bloom. Heavy plants such as the tall elatum delphinium cultivars are best supported with canes, either three to four to each clump or a separate cane to each stem. There are several proprietary supports based upon circles or squares of stout galvanised wire with or without a grid of cross wires. These are ideal for such plants as peonies which need support only in their lower halves. Whatever means of support are employed they must be put into position while growth is small, ideally mid to late spring.

Weeding must be attended to early in the season, especially in the first year after planting. Once the plants are growing vigorously and meet together, weeds are never a problem. Each spring a mulch of organic matter should be applied and on the poorer soils a dressing of general fertiliser such as Growmore at 90 g per sq. m.

During the late autumn to winter period all supports should be removed and the dead stems cut down and burnt. Overlooked weeds can also be removed. In cold areas there is something to be said for delaying this tidying operation until early spring, as the tops give the plants beneath some protection.

Providing they are growing vigorously and healthily, hardy perennials are remarkably free of pest and disease troubles. The primary troubles are listed below under the observable symptoms. Where chemical sprays are recommended they must be used to makers' instructions. Applied at too weak a strength it will not kill the pest; if too strong it may damage the plant as well. Only the infected plant should be treated. To spray the whole bed or border because a few plants are suffering is wasteful and will almost certainly kill some beneficial insects as well. It must be remembered that most insects have predators that feed upon them and pests are no exception. At present there is no approved technique of applying the use of such biological control to hardy perennials efficiently. There is however much to be said for getting familiar with the common and useful predators, e.g. ladybirds and hover flies that prey upon greenfly and other aphids. Insect-eating birds should also be encouraged whenever possible.

Pests and Diseases

Leaves and Stem Tips Deformed

Grossly to mildly malformed leaves and stems are usually the result of piercing and sucking insects. Most commonly met with are the various kinds of aphids, mainly greenfly and blackfly. These tiny, soft, oval-bodied, sometimes winged insects multiply rapidly but are easily killed with derris or malathion. Small attacks can often be dealt with by squashing between thumb and forefinger or sponging with warm sudsy detergent water. If the deformation of leaves is accompanied by a rather tattered appearance caused by small irregular holes this is the result of capsid bug feeding. Capsids are several times larger than aphids, fast moving and secretive. The observable damage is the result of much earlier feeding by piercing the tender shoot tips. If this sort of damage regularly occurs, a preventative series of monthly spray applications, using fenitrothion or HCH (BHC), should start in late spring just as vigorous growth gets underway. Blobs of spit-like froth are the shelters of the immature (nymphal) stages of the frog-hopper. This sucking creature can cause stunting and crippling of stems, but damage varies. Small infestations can be squashed. Larger attacks can be dealt with by forcefully spraying with malathion or derris.

Leaves Eaten

Sections eaten out of leaf margins denotes that caterpillars or earwigs are feeding. Where damage is slight it is worthwhile looking for the pest and dealing with it in an approved manner. Earwigs feed only by night and hide by day. They can be trapped in rolls of corrugated cardboard or small containers of dry straw. These traps must be checked daily and the earwigs killed. A routine spraying of HCH (BHC) at 10-14 day intervals during the main growing season will greatly reduce severe attacks. A more irregular feeding, especially on young leaves near ground level is usually the work of slugs and snails. Silvery slime trails should confirm this. One of the approved slug killers should be applied; Draza pellets are recommended.

Leaves and Shoots Wilting

Severe wilting is invariably the result of trouble at the root. The commonest cause among hardy perennials is due to the roots being eaten by garden swift moth and other soil-dwelling caterpillars, also often referred to as cutworms. But see also comments under *Flowers Withering* (below). Swift-moth caterpillars are a dirty white and wriggle actively. The cutworm group are in shades of brown or yellowish-brown and roll up when disturbed. Control is difficult, but soaking the base of the plant and the ground around with malathion or liquid HCH (BHC) is usually reasonably effective.

Leaves with Whitish or Greyish Discoloration

The leaves of single shoots or whole plants may be completely covered with or bear patches of a whitish, somewhat powdery film. This is mildew, and as the attack develops leaves die off rather earlier than usual, weakening the plant and rendering it unsightly. Michaelmas daisies are particulalry prone to this fungal disease but many other plants may get a touch of it from time to time. Late summer to autumn is the worst time. Control is not always easy but spraying with Benlate as soon as the mildew is observed is usually successful.

Flowers and Buds Deformed or Eaten

The same pests of leaves and young shoots can attack flowers. For control, see the headings above.

Flowers Withering or Failing to Develop

Beds and borders in the lee of hedges and walls may be in rain shadow and be drier than expected. This may result in some wilting of leaves, at least in hot sun, and the failure to develop flower buds. Regular watering during dry spells is the only answer.

If, in peonies, flower-bud withering is accompanied by browning of leaves or whole shoots, peony blight or wilt is present. This is a form of grey mould (botrytis) and a fuzzy grey-white 'mould' is usually seen on the dead buds and stem bases. Spraying with captan, thiram or zineb should be carried out as soon as possible and dead growth removed and burnt. If the disease occurs regularly, begin spraying each year as soon as the young leaves expand, continuing at 14-day intervals until flowering is completed.

A-Z List of Genera and Species

Acanthus (Bear's Breech) (*Acanthaceae*)

Fifty species of shrubs and perennials from Asia, Africa and S. Europe comprise this genus, some of the hardy perennials providing statuesque specimen plants with boldly handsome foliage and spikes of hooded flowers from among decoratively spiny bracts. All species have intriguing seed capsules which explode when ripe. The hardy species thrive in any fertile, well-drained soil, preferably in sheltered sunny or partially shaded sites. Propagation is by division, root cuttings or seed, from late winter to spring. *A. balcanicus* (*A. longifolius*) (Balkan Peninsula to Romania and Yugoslavia) is like a shorter *A. mollis*, and inferior to it as a garden plant, with longer, more gappy leaves. *A. dioscoridis* (Turkey to India) resembles a dwarf form of *A. mollis* with leaves to 30 cm and flower spikes to 45 cm. *A. mollis* (S. Europe to Turkey) is the most commonly grown species with clumps of deeply lobed obovate leaves to 60 cm long and flowering stems 90-120 cm tall, bearing white or purple-flushed flowers in summer. The more robust *A. m. latifolius* is the form usually met with in British gardens. *A. perringii* (of gardens) is rather like a dwarf *A. mollis* with toothed grey-green leaves and flower spikes to 45 cm tall. *A. spinosus* (Italy to Greece) ranks highest in garden worthiness with its glossy dark-green, deeply dissected leaves, each lobe spine-tipped and 1.2-1.5 m-tall spires of mauve-purple bracts and white flowers in late summer. *A. s. spinosissimus* has more finely dissected leaves with whitish spines and is marginally less hardy. The plant listed as *A. caroli-alexandri* is, in effect, a small version of *A. spinosus*; in some gardens it can be invasive.

Achillea (Yarrow) (*Compositae*)

About 200 species of perennials from the north temperate zone, several of the taller sorts being indispensable for the summer garden.

Most of them have robust or wiry self-supporting stems; dissected, often ferny foliage and flattened terminal clusters of tiny button-like flower heads which dry well if cut in full bloom. Yarrows need a sunny site, but thrive in ordinary soil. They are best planted in autumn or spring. Propagation is by division at planting time, preferably spring. *A. clypeolata* (of gardens - not the true species from Greece which is seldom cultivated), is probably of hybrid origin, this clump-forming evergreen plant has elegant, silvery-grey leaves and bright-yellow flowers on 45-60 cm-tall stems. In the Lye End nursery of Miss R. B. Pole, former Chairman of the Hardy Plant Society, it hybridised with *A. filipendulina* and gave rise to 'Coronation Gold', a sturdier, taller, greener plant with broader heads of richer yellow; 'Lye End Lemon' is similar but with lemon-yellow flowers and the cream 'Lye End Ivory'. *A. filipendulina* (*A. eupatorium*) (Caucasus), is probably the most generally garden worthy of the border yarrows; this robust, 1-1.2 m-tall clump-former has ferny, green foliage and wide heads of bright yellow; 'Gold Plate' is a richer hue. *A. mille-folium* is the common yarrow of the British countryside, gracing roadsides and downland and also posing problems as a lawn weed with its running rhizomes. As a garden plant it must be treated with caution, but in its pink and cerise forms is undeniably attractive. 'Cerise Queen', 'Red Beauty', 'Fire King' are all about 60 cm tall and similar in flower, the latter two of a deeper tint. The rich green mossy leaves are evergreen. *A. ptarmica* (Europe to Siberia) is another British native of invasive habits and should be admitted to the garden only in its double forms, 'The Pearl' ('Boule de Neige') and 'Perry's White'. The latter has larger, whiter flowerheads, but the plant needs support. Best known as sneezewort, *A. ptarmica* forms wide clumps 45-60 cm tall and has small, narrow, undivided leaves. *A. serrata* (*A. decolorans*) is represented in gardens by the double cultivar 'W.B. Child'. This probable hybrid can best be described as a blend of *A. ptarmica* and *A. millefolium* with white and green flowerheads and narrow, sharply toothed leaves on stems to 60 cm. *A.* X *taygetea* is similar to *A. clypeolata* of gardens and is thought to be a hybrid of that species with *A. millefolium*. It has greener leaves on stems to 60 cm tall and pale-yellow flowers, brightest in 'Flowers of Sulphur' ('Schwefel-blute'). Crossing with *A. clypeolata* has given 'Moonshine', a fine vigorous hybrid from Blooms of Bressingham which blends the best characters of its parents.

Aciphylla (Speargrass, Wild Spaniard) (*Umbelliferae*)

None of the 40-odd species of this largely New Zealand genus are well known in Britain, though the large ones are of uniquely picturesque appearance. They form compact clumps of compound leaves, the narrow leaflets of which are spine-tipped. The often spike-like in-

21

florescences are composed of numerous small umbels of yellow to white flowers. They are not always easy to please and can be slow growing. A moist but well-drained peaty, gritty soil usually gives the best results. Planting is best in spring. Propagation is by seeds when ripe, the seedling potted singly when the first true leaf shows. Species worth trying are: *A. aurea* (1 m tall), *A. glaucescens* (50 cm), *A. horrida* (80-100 cm), *A. scott-thomsonii* (2-3 m) and *A. squarrosa* (1 m).

Aconitum (Monkshood, Wolfbane) (*Ranunculaceae*)

Of the 300 north temperate species that comprise this genus only a handful of the most decorative are grown. Closely allied to *Delphinium*, they are easily distinguished by the helmet-shaped, petal-like sepal at the top of each flower. They need fertile, moisture-retentive soil in sun or partial shade and can be planted from autumn to spring. Propagate by seeds in spring or by division at planting time. *A. amplexicaule* (Nepal), this promising species produces clusters of lustrous purple-blue flowers on stems to 1 m in summer. *A.* X *cammarum*, sometimes listed as *A. bicolor*, this name covers a group of hybrid cultivars derived from *A. napellus* and *A. variegatum*. Among the best are 'Blue Sceptre', 90 cm tall with blue-purple and white flowers; 'Bressingham Spire', 90 cm, violet-blue; 'Bicolor' 1.5 m, blue-violet and white. *A. carmichaelii* (*A. fischeri*) (Kamtschatka) is one of the finest early autumn species with branched spikes of light blue on stems to 1.2 m; *A. c.* 'Arendsii' has deeper blue flowers; while *A. c. wilsonii* grows to 1.8 m. *A. c. wilsonii* 'Barkers' is the best form and *A. c. w.* 'Kelmscott' has violet-blue flowers. *A. napellus* (Europe to Asia), this is the common monkshood, a variable early summer species with erect spikes of purple-blue flowers on stems 1-1.5 m tall. *A. n.* 'Album' is white, while *A. n.* 'Carneum' has soft-pink flowers, a shade rare in the genus. *A. orientale* (Caucasus to Iran), much like a more sturdy version of *A. vulparia* with longer spikes of pale-yellow flowers. *A. septentrionale* (Scandinavia, N. Russia), this large-leaved plant attains 90 cm in height and bears erect racemes of purple flowers in summer; *A.s.* 'Ivorine' has cream flowers (sometimes classified under *A.* X *cammarum* (*A. bicolor*)). *A. uncinatum* (E. USA) has reclining stems to 80 cm and blue flowers in loose panicles in summer; it needs support. *A. variegatum* (E. Alps), this late summer blooming plant has somewhat zigzag stems that can reach 1.5-2 m and bear loose racemes of violet-blue, cream or bicoloured flowers; *A. v. bicolor* is somewhat shorter with purple-blue and white blooms. *A. volubile* (Altai Mountains) is a true climber with twining stems to 3 m or more and violet-purple flowers late summer to autumn. *A. vulparia* (*A. lycoctonum* (Europe to Asia) is the wolfbane of Europe. It is a slender species with well branched stems to 1 m or more that need support. The cream to yellow flowers have curiously elongated helmets and open in summer.

Acorus (Sweet Flag) (*Araceae*)

Two widespread species comprise this genus, both rhizomatous and iris-like but bearing minute greenish flowers in a spadix hidden by the leaves. They need moist to wet soil and thrive in sun or partial shade. Planting is best in spring and propagation is by division at the same time. *A. calamus* (Asia, N. America, naturalised in Europe), the common sweet flag has creeping rhizomes and sword-shaped leaves up to 1 m tall and grows best in water with a natural mud bottom. *A. c.* 'Variegatus' has the leaves cream-striped. *A. gramineus* (India to Japan) has grassy leaves 30-50 cm long and a more compact habit of growth. *A. g.* 'Variegatus' has cream striped leaves; *A. g. pusillus* is smaller and more tufted, while *A. g. p. minimus* is even smaller; all will grow in ordinary moist soil.

Actaea (Baneberry) (*Ranunculaceae*)

Half of the ten known species of baneberry are cultivated but only two to three are generally available. All are clump-forming with elegant compound leaves, and spikes of fluffy cream or white flowers followed by showy but poisonous red or white berries. They need moisture-retentive ordinary soil and thrive in shade or sun. Planting is best in autumn or spring. Propagation is easiest by division at planting time or seeds can be sown when ripe. Dried seeds usually take one year or more to germinate and the young plants begin to flower in their third year. *A. alba* (*A. pachypoda*) known as dolls' eyes and white baneberry, is the most intriguing and probably the most decorative species, with bright-green, neatly dissected foliage and 60-90 cm-tall stems bearing white flowers in spring. The berries are like white beads, each one poised at the end of a swollen red stalk. *A. asiatica* (E. Asia) is much like a more robust *A. spicata*, with smaller, shining black berries. *A. rubra* (red baneberry) (N. America) resembles *A. alba* but bears red berries on slender stalks; *A. r. neglecta* is white fruited. *A. spicata* (Europe, Asia), is the only species native to Britain where it is also known as herb Christopher. It is rather like *A. alba*, but with lustrous black berries up to 1 cm in diameter.

Adenophora (*Campanulaceae*)

This genus of 60 species from Europe and Asia is so closely related to *Campanula* that the novice has difficulty in seeing the differences. The species in cultivation are tufted or closely clump-forming with erect racemes of pendent bell-flowers. They grow in ordinary soil that is reasonably fertile and moisture retentive and tolerate moderate shade. Planting is best in autumn or spring and propagation is by cuttings of basal shoots, or by seeds in spring. *A. bulleyana* (China) in one of the tallest species reaching to 1.2 m, the stems bearing oblong-ovate leaves and branched racemes of pale-blue bells in late summer. *A. potaninii* resembles the previous species but is usually shorter and bears its violet-blue flowers in summer. *A. tashiroi* (*A. polymorpha tashiroi*) (Japan, Korea) rarely exceeds 30 cm and carries its larger blue flowers in short terminal racemes in late summer.

Adiantum (Maidenhair Fern) (*Adiantaceae*)

Although only two of the 200 species of maidenhair fern are reliably hardy, they happen to be among the most decorative and deserve to be grown more often. Both are easily grown in shade or partial shade providing the soil is not too dry and is preferably enriched with leaf-mould or peat. Planting is best in spring and propagation is by division at the same time. *A. pedatum* (N. America, Asia) is the toughest of all the maidenhair ferns and totally hardy in Britain. It is clump-forming and deciduous, each 25-40 cm-long glossy black stalk topped by a radiating filigree of bright-green leaflets. *A. p. aleuticum* has the young leaves pink-flushed and the similar *A. p.* 'Imbricatum' has shorter, broader leaflets that just overlap. All will grow even in chalky soil if laced with humus. *A. venustum* (Himalayas) resembles the tropical maidenhairs so popular as pot plants, but spreads by slender rhizomes and seldom grows above 20 m tall. It is evergreen in mild winters but even if the fronds are killed by frost, they stay a warm russet brown until the young bronzy-pink fronds overtop them in early spring.

Adonis (*Ranunculaceae*)

About 20 species of annuals and perennials comprise this genus, some of the latter being invaluable for their very early anemone-like flowers and ferny foliage. They need well-drained but moisture-retentive fertile soil and a site that is sunny at least in late winter and spring. Planting in autumn is best, but possible also in late winter. Propagation is by division at planting time or by sowing seeds when ripe. *A. amurensis* (China, Japan), this is the first to bloom, its many petalled yellow flowers opening as early as February in a mild season. Flowers appear on short stems which gradually elongate to 20-30 cm. Several cultivars have arisen in Japan and some of these are usually available in GB; 'Fukujukai' has larger, brighter yellow blooms; 'Nadeshiku' is a shade of lime yellow with a satiny sheen, the petals fringed; 'Pleniflora' ('Flore-pleno') has double flowers. *A. brevistyla* (Bhutan, Tibet, China) is distinct in having white flowers which are bluish flushed or striped in bud, but otherwise it is not particularly

Figure 4:
Adonis amurensis
'Nadeshiku'

garden worthy. *A. pyrenaica* (Pyrenees) grow 25-40 cm tall with large flowers having 12-20 golden-yellow petals in early summer. *A. vernalis* (Europe) is similar to *A. pyrenaica* but has earlier flowers with fewer petals. *A. volgensis* has coarser foliage and a more branched habit, otherwise resembles *A. vernalis*.

Agapanthus (African lily) (*Alliaceae*)

Depending on the botanical authority, there are five to twelve species of African lily, all from S. Africa. They form dense clumps of arching strap-shaped leaves which are overtopped by rounded heads of lily-like blue or blue-purple flowers. Any well-drained soil is suitable and a sunny site is essential. The evergreen kinds are not generally hardy, but the deciduous ones below usually come through all winters. Plant in spring. Propagation is by division at planting time or by sowing seeds under glass in spring, the young plants kept in a frame for the first winter. *A. campanulatus* produces flowering stems to 90 cm or more in height, with blossoms in shades of blue or white in late summer. *A. c. patens* is smaller and slenderer with more widely expanded flowers; it is probably identical with the plant sometimes listed as *A. umbellatus globosus*. *A.* X Headbourne Hybrids are the best known and most frequently grown of the African lilies, being hybrids largely derived from *A. campanulatus* and *A. inapertus* and probably *A. praecox* (*A. umbellatus* and *A. africanus*). Several cultivars are grown and mixed seed strains are readily available. The following are worth while seeking out: 'Isis', 'Molly Howick', 'Dorothy Palmer', 'Midnight Blue', 'Cherry Holley' and 'Loch Hope' (all shades of deep blue). Lighter blues include 'Blue Moon', and 'Luly'. *A. inapertus* is probably the most distinctive species with blue-green foliage and pendent flowers on stems to 1.8 m. *A. inapertus pendulus* (*pendulinus*) has much broader leaves and more tubular darker blue flowers. *A. 'weillighii'* covers another hybrid race largely derived from *A. inapertus* and is best combined with the Headbourne group.

Agastache (*Labiatae*)

Although 30 species from N. America, Mexico and Asia are known, only one is likely to be seen in cultivation. *A. mexicana* (*Cedronella* and *Brittonastrum mexicanum*) (Mexico) is a clump-former to 75 cm tall with glandular, lance-shaped leaves and whorled spikes of two-lipped, red tubular flowers in summer. Any well-drained soil in a sunny, preferably sheltered site is suitable. Propagation is by division or seeds under glass in spring.

Agrostemma coronaria — see *Lychnis coronaria*.

Ajuga (Bugle) (*Labiatae*)

Of the 40 species in this genus three are cultivated as front-of-border and ground-cover plants. They are either clump or mat-forming with obovate leaves and stiff spikes of blue-purple to blue flowers each one with a prominent three-lobed lip. Ordinary garden soil that does not dry out unduly and a site in sun or shade is suitable. Planting can take place from autumn to spring. Propagation is by division at planting time. *A. genevensis* (Europe to SW Asia) is clump-forming and white hairy with stems to 30 cm and rich bright-blue flowers in spring; 'Jungle Beauty' has smoother, larger leaves and deeper flowers and may be a hybrid between *A. genevensis* and *A. reptans*. *A. pyramidalis* (Europe) can exceed 30 cm in height and has spikes of red-purple bracts and violet-purple flowers. It spreads by emitting shoots from far-spreading roots and can be invasive, especially in peaty soils. *A. p.* 'Crispa' (*A. metallica* 'Crispa') has crinkly leaves with a metallic green-purple lustre. *A. reptans* (Europe to SW Asia) is the mat-forming common bugle with smooth leaves and 15-30 cm spikes of blue-purple flowers in spring and early summer. It has given rise to several garden-worthy cultivars: 'Alba' is white-flowered; 'Atropurpurea' ('Purpurea') has red-purple flushed leaves; 'Burgundy Glow' is similar but nearer to wine-red; 'Delight' is variegated with white and pink; 'Multicolor' ('Rainbow' 'Tricolor') has leaves bronze-flushed with a mottling of yellow, suffused pink; 'Pink Elf' is dwarf with pink flowers and 'Variegata' has each leaf splashed grey-green and white.

Alcea — see *Althaea*.

Alchemilla (Lady's Mantle) (*Rosaceae*)

Only one of the 250 kinds of lady's mantle is large enough for the herbaceous garden and this happens also to be the finest. *A. mollis* (Carpathians to Turkey) is a clump-former with toothed, softly hairy, mantle-shaped leaves to 15 cm wide which, in early summer, are over-topped by a foam of tiny lime-green flowers much beloved by the flower arranger. It thrives in sun or shade in ordinary soil and can be propagated by division or seeds. Self-sown seedlings invariably appear if the soil does not get too dry.

Alstroemeria (Peruvian Lily) (*Alstroemeriaceae*)

Most of the 60 species in this genus (all S. American) are too tender for general planting outside, though some will survive at the foot of a south wall. They are tuberous rooted, producing erect stems and clad with narrow, upside-down leaves and topped by clusters of lily-like flowers generally in pastel shades though often strikingly spotted or streaked. The following species and hybrids are hardy in well-drained soil in sunny sheltered sites. They should be planted in spring. Propagation is by careful division at planting time or by sowing seeds under glass in spring. The latter are best sown singly in small pots, or pricked off singly when very small. *A. aurantiaca* (Chile) is the best known and hardiest, eventually forming sizeable colonies of 90 cm stems, and bright orange, red-streaked flowers in summer. *A. a.* 'Dover Orange' is a richer shade of orange; 'Aurea' is golden-yellow, while 'Lutea' is a true yellow. *A. brasiliensis* (C. Brazil) needs a sheltered site but is otherwise hardy, producing stems to 1.2 m, very narrow leaves and red-flushed yellow flowers with mahogany spots. *A. chilensis* (Chile) also needs a sheltered place and bears pink to creamy-white blossoms. The true species is seldom obtainable, one of the Ligtu Hybrids sometimes masquerading in its place. *A. hookeri* (Chile) is rather like a 30 cm-tall pink-flowered *A. ligtu*. *A. ligtu* is not unlike *A. aurantiaca* but more graceful and with pink to pale-red flowers streaked crimson. The true species is seldom offered, being now largely replaced by the more colourful and vigorous Ligtu Hybrids in shades of pink to orange-red, yellow and white.

Althaea (*Alcea*) (Hollyhock) (*Malvaceae*)

Traditional cottage-garden plants, the tall hollyhocks with their spires of varied-hued hibiscus-shaped flowers are familiar to all. They thrive in ordinary soil and are best in full sun. Propagation is by seeds sown in spring, the young plants set out in their permanent sites when two or three true leaves have formed. Modern cultivars can be short lived and it is well worth while seeking out some of the older sorts that are nearest to the species. *A. rosea* (China) is best known, with its broad, shallowly lobed leaves and stems to 3 m or more. Less readily obtainable are *A. ficifolia* (yellow or orange) and *A. cannabina* (pink), less massive species with fingered leaves which form clumps when mature.

Alyssoides (*Cruciferae*)

Four species make up this genus but only one is cultivated. *A. utriculata* (S. Europe) looks like a blend of alyssum and wallflower, with stems to 40 cm bearing oblong to spathulate leaves and racemes of small, bright-yellow fragrant flowers in spring and summer. Its main attraction however is in the inflated seed pods which can be used in dried flower arrangements. Any well-drained soil in a sunny site is suitable. Propagation is by sowing seeds in spring or by cuttings in late summer.

Amsonia (Blue Star) (*Apocynaceae*)

Most of the 25 species in this genus are undistinguished, but one has a quiet attraction and is worthy of a place in the border. This is *A. tabernaemontana*, a clump-former from N. America with erect stems to 60 cm clad with elliptic to ovate leaves and topped by heads of pale-blue starry flowers in summer. *A. t. salicifolia*, often offered as a species in its own right, is less erect and has slender willow-like leaves which are glaucous beneath. Plants can be set out at any time from autumn to spring. Propagation is by division or by seeds in spring.

Anaphalis (Pearly Everlasting) (*Compositae*)

The 35 species in this genus are typified by their terminal clusters of small, summer-borne everlasting flowers which can be dried for winter decoration. The individual flowerheads are daisy-like, but lack true petals, their place being taken by white or cream chaffy bracts. All species are easily grown in ordinary well-drained soil in a sunny site; some are rhizomatous and can be invasive. Planting can take place from autumn to spring. Propagation is by division at planting time, but preferably in spring. *A. cinnamomea* (*A. yedoensis*) (mountains of India and Burma) is possibly the most handsome of the taller species with erect stems to 75 cm clad with lance-shaped leaves that are fringed and covered beneath with white felt. It is rhizomatous and forms wide colonies. *A. margaritacea* (N. America, E. Asia) reaches 60 cm in height and has very narrow leaves, grey-downy beneath, and pearly-white flowers. *A. nubigena* (China and Tibet) is the smallest cultivated species and suitable only for the very front of the border. Seldom above 20 cm, it has lanceolate leaves, grey-felted beneath and numerous flowers in small clusters. *A. triplinervis* (Himalayas) forms dense clumps to 45 cm tall which bear obovate leaves that are grey-felted beneath, cottony above and are prominently three-veined. *A. t.* 'Summer Snow' is dwarfer, with whiter flowerheads.

Anchusa (Alkanet) (*Boraginaceae*)

Fifty species of annuals and perennials make up this genus. Most are rather weedy but one is indispensable in the perennial garden, providing an abundance of rich blue flowers in early summer. This is *A. azurea* (*A. italica*), which despite its *italica* synonym, comes from the Caucasus. It is a hispid plant 90-150 cm tall having narrow leaves and large terminal clusters of blue to blue-purple flowers. *A. a.* 'Little John' is short and sturdy to 45 cm, with deep-blue flowers 'Loddon Royalist' has gentian-blue flowers on 90 cm stems, while the tall 'Opal', up to 2 m, is sky blue. If a really dwarf anchusa is required, *A. angustissima*, from Turkey, grows to about 30 cm tall and produces bright-blue flowers from late spring. It is sometimes confused with the very dwarf *A. caespitosa*, a rare species for the scree garden. For *Anchusa myosotidiflora*, see *Brunnera macro-*

phylla. A. sempervirens (now *Pentaglottis sempervirens*) has large, coarse leaves, a deeply delving ineradicable tap root, bright but small blue flowers and an over-free self-seeding habit. There are deep and very pale-blue forms, all for the wild garden only. All the anchusas thrive in ordinary soil, for *A. azurea*, ideally enriched with decayed manure. Planting is best in autumn or spring. Propagation is by root cuttings in late winter, division or by sowing seeds spring.

Anemone (Windflower) (*Ranunculaceae*)

The 150 species of anemone are of cosmopolitan distribution and vary much in form and stature. Their often showy flowers are composed of 5-20 or more petal-like sepals known as tepals. Many species are dwarf, arising from tuber-like or slender rhizomes, and flower early. They can be useful at the front of a mixed border but are generally too small and ephemeral elsewhere. Some species are fibrous rooted, tall and bloom in summer and autumn. Among this group are several indispensable border perennials. All thrive in ordinary soil, tolerate a fair amount of shade and can be planted from autumn to spring. Division at planting time or by sowing seeds when ripe or in spring are easy means of increase. *A. hupehensis*: plants grown under this name are invariably cultivars of *A. hybrida*, though the true plant is occasionally available. It grows to 60 cm and has trifoliate leaves, each leaflet being unequally three-lobed and toothed. The flowers which open in late summer are always five-tepalled, red-flushed in bud, opening lilac-pink. *A. h.* 'Superba' is more vigorous and is the clone most likely to be encountered in cultivation though not easy to acquire. *A. h.* 'September Charm' is similar but superior and may be of hybrid origin. It grows to 75 cm and has rose-pink flowers some of which are composed of six or seven tepals. *A. h. japonica* is distinguished by having flowers of many narrow tepals, but it is rare and less desirable than its hybrid cultivars. *A.* X *hybrida* (*A. elegans, A. japonica* of gardens), this name covers all the so-called Japanese anemones but in fact, blends the characters of *A. hupehensis japonica* and *A. vitifolia*. It most resembles the first parent but is taller, with leaflets often having seven lobes and flowers usually with seven to nine or more tepals. All the following cultivars are very garden worthy, blooming in late summer and autumn. In moist fertile soils they can be invasive: 'Bressingham Glow', compact habit to 60 cm, almost double, rosy-red; 'Lorelei', pale pink, about 1 m tall; 'Louise Uhink', large semi-double flowers on 1 m stems; 'Margarete', rich pink, almost double, 1 m; 'Mont Rose', rose-pink, double, 75 cm; 'Profusion', one of the smallest, 45-60 cm, bearing almost double deep-pink flowers; 'Queen Charlotte', semi-double, rose-pink, darker in bud, 1 m tall; 'Whirlwind', semi-double, pure white, to 1.2 m. *A.* X *lesseri* (*A. multifida* X *A. sylvestris*) is a variable hybrid of tufted habit with glossy palmate leaves and freely borne small flowers in shades of white, yellow, purple, pink, red, though only the last mentioned colour is commonly available. *A. narcissiflora* is one of the joys of the mountains of Europe and Asia where it can occur in localised profusion. Clump-forming to 60 cm it produces palmate, deeply toothed leaves and clustered white flowers often purple-flushed in bud. *A. rivularis* (Himalayas) has a tuberous rhizome and three-lobed leaves but is otherwise like *A. narcissiflora* with lustrous, bluish-flushed buds. *A. sylvestris* is also known as the snowdrop anemone or windflower. From Europe and W. Asia, it has deeply lobed leaves and nodding, fragrant solitary white flowers from spring onwards. It can be invasive on light soil. *A. tomentosa* (Himalayas and China), this is much like a very robust form of the next species and is often confused with it; as 'Robustissima' it may be listed in catalogues as a cultivar of *A. vitifolia*. It grows to 1.2 m and has soft pink flowers from late summer onwards. The true *A. vitifolia* reaches only 60 cm and has vine-like leaves and white flowers. *A. v.* 'Alba Dura' has purple buds and may be of hybrid origin.

Anthemis (Golden Marguerite) (*Compositae*)

Although many of the 200 species in this genus are annuals and weeds it also includes the golden marguerite and its hybrids, indispensable daisies for the perennial garden. They thrive in ordinary soil in sun and can be planted any time from autumn to spring. Propagation is by division, ideally in spring. *A. tinctoria* is the main species, forming dense clumps 60-90 cm tall with dissected leaves, and yellow daisies in summer. Crossed with the orange *A. sancti-johannis*, a rarely grown species from Bulgaria, it has given rise to most of the popular cultivars, e.g. 'Grallach Gold', bright orange-yellow; 'E.C. Buxton', lemon yellow. These and other cultivars need regularly dividing to maintain vigorous plants.

Anthericum (St Bernard's Lily) (*Liliaceae*)

Very few of the 300 members of this widespread genus are hardy or particularly decorative, and only one is commonly available. *A. liliago* (S. Europe to Turkey) is the St Bernard lily, a clump-former to 60 cm with grey-green, grassy leaves and wands of starry pure-white flowers in early summer. The plant listed as *A. algeriense* is almost certainly a robust form of *A. liliago*, with stems to 90 cm. *A. ramosum* (Europe) is the same height but bears its smaller flowers in airy panicles.

Aquilegia (Columbine) (*Ranunculaceae*)

Depending on the botanical authority there are 70-100 species of columbine scattered around the northern hemisphere. Several of these are very desirable hardy perennials and some have given rise to very popular cultivars and strains. They require moisture-retentive but well-drained, ideally humus-rich soil and thrive in partial shade or sun. Planting can be done in autumn or spring. Propagation is by division at planting time, or by seeds when ripe, or in spring. *A. alpina* (Switzerland) is a connoisseur's plant and should be tried more often in its wild form with its shapely deep-blue flowers poised on 30 cm stems (see also under 'Hensol Harebell'). *A. atrata* (C. Europe) has dark violet-purple to almost black flowers but otherwise resembles *A. vulgaris*. *A. caerulea* (W. North America) varies from 30-60 cm in height, with erect, long-spurred blossoms of blue and white. *A. canadensis* (N. America) is one of the brightest and most elegant. It has stems 30-40 cm tall and yellow flowers with large red spurs; there are many inferior forms and hybrids. *A. chrysantha* (SW USA) is one of the tallest with stems 90-120 cm, bearing flowers in tones of pale and deep yellow. It is not often grown but is an important parent of the long-spur hybrids – see *A.* X *hybrida*. *A. formosa* (W North America) is another parent of the long-spur hybrids, but well worth growing in its own right, each branching 60-90 cm stems bearing flights of flowers similar to those of *A. canadensis*, but later with larger, widely flared petals of orange-red. *A.* 'Hensol Harebell' combines the best qualities of its parents *A. alpina* and *A. vulgaris*. The true plant is deep purple-blue and up to 90 cm tall, but other shades and statures are sometimes listed under this name. *A.* X *hybrida* covers crosses between *A. chrysantha*, *formosa, caerulea* and *vulgaris* which have resulted in the long-spurred and short-spurred hybrids, each with several strains and cultivars. The long-spurred are most popular and decorative and come in a wide colour range, e.g. 'McKana' and 'Monarch'. 'Crimson Star' and 'Snow Queen' are single-colour seed strains. *A. longissima* (Texas to Mexico) is another neglected species with stems 60-70 cm tall bearing long-spurred, pale-yellow flowers. *A. pyrenaica* (Pyrenees, N. Spain) is cast in the mould of *A. alpina* but has smaller flowers of purple-blue. *A. viridiflora* (Siberia, China) is essentially a collector's or flower arranger's plant, its 30-40 cm stems carrying shapely fragrant blossoms in tones of green and yellow-green to brownish-purple. *A. vulgaris* (Europe) is the common columbine so frequent in the older gardens where it can become almost a weed. It bears its rather squat flowers in great profusion in a range of colours. Best known is the semi-double granny's bonnets with flowers like classical ballet skirts; *A. v.* 'Clemataquila', 'Clematiflora' and 'Stellata' are all spurless mutants of similar form.

Armeria (Thrift) (*Plumbaginaceae*)

Surprisingly enough there are 80 species in this genus, all variations on a theme of the very familiar thrift. They thrive in ordinary well-drained soil and can be planted from autumn to spring. Propagation is by division at planting time, or by seeds in spring. *A. alliacea* (*A. arenaria*, *A. plantaginea*) (West Europe) is a robust species to 50 cm with broad grassy leaves and flowers in shades of red-purple or white, in summer. *A. maritima* only just qualifies as a front of the border plant, its stems usually less than 25-30 cm; superior cultivars are: 'Alba' (white), 'Bloodstone' (deep red), 'Corsica' (light brick-red), 'Perfection' (bright pink, large), 'Vindictive' (deep pink). *A. pseudar-meria* (*A. formosa*, *A. latifolia*) (Portugal) is akin to *A. alliacea* but has oblanceolate leaves and larger, usually white, flowerheads. It has crossed with *alliacea* and possibly *maritima* to give the brilliant pink 'Bees Ruby', and such seed strains as Formosa Hybrids.

Arnebia echioides (Prophet Flower) (*Boraginaceae*)

Of the 25 known species, this is the only one in general cultivation and it is all too seldom seen. Barely 30 cm tall, it makes a bright splash of yellow at the front of the border in early summer. When newly open each flower shows five basal black spots (the prophet's fingerprints) which gradually disappear in an intriguing fashion. It needs a fertile, well-drained soil and a sunny site and can be planted in autumn or spring. Propagate by root cuttings in late winter, by sowing seeds in spring or heel-cuttings of non-flowering shoots in late summer.

Arnica montana (Mountain Tobacco) (*Compositae*)

The only member of its 32-strong genus, this is a handsome daisy ally which deserves to be tried more often. From a tuft of bold, oblong lanceolate leaves arise stems 30 cm or more tall, each topped by an 8 cm-wide orange-yellow daisy in early summer. It needs a humus-rich well-drained soil that does not dry out and should be planted autumn or spring. Propagation is by division or by sowing seeds in spring.

Artemisia (Wormwood) (*Compositae*)

About 400 members of this varied genus are recognised, including annuals, perennials and shrubs mostly from the northern hemisphere. They are grown mainly for their often dissected foliage which is usually grey or silvery hairy. They grow in ordinary, well-drained soil and need a sunny site. Planting is best in autumn and spring. Propagation is by division at planting time. *A. absinthium*, common wormwood (Europe), is really a sub-shrub with a woody base and annual stems to 90 cm. In the best form, 'Lambrook Silver', the leaves are silvery grey. It should be cut back to near ground level each late winter and may be propagated by basal cuttings in late spring, or by seeds. *A. canescens*, see comment under *A. splendens*. *A. discolor* (W. North America) is a suckering, sub-shrubby plant that can be invasive, but is very decorative, with erect stems to 45 cm and white-hairy, pinnate or bipinnate leaves. *A. gnaphalodes* – see under *A. ludoviciana*. *A. lactiflora* Chinese mugwort (China, India) forms dense clumps to 1.8 m in height and is a true border perennial. Unlike most artemisias it is grown for its large, plume-like heads of tiny cream flowers in late summer. *A. ludoviciana*, western mugwort, white sage (C. North America), is a white woolly rhizomatous perennial to 1.2 m tall. It differs from most of the species discussed here, in having undivided, lance-shaped leaves with or without a few lobes or teeth. *A. l. gnaphalodes* is scarcely different, smaller and with some leaves oblanceolate; 'Silver Queen' is similar but more silvery. *A. maritima*, sea wormwood, (coasts of W. and N. Europe) much resembles a more silvery and smaller version of *A. absinthium*. *A. m. nutans* (*A. nutans* of some catalogues) is slenderer and more graceful – not to be confused with the much larger true *A. nutans*, a rare sub-shrub from USSR. *A. palmeri* (of gardens) is a smaller version of *A. ludoviciana* (the true species has pinnately cut leaves and is seldom cultivated). *A. pontica* (C. and E. Europe) varies from 40-80 cm tall, depending on soil and situation, and has densely white-downy, pinnatifid or bipinnatifid leaves. *A. purshiana* is now considered to be a variant of *A. ludoviciana*, usually of lesser stature and with whiter, lanceolate to ovate leaves. *A. splendens* (Turkey) forms hummocks to 30 cm or more composed of silvery, dissected and curled leaves. It is often confused with the allied *A. canescens* (to 45 cm tall). *A. stellerana*, beach wormwood (NE Asia, naturalised in N. Europe and NE North America). This is a rhizomatous perennial 30-60 cm tall with white felted leaves, and makes a fine substitute for *Senecio cineraria* (*Cineraria maritima*) in cold gardens. *A. vallesiaca* (Switzerland, France) has affinities with *A. splendens/canescens*, but the leaves arch outwards from their 40-50 cm-tall stems.

Aruncus dioicus (Goat's Beard) (*Rosaceae*)

Of the twelve species recognised, only this one is commonly grown. Formerly known as *Spiraea aruncus* and *Aruncus sylvester* and found throughout the northern hemisphere, it makes a massive clump of bold, fern-like foliage topped by large airy plumes of minute creamy-white flowers in summer. Well-grown plants will reach 2 m in height and can be used very effectly as isolated specimens. *A. d. astilboides* is a dwarf replica to 60 cm, while *A. d. triternatus* is a miniature from Nepal, to only 30 cm. *A. d.* 'Kneiffii' is more curious than beautiful, with very narrow, irregularly shaped leaflets and stems to 1 m tall. Ordinary but preferably moisture-retentive soil is suitable, and a site in either sun or shade. Planting can be carried out from autumn to spring. Propagation is by division at planting time or by sowing seeds in spring.

Arundo donax (Giant Reed) (*Gramineae*)

Despite the vernacular name, this is a true grass and the giant of its genus. Evergreen and clump-forming from a woody base, it produces stems to 3 m or more, clad with strap-shaped, grey-green leaves. The plumy, typically grassy flowering panicles are seldom produced in Britain. *A. d.* 'Versicolor' ('Variegata') is smaller, with white striped leaves, but not very hardy. Although fairly hardy, this giant grass needs a sheltered, sunny site to thrive well, and moisture-retentive but otherwise ordinary soil. It should be planted in spring. It is propagated by division at planting time or by cuttings of sideshoots in a sand-frame in summer.

Asclepias (Milkweed) (*Asclepiadaceae*)

Most of the 120 sorts of milkweed are either shrubby or too tender for outside planting but a few N. American species make interesting additions to the hardy perennial garden. They need fertile, moisture-retentive soil and sunny, at least moderately sheltered, sites. Planting should be in spring. Propagation is by careful division at planting time, or by sowing seeds under glass in spring. Most species exude a poisonous milky latex when cut or broken. *A. incarnata*, swamp milkweed, forms small clumps of erect stems that can attain 1.5 m in height, each stem clad with pairs of pointed leaves and terminal clusters of pink flowers in summer. It grows well in wet soil. *A. speciosa* is rhizomatous with stems 1-2 m tall and large, oval, grey-green leaves. The horned, greenish-purple flowers appear in late summer to autumn. *A. syriaca* (*A. cornuti*), common milkweed, is similar to *A. speciosa*, but with dull-purple flowers. *A. tuberosa* is tuberous rooted and clump-forming, with deep-orange flowers on 45 cm stems. It is however unreliably hardy and fails to thrive in some gardens.

Asphodeline (Yellow Asphodel) (*Liliaceae*)

One, sometimes two species represent this 15-strong genus, from the Mediterranean and W. Asia. They are clump-forming, with erect stems clad in grassy foliage and terminating in racemes of starry flowers in late spring and early summer. Any well-drained soil in a sunny site is suitable. Late summer is the best planting time or during mild spells throughout the autumn and winter. Propagate by division at planting time, or by seeds under glass in spring. *A. liburnica*

(SE Europe) is like the more familiar next species but somewhat smaller and slenderer with paler flowers a little later. *A. lutea*, king's spear (E. Mediterranean), grows to 90 cm, with grey-green leaves and bright-yellow flowers, each tepal with a green central stripe. Large berry-like capsules follow.

Asphodelus (Asphodel) (*Liliaceae*)

Although related to *Asphodeline* and having the same geographical distribution, the twelve true asphodels are easily distinguished by their much longer leaves in dense basal clumps and almost leafless flowering racemes. Culture is as for *Asphodeline*. *A. aestivus* (*A. microcarpus*, *A. ramosus*) (S. Europe) is similar to the better-known *A. albus*, but with flowers to 2 cm wide which are often pink-flushed in bud. *A. albus*, white asphodel (S. Europe) forms robust clumps 60-90 cm tall with white flowers to 5 cm wide in late spring. *A. cerasiferus* (S. Europe) is akin to *A. albus* but has branched racemes.

Asplenium scolopendrium (Hart's Tongue) (*Aspleniaceae*)

Better known as *Phyllitis scolopendrium* or *Scolopendrium vulgare*, this fern is the only member of a 650-species-strong genus hardy and large enough to take its place in the perennial garden. It is clump-forming with arching, glossy, tongue-like leaves to 30 cm or more long, somewhat wavy-margined and carried on strong stalks. Several mutant forms have arisen, some with crested tips or irregular lobes which add nothing to its beauty. Plants listed as *A. s.* 'Crispum' and 'Undulatum' are however exceptions to this comment, having beautifully crimped or waved leaf margins. Hart's tongue grows in all soils that are not too dry and is best in shade; it will grow even where the sun's rays never penetrate. Planting can be carried out from autumn to spring with propagation by division at the same time.

Aster (Michaelmas Daisy) (*Compositae*)

Among the 500 species in this genus are several mainstays of the perennial garden, providing colourful daisy flowers from late summer to the end of autumn. They are clump-forming with erect stems and give the best effect planted in groups. Ordinary soil that does not dry out excessively is best and a sunny or lightly shaded site. Planting can take place from autumn to spring, and propagation by division in spring is easy. For the best flowers on *A. novi-belgii* cultivars, plants should be divided into rooted single shoots annually. The following are all N. American and flower late summer to autumn unless otherwise stated. *A. acris* – see *A. sedifolius. A. amellus* (C. and S. Europe) is a hoary green plant to 60 cm with solitary purple and yellow daisies to 8 cm wide; several cultivars are available, including 'King George' (violet-blue) and 'Brilliant' (bright pink). *A. cordifolius* spreads by rhizomes and eventually forms wide clumps of stems to 1.2 m tall bearing heart-shaped leaves and large clusters of small, pale violet-purple flowers. *A. c.* 'Silver Spray' is white. *A. divaricatus* (*A. corymbosus*) has slender, deep-purple, somewhat zigzag stems to 60 cm, narrowly to widely heart-shaped leaves and white flowers with yellow discs that age purple. *A. ericoides* is a bushy plant to 1 m tall having spathulate basal and linear stem leaves; tiny white or blue-tinted flowers appear in great profusion in autumn; *A. e.* 'Esther' is pink, 'Cinderella', blue; 'Ringdove', rosy-mauve. *A. farreri* (W. China, Tibet) forms clumps of narrowly spathulate leaves and erect, sparsely leafy 45 cm stems topped by solitary, blue-purple, orange-yellow-centred daisies to 7 cm wide, in early summer. *A.* X. *frikartii* 'Mönch' (*A. amellus* X *A. thomsonii*) grows to 80 cm and combines the best of both parents, bearing clusters of satiny lavender-purple and orange-yellow flowers in early autumn; *A.* X *f.* 'Flora's Delight' is dwarfer, to 50 cm. *A. horizontalis* — see under *A. lateriflorus*. *A. hybridus luteus* — see X *Solidaster luteus*. *A. lateriflorus* (erroneously as '*laterifolius*' in some catalogues) grows 60-90 cm tall with wide-spreading branches, lanceolate leaves and purple-centred white or pink-tinted flowers in autumn. *A. l. horizontalis* (of gardens) has longer branches and slightly larger flowers. *A. linosyris* (*Crinitaria linosyris*, *Lynosyris vulgaris*) differs from most other species in having flowers with prominent yellow discs and no ray florets; its wiry stems reach 50-60 cm in height. *A. novae-angliae* is one of the familiar Michaelmas daisies having hairy, woody-based stems 1.3-2 m tall, stem-clasping, harsh-textured lanceolate leaves and 3-5 cm-wide flowers with numerous narrow rays; several fine cultivars in shades of pink and purple are available. *A. novi-belgii* (common Michaelmas daisy) is represented in gardens by cultivars mostly of hybrid origin with such allied species as *A. dumosus* and *A. laevis*. All have smooth stems and leaves and vary greatly in stature and flower size. Many cultivars are available ranging in height from 25 cm to 1.5 m and in shades of white, pink, red, purple and blue. *A. paniculatus* (*A. simplex* and *A. tradescantii* of gardens) much resembles a larger replica of *A. ericoides* with white flowers. *A. sedifolius* (*A. acris*) (S. and E. Europe) grows 60-90 cm tall and produces a profusion of bright blue-mauve flowers in late summer — a lovely prelude to the Michaelmas daisy season. *A. s.* 'Nanus' is dwarf and compact to 45 cm. *A. thomsonii* (W. Himalayas) is seldom seen, being largely represented in cultivation by the 45 cm-tall *A. t.* 'Nanus' which rather resembles a smaller, paler version of *A.* X *frikartii*; *A. thomsonii* itself grows 60-90 cm tall. *A. tongolensis* (W. China) (*A. subcaeruleus*, *A. yunnanensis*) is, in effect, a finer version of *A. farreri*; *A. t.* 'Berggarten' and 'Napsbury' are finer still, with deep blue-purple, orange-centred flowers. *A. turbinellus* is a slender, elegant Michaelmas daisy to 1 m or more, with stem-clasping leaves and violet-blue flowers in autumn.

Astilbe (False Goatsbeard) (*Saxifragaceae*)

Eastern Asia and E. North America are the home territories of the 25 known astilbes. All are pleasing in their ways and some are outstandingly beautiful with their dissected, often fern-like foliage topped by frothy plumes of tiny flowers. Moisture-retentive fertile soil is essential, and ideally a site in partial shade, though full sun is tolerated if the soil is permanently moist. Planting can take place in autumn or spring. Propagation is by division at planting time, or by sowing seeds in spring. Seedlings usually take two years to flower. *A.* X *arendsii* covers the popular hybrid group raised in Germany at the turn of the century, between *A. A. davidii*, *astilboides*, *japonica* and *thunbergii*. They vary from 45-150 cm in height with shapely summer-borne white, pink or purple plumes, and often dark or coppery-tinted foliage; several cultivars are listed, all very garden worthy. *A. chinensis* (*A. sinensis*) (China) grows to 90 cm with white, pink or purple-flushed flowers in summer; it is seldom grown, being represented in gardens mainly by *A. c. pumila*, a 45 cm-tall plant with dense clusters of mauve-pink flowers and a colonising habit which makes it useful as a front of the border subject. *A. c. davidii* is usually listed as a species in its own right, having stems to 1.2 m, more dissected leaves and red-purple flowers. *A. taquetii* (E. China) rather resembles a finer *A. chinensis davidii*, with bolder, brighter floral plumes and broader leaves.

Astrantia (Masterwort) (*Umbelliferae*)

Of the ten recognised species of masterwort three to four are available. All are quietly attractive and much in demand by flower arrangers. They are distinct from most other members of the carrot family in having their umbels of tiny flowers surrounded by a ruff of petal-like, coloured bracts. Ordinary soil is suitable, ideally laced with leafmould or compost, and a site in sun or partial shade. Planting can take place from autumn to spring. Propagation is by division at planting time, or by sowing seeds when ripe or in spring. *A. carniolica* (Italy, Austria, Yugoslavia) is a slender plant to 30 cm or more with basal leaves composed of five to seven leaflets and white or pink-flushed flowerheads; there is confusion with *A. major*, and robust plants with obovate to lanceolate leaves are invariably that species. *A. major* (C. and E. Europe) is the best-known species, a clump-former 60-90 cm tall with branched stems and greenish-white, sometimes pink or purple-tinted flowerheads in summer. *A. m. rubra* has plum-red heads; 'Sunningdale Variegated', yellow-splashed and striped leaves; *A. m. carinthiaca* (*A. m. involucrata* of gardens) has much larger floral bracts; the cultivar 'Shaggy' is a white-bracted form of this. *A. maxima* (*A. helleborifolia*) (Caucasus, Turkey) has trifoliate leaves and slender stems 40-60 cm tall, bearing a few rose-pink heads in summer.

Athyrium (Lady Fern) (*Athyriaceae*)

Although of world-wide distribution in temperate climates, and often extremely decorative, very few of the 180 species in this genus are cultivated. The two mentioned here are excellent shade plants, growing in ordinary soil that does not dry out. They can be planted from autumn to spring and are easily propagated by division. *A. felix-femina* (common lady fern) occurs throughout the north temperate zone and on tropical mountains. It is clump-forming with finely dissected, tapered, bright-green fronds to 1 m long. They make a fine contrast for the bold paddles of hosta and bergenia. There are cultivars with crested or tasselled fronds but they lack the simple elegance of the species. *A. goeringianum* 'Pictum' has fronds 30 cm long which are charmingly banded silver-grey.

Avena – see *Helictotrichon*.

Ballota (Horehound) (*Labiatae*)

Only two members of this genus of 35 species are much cultivated. Both are sub-shrubby but are invariably associated with hardy perennials in the garden. They need well-drained soil and a sunny site. Planting is best in spring and propagation by cuttings in spring or late summer. *B. acetabulosa* (Greece, Crete) can reach 60 cm in height and more in width, its stems and paired, heart-shaped leaves densely white-woolly. The small, two-lipped rose, purple and white flowers are not showy. *B. pseudodictamnus* (S. Aegean) is confused with *B. acetabulosa* but easily distinguished by the yellowish caste to its equally woolly leaves.

Baptisia (False Indigo) (*Leguminosae*)

All the 35 species of false indigo are native to N. America. They are erect, branched plants with trifoliate leaves and short lupin-like spikes of pea flowers. They thrive in humus-rich soil in sun or partial shade and can be planted in autumn or spring. Propagation is by division at planting time, or sowing seeds in spring. *B. australis* (*B. exaltata*) is the only species generally available. About 1.2 m tall, it has bluish-green leaves and flowers of soft indigo-blue. Worth looking out for are *B. leucantha* (white) and *B. tinctoria* (yellow). All flower in summer.

Barbarea (*Cruciferae*)

As American land or winter cress, two members of the 20 species in this genus are cultivated as salad plants. A variegated form of one makes an unusual foliage plant for the perennial garden. *B. vulgaris* 'Variegata' produces neat rosettes of pinnately lobed leaves which are rather inelegantly marbled creamy yellow. The spikes of small yellow flowers are best removed unless seeds are required. Unusually for a variegated plant it comes at least partially true from seed. A moisture-retentive soil and a position in sun or partial shade are best. Propagate by seeds or by taking small side rosettes as cuttings in spring.

Belamcanda (*Iridaceae*)

There are only two species in this E. Asian genus, one of which is sometimes cultivated. *B. chinensis* is an iris-like plant to 50 cm tall with slender branched stems bearing orange-red to orange-yellow purple-brown spotted flowers in summer. They are rather like those of a large sisyrinchium. Iris-like capsules of glossy black seeds follow. A well-drained but moisture-retentive soil is needed, and a sheltered site in partial shade is preferred, though full sun is tolerated. Planting is best in spring. Propagate by division or by sowing seeds in spring.

Bergenia (*Megasea, Saxifraga*) (*Saxifragaceae*)

Six species and many more hybrid cultivars comprise this useful and decorative genus. Their paddle-shaped evergreen leaves make good ground cover at all times and the showy flowers are often produced in abundance. Ordinary soil is suitable, ideally laced with humus, and a partially shaded site preferred though they also thrive in sun. Planting can take place from autumn to spring. Propagate by division at planting time or by cuttings of stem sections in late winter. Seeds can be sown in spring but usually take two years to flower. A selection of the best hybrid cultivars follows the species described below. *B. ciliata* (W. Himalayas) has conspicuously hairy leaves to 25 cm long and white flowers which age reddish. *B. c. ligulata* differs in its smooth leaves with only a fringe of hairs on the margins; both it and *B. ciliata* can be partially deciduous and are unreliably hardy. *B. cordifolia* (Siberia) has rounded leaves with a heart-shaped base and somewhat crinkly margins. Pale to deep rose-pink flowers are borne in panicles to 40 cm tall in spring. *B. c.* 'Purpurea' has purple-flushed foliage especially in winter, and darker flowers. *B. crassifolia* (Siberia) is similar to *cordifolia* but the more oval leaves have wedge-shaped to rounded bases. Rose-purple flowers are borne on stems to 30 cm tall and often start to open among the leaves in late winter. *B. c. pacifica* has deep purple flowers. *B. purpurascens* (*B. delavayi,*

B. beesiana) (Himalayas to W. China) in bloom is the tallest of the species, achieving 40-60 cm, the nodding red-purple to deep-pink flowers being carried on reddish stems above convex, red-flushed leaves. *B. p.* 'Ballawley' ('Delbees') is a vigorous magenta-flowered plant which arose between the entities *B. delavayi* and *B. beesiana* before they were amalgamated. *B.* X *schmidtii* (*B. ciliata* X *B. crassifolia*) is much like *B. crassifolia* but with larger pink flowers and hairy leaf margins. *B.* X *smithii* (*B. cordifolia* X *B. purpurascens*) favours *B. cordifolia* with reddish or purple-margined leaves; several cultivars of this parentage are available, including 'Bressingham Bountiful' (fuchsia-pink), 'Margery Fish' (glowing pink), 'Sunningdale' (deep purple). *B. strachyi* (W. Himalayas, Afghanistan) is the smallest species with more erect paddle-shaped leaves and white flowers ageing pink; the flower buds are frost tender. Several bergenia cultivars are of complex or unknown parentage. Among the best are: 'Abendglut', ('Evening Glow') with deep-purple flowers and maroon winter leaves; 'Morgenrote' ('Morning Red'), red purple, and 'Silberlicht' ('Silver Light') having white petals that age pinkish from red-brown calyces.

Berkheya macrocephala (*Compositae*)

Out of 90 species – all African – this is the only one in general cultivation. It is a clump-forming plant with handsome, if rather spiny, thistle-like leaves on stems to 90 cm. The bright-yellow daisy flowers are surrounded by spiny bracts, and open in summer. Well-drained, fertile soil and a sunny site are required. Planting is best in spring and propagation by division or seeds at the same time. The less hardy *B. onopordifolia* is sometimes available, but though not without attraction it is inferior to *B. macrocephala*.

Betonica – see *Stachys*.

Blechnum (Hard Fern) (*Blechnaceae*)

The 220 species in this genus of ferns have a world-wide distribution. Most of them are not hardy in Britain and of those that are, few are readily available. Those described here are attractively evergreen and combine well with shade-loving flowering perennials. They need moisture-retentive but well-drained soil, ideally enriched with peat or leafmould; they thrive in shade or sun. Planting is best in autumn or spring with propagation by division at the latter time. *B. chilense* (temperate S. America) can, when well established, produce its fingered, crimped fronds to 60-90 cm in height. The young fronds are coppery and particulalry appealing. Best in partial shade, it slowly forms wide colonies. It is much confused in the trade with the similar but half-hardy *B. tabulare* (*Lomaria magellanica*) which produces its rosettes of leaves on short, erect, trunk-like rhizomes, *B. spicant* is the common hard fern of Britain, producing clumps of rich glossy-green, ladder-like leaves 30-45 cm long. It eventually forms colonies. *B. penna-marina* (south temperate zone) is similar but much smaller, forming wide, dense colonies which can be invasive.

Bletilla striata (*Orchidaceae*)

Also known as *Bletia hyacinthina*, this is one of the few hardy terrestrial orchids that is comparatively trouble free. Clump-forming, it has narrow, pleated leaves to 30 cm long and erect wiry stems up to twice this, bearing several rose-purple flowers in summer. The bulb-like pseudo-bulbs should be planted about 5-6 cm deep in humus-rich soil in sunny or partially shaded sites in spring. Propagation by division after flowering, or in spring as young growth commences.

Bocconia – see *Macleaya*.

Bouteloua (Signal Arm Grasses) (*Gramineae*)

Very few of the 40 species in this genus of grasses are cultivated. They are modest plants but intriguingly decorative with their erect, slender stems bearing one to several one-sided flower spikes like stiff arms. Ordinary well-drained soil and a sunny site are required. Planting is best in spring with propagation by division, or by sowing seeds at the same season. *B. gracilis*, blue grama (S. USA, N. Mexico) is densely tufted with very narrow leaves and one to three long, purplish-brown flower spikes on stems to 45 cm tall in late summer. It is sometimes listed as *B. oligostachya*. *B. curtipendula* (E. USA to Mexico) can form wide clumps when happily situated. The 60 cm-tall stems bear several to many short, spreading or reflexed flower spikes.

Boykinia (*Saxifragaceae*)

About eight species of clump-forming plants form this Japanese and N. American genus. They have an overall resemblance to *Heuchera* but the flower clusters have fewer, larger flowers. Ordinary soil that does not dry out, and partial shade provide suitable cultural requirements. Planting can take place from autumn to spring. Propagation is by division at planting time or by sowing seeds in spring. *B. aconitifolia* (E. USA) has long stalked, five to seven lobed leaves of kidney-shaped outline and flowering stems to 45 cm or more bearing pure-white blossoms in summer. *B. tellimoides* (*Peltoboykinia tellimoides*) (Japan) differs from *B. aconitifolia* in its rounded, shallowly lobed, peltate leaves and creamy flowers. *B. t. watanabei* has deeper lobed leaves and pale-yellow flowers.

Brittonastrum – see under *Agastache*.

Brunnera macrophylla (*Boraginaceae*)

Still often listed as *Anchusa myosotidiflora*, this is an easy to please, decorative and useful perennial. Its immediate appeal is in its showers of small, light-blue flowers exactly like forget-me-nots during spring and summer, but backed by substantial heart-shaped leaves which make good ground cover. *B. m.* 'Variegata' has the leaves broadly white margined, and forms with silvery grey markings occur, e.g. 'Langtrees'. It is best in partial shade in a soil that does not dry out, but it will grow almost anywhere. Planting can take place autumn to spring and propagation by division at the same time.

Bulbinella hookeri (*Liliaceae*)

This is the only member of a 20-strong, southern hemisphere genus which is hardy and easy going enough for the perennial garden. A native of New Zealand, it resembles exactly a yellow-flowered 40-60 cm tall *Asphodelus albus* and blooms in summer. Moisture-retentive, preferably neutral to acid soil is preferred, with a site in sun or partial shade. Planting in early summer or spring is best and propagation is by division, or by sowing seeds during the latter season.

Buphthalmum (Yellow Ox-eye Daisies) (*Compositae*)

At least two of the six members of this genus provide showy yellow daisy flowers. They grow best in moisture-retentive, humus-rich soil in sun or partial shade. Planting can take place from autumn to spring. Propagation is by division, ideally in spring. *B. salicifolium* (C. Europe) is the common ox-eye, forming clumps of narrow leaves and erect, branched stems 45-70 cm tall topped by 5 cm-wide yellow daisies in summer. *B. speciosum* (*Telekia speciosa*) (SE Europe) is a massive clump-former, with broad aromatic leaves to 30 cm long and branched stems to 1.5 m or more tall. The flowers are deep yellow and open in summer over a long period. It makes a fine isolated specimen plant.

Calamintha (Calamint) (*Labiatae*)

About six aromatic sub-shrubs and perennials comprise this genus, two of which provide modestly pleasing tufted plants for the front of the border. They grow in ordinary soil and are best in sun. Planting can take place from autumn to spring. Propagation is by division or by sowing seeds in spring. *C. grandiflora* (*Satureja grandiflora*) (Spain to Turkey) makes a bush to 45 cm tall, with coarsely toothed leaves and light pinkish-purple sage-like flowers in profusion summer to autumn. *C. nepeta* (*C. nepetoides*, *Satureja calamintha*) (mountains of S. and C. Europe) is erect to 40 cm or so, with sprays of lilac or white thyme-like flowers in late summer.

Caltha (Marsh Marigold) (*Ranunculaceae*)

Most of the 30 species in this genus are moisture lovers and inhabit the cooler parts of both hemispheres. The species described are variations on a theme of the marsh marigold or kingcup, a familiar plant of moist meadows and marshy places in Great Britain. In cultivation they will grow in any moist soil but are best where conditions stay wet. A sunny site is best. Planting can be carried out any time after flowering until the following spring. Propagate by division at planting time or by seeds when ripe. *C. howellii* (*C. biflora*) and *C. leptosepala* (W. USA) are white flowered and not very exciting. *C. minor* (N. Europe) is a small version of *C. palustris*, barely to 30 cm tall; *C. p. radicans* has running rooting stems. *C. palustris* is probably the finest species, a clump-former with robust stems 30 cm or more high, with glossy kidney-shaped leaves and satiny rich-yellow flowers. *C. p. alba* is white; *C. p.* 'Florapleno', 'Multiplex' and 'Monstrosa Plena' ('Plena') are fully double, and 'Plurisepala' ('Semi-Plena') is semi-double. *C. polypetala* (Caucasus, Turkey) resembles a robust *C. palustris*, sometimes to 60 cm tall.

Campanula (Bellflower) (*Campanulaceae*)

Most of the 300 species of bellflower are too small for inclusion here but among those that are tall enough there are several indispensable border perennials. They thrive in ordinary soil, ideally laced with humus, and in sunny or partially shaded sites. Planting can take place from autumn to spring. The following are summer-flowering unless otherwise stated. Propagation is by division at planting time or by sowing seeds under glass in spring. *C. alliariifolia* (Caucasus, Turkey) has heart-shaped basal leaves, and one-sided wand-like spikes to 60 cm tall, bearing creamy-white, nodding bells. *C.* X *burghaltii* (*C. latifolia* X *C. punctata*) can reach 60 cm, with large lavender to pale-lilac-grey bells. *C.* 'Van Houttei' is similar but darker. *C. carpatica* (Carpathian Mountains) is a variable species, the tallest forms — 30 cm or more — making eye-catching front-of-the-border plants, with their profusion of large, upwards-facing flowers in shades of blue, purple and white. *C. glomerata* (Europe) varies greatly in stature and flower colour but is always clearly identifiable by its dense terminal clusters of upward-facing bells. It spreads by rhizomes and can be invasive. Robust and very handsome are the 50-60 cm-tall *C. g. dahurica* (violet purple) and its deeper coloured, even more vigorous form 'Superba'. Almost as tall, and pure white is 'Crown of Snow' ('Schneekrone'); shorter sorts in shades of paler purple and white are available. *C. grandis* (*C. latiloba*) (Siberia) is close to *C. persicifolia* but has lavender-blue, stalkless flowers which face rigidly outwards on stiffer stems. 'Alba' is a white version; 'Percy Piper' is darker and more vigorous. *C. lactiflora* (Caucasus) forms dense clumps of erect stems to 1.5 m, each one topped by broad clusters of milky-blue, widely expanded bells. *C. l.* 'Alba' is white; 'Loddon Anna', lilac-pink; 'Prichards', violet-blue, while 'Pouffe' is very dwarf to about 25 cm. *C. latifolia* (Europe, W. Asia) is a clump-former to 1.5 m tall with heart-shaped basal leaves and erect racemes of large, nodding flowers in shades of violet-blue. *C. l.* 'Alba' is pure white and very effective as a specimen plant for a shady corner; 'Gloaming' is tinted mauve while 'Brantwood' and *C. l. macrantha* have wider violet-purple flowers. *C. persicifolia* is the popular peach-leaved bellflower from Europe and Asia. It forms wide clumps of dense narrow leaves and strong but slender stems to 90 cm, bearing wide, nodding bells of violet-blue. The evergreen leafage makes useful ground cover for sun or partial shade. *C. p.* 'Alba' and 'Snowdrift' are white, and 'Telham Beauty' has larger, darker blooms; 'Fleur de Neige' is double. *C. p.* 'Planiflora' and 'Planiflora Alba' are dwarf mutants to about 30 cm tall. *C. punctata* (E. Siberia, N. Japan) can be invasive on light soils but makes an intriguing front-of-border subject with its erect stems to about 30 cm, and large, tubular flowers to 5 cm long. Cream is the usual colour but mauve or pink-flushed forms are common, all thickly sprinkled inside with red dots. *C. pyramidalis*, chimney bellflower (N. Italy, Yugoslavia, Albania) though hardy in well-drained soil and sheltered, sunny sites is often thought of as a cool greenhouse pot plant with its 2 m tall spires of starry pale-blue or white flowers. *C. rapunculoides* (Europe) can only be described as a lovely pest. Once established in the garden its mixture of fleshy storage, and slender, fast-creeping, roots are impossible to eradicate entirely without resort to the more dangerous herbicides. It has long-stalked, coarsely toothed basal leaves and stiff but slender stems 45-90 cm tall bearing nodding, violet-blue flowers. Anyone who grows bellflowers from seed should beware of this plant which is often distributed under the names of choicer species – and of *Symphyandra* as well. *C. sarmatica* (Caucasus) has downy grey-green leaves and velvety grey-blue flowers on 30-45 cm stems; a clump-forming plant of distinction and worthy of more frequent planting. *C. trachelium* is the nettle-leaved bellflower from Europe and N. Africa to Siberia, a 60-90 cm-tall plant with harsh-textured, boldly toothed leaves and branched clusters of blue-purple to lilac bells. It spreads underground and can be invasive. *C. t.* 'Alba' is white; 'Bernice' double lilac. *C.* X 'Van Houttei' – see comments under *C.* X *burghaltii*.

Cardamine (*Cruciferae*)

About 160 species form this genus but only a handful are suitable for the perennial garden. They need moisture-retentive but otherwise ordinary soil and grow in sun or partial shade. Planting can take place from autumn to early spring. Propagation is by division at planting time, or after flowering, or by seeds when ripe or in spring. *C. asari-folia* (mountains of Europe) eventually forms mats of quite large, bright-green kidney-shaped, wavy leaves which are useful as ground cover. From spring to early summer, 25-40 cm-tall stems dispense a sequence of small, pure-white flowers, the first opening low down among the new leaves. *C. pratensis*, cuckoo flower, lady's smock (Europe) is the familiar springtime plant of moist meadows and roadsides, with pinnate leaves and stems 30-40 cm tall. *C. p.* 'Flora Pleno' has pleasingly double, longer-lasting flowers with leaves which produce plantlets when mature, thus providing an easy means of increase. *C. p.* 'Bountiful' is a larger, more vigorous and floriforous form of the wild plant. *C. raphanifolia* (*C. latifolia*) (mountains of S. Europe) resembles in some ways *C. asarifolia*, forming similar mats, but the leaves are pinnate (with a large terminal leaflet) and the flowers reddish-purple in taller racemes.

Carex (Sedge) (*Cyperaceae*)

Depending on the botanical authority, there are 1,500-2,000 different sedges of cosmopolitan distribution, mainly from wet soils and temperate climates. Only a few are widely grown, but several others have garden potential and are worth seeking out. They are grass-like plants grown primarily for their foliage, though some species have attractive catkin-like flowering and seeding heads. Moisture-retentive soil and sunny sites provide good growing conditions and spring is the best time to plant. Propagation is by division or by sowing seeds in spring. *C. buchananii* (New Zealand) forms dense tufts of slender, arching leaves to 40 cm which are bronzy beneath and pinkish or creamy-green above, the *en masse* effect being a unique shade of pinkish-brown. *C. elata* (*C. stricta*), tufted sedge (Europe, W. Asia) is clump-forming, with arching leaves 40-80 cm long. *C. e.* 'Aurea' has the young leaves golden yellow gradually ageing to green; also known as 'Bowles Golden' (after Edward Augustus Bowles who found it in the Norfolk Broadland) and sometimes listed erroneously in catalogues under *C. riparia*. *C. grayi* (E. North America) is grown primarily for its unique seeding heads which are almost globular, about 4 cm long and composed of rigidly inflated, beak-like green to bronze-tinted calyces, a must for the flower arranger who seeks the unusual. *C. morrowii* (Japan) forms low, arching clumps of deep glossy-green leaves 20-40 cm long. *C. m.* 'Variegata' has white-striped leaves but is not reliably hardy in cold winters. *C. m.* 'Evergold' is probably of hybrid origin and is hardy; each leaf bears a broad yellow stripe. *C. pendula* (Europe, W. Asia) is the great drooping sedge, forming tufts of long leaves and arching stems to 1.5 m long and bearing pendulous catkin-like seed spikes. Good for moist shade. *C. riparia*, greater pond sedge (Europe, W. Asia) is rhizomatous and can be invasive, its 1.5 m stems bearing semi-erect, deep-brown catkin-like flower spikes; it is best restricted to the margins of a large, informal pond. *C. r.* 'Variegata' has leaves white striped and is less vigorous. *C. r.* 'Aurea' — see under *C. elata*.

Carlina (Everlasting Thistle) (*Compositae*)

About 20 species of thistle-like plants form this genus. The flower-heads differ from those of the true thistles in having long, petal-like bracts which are strawy in texture. They require well-drained, preferably limy soil and a sunny site. Planting is best in early autumn or spring just as young growth starts. Propagation is by seeds sown when ripe or in spring. Root disturbance is resented at all stages. *C. acanthifolia* (Pyrenees to N. Greece) strictly should not be included as the flowerheads are stemless and the plants are monocarpic. However, it is so eye-catching with rosettes of 30 cm-long ornate leaves and great central lemon-yellow flowers to 14 cm wide that it is well worth the trouble of regular seed raising. *C. acaulis simplex* (*C. a.* 'Caulescens' of gardens) is a true perennial forming clumps of stems 30 cm or more high. Each stem bears one to six silvery bracted flower-heads in summer. *C. a. acaulis* has stemless or very short-stalked blooms.

Catananche caerulea (Blue Cupidone) (*Compositae*)

This is the only garden-worthy member of the five species which form the genus. Native to S. Europe from Portugal to Italy, it forms tight clumps of almost grassy leaves above which rise wiry, branched stems 50-80 cm tall. The solitary flowers are similar to those of chicory but are mainly lavender-blue and emerge from papery 'everlasting' bracts. *C. c.* 'Bicolor' has blue-and-white, while 'Major' has larger, brighter-hued flowers. It grows in any well-drained soil in a sunny site and is best planted in early autumn or spring. Propagation is by seeds in spring, or by root cuttings in late winter.

Cautleya (*Zingiberaceae*)

Five species are recognised in this genus, all from the Himalayan region. Unlike most members of the ginger family, it contains hardy species which can add a touch of the exotic to cool, temperate gardens. A fertile, moisture-retentive but well-drained soil is required and a sunny or partially shaded site sheltered from strong winds. Planting is best in spring, and propagation by careful division at the same time. Seeds also may be sown under glass in spring. *C. lutea* (*Roscoea lutea*) forms small colonies of erect, slender leafy stems to 45 cm tall topped by spikes of yellow, orchid-like flowers with purple-red calyces in late summer. *C. spicata* is more robust, with stems to 60 cm, richer-yellow flowers and green to red calyces. It is represented in gardens by *C. s.* 'Robusta' (*C. robusta* and *C. s.* 'Autumn Beauty' of catalogues) which has maroon calyces and black seeds in almost white capsules.

Cedronella – see *Agastache*.

Centaurea (Knapweed, Hardheads) (*Compositae*)

The 600 species of centaurea include some shrubs and sub-shrubs and such annuals as the familiar cornflower. At least some of the perennials mentioned here should be in the garden of every hardy planter. Any fertile, well-drained, but not dry soil is suitable, and a site in the sun. Planting can take place from autumn to spring. Propagate by division at planting time, or by seeds in spring. The following flower in summer: *C. dealbata* (Caucasus) can attain 90 cm in height, with long-stalked ferny leaves that are pale green above, grey-white beneath, nicely foiling the lilac-pink flowers. *C. d.* 'Steenbergii' has rose-crimson flowers, is more vigorous and can spread moderately invasively underground. See *C. hypoleuca* for the cultivar 'John Coutts'. *C. glastifolia* (*Chartolepis glastifolia*) (S. and SE USSR) can best be described as a somewhat slenderer version of *C. macrocephala* with smaller lemon-yellow flowers. *C. hypoleuca* (Turkey, Transcaucasia), is similar to *C. dealbata* but has leaves with a large, terminal leaflet and slightly smaller pink flowers. *C. h.* 'John Coutts' has deep-rose flowers (formerly wrongly identified as a form of *C. dealbata*.) *C. macrocephala* (Caucasus) is the giant of the genus forming clumps to 1 m tall, each stem terminating in a deep-yellow flower 8 cm wide. *C. montana*, mountain knapweed (European mountains) often opens its large, purple-blue cornflowers in late spring and continues through the summer. It forms clumps 45-60 cm tall and spreads by rhizomes. *C. m.* 'Alba' is white flowered, 'Rosea' ('Carnea') is pink, 'Rubra' rose-red and 'Parham' rich amethyst. *C. pulcherrima* (*Aethiopappus pulcherrima*) (Caucasus) grows 60-75 cm tall with pinnate leaves and bright rose-pink flowers. *C. pulchra major* (of gardens) has lobed leaves, stems to 60 cm or more and purple-rose flowers; it is reputedly not reliably hardy, needing a sheltered site. *C. ruthenica* (E. Europe) has rich-green leaves cut into narrow lobes, stems to 1 m and pale-yellow flowers in late summer.

Centranthus (*Kentranthus*) **ruber**, (Red Valerian) (*Valerianaceae*)

This is the only one of the twelve species ever cultivated and it usually seems happier on old walls and stony banks than in the garden. A native of C. and S. Europe, N. Africa and Turkey and naturalised elsewhere, it is a bushy, woody-based plant 45-90 cm tall with paired, smooth leaves and profuse clusters of tiny, spurred flowers in shades of red, pink and white from early summer to autumn. *C. r.* 'Atrococcineus' has dark, almost coppery-red flowers. Ordinary well-drained soil and sun are its essential requirements. Planting is best in spring or summer. Propagation is by basal cuttings, or by sowing seeds in spring.

Cephalaria gigantea (*Dipsacaceae*)

Although 65 species of annuals and perennials are listed for this genus, only one has become popular. Often catalogued as *C. tatarica*, it is a clump-former from Siberia, rather ungainly of habit, but effective at the back of a border where its primrose-yellow scabious flowers can sway on their slender stalks 1.5-2 m in the air. Fertile soil and a sunny site are essential. Plant from autumn to spring. Propagate by division, or by seeds in spring.

Ceratostigma plumbaginoides (*Plumbaginaceae*)

In a genus of eight species of shrubs, this is the odd man out, dying back to ground level each winter and behaving as the perfect herbaceous perennial. It is a spreader, running underground to form wide colonies of 30 cm-tall stems set with spoon-shaped leaves that usually redden in autumn. The sky-blue plumbago-like flowers are carried in terminal clusters in late summer and autumn. Ordinary well-drained soil is suitable and a sunny site. Planting is best in spring with propagation by division at the same time.

Cheiranthus (Wallflower) (*Cruciferae*)

About ten species of wallflower are recognised though there is confusion with the very closely allied *Erysimum*. The taller members are sub-shrubby and short lived, but fit in usefully towards the front of mixed borders. They grow in ordinary, preferably limy, well-drained soil in sun. Planting is best summer to early autumn or spring. Propagate by seeds in spring, or by cuttings with a heel in summer. *C.* 'Bowles Mauve' ('Bowles Purple') is of uncertain origin, perhaps a hybrid between or with one of the Canary Islands species. Up to 60 cm tall, it has narrow, greyish leaves and long racemes of mauve-purple flowers off and on for most of the year. It is not reliably hardy in exposed sites or cold winters. *C. mutabilis* (Canary Islands, Madeira) is similar to 'Bowles Mauve', but the flowers open pale yellow and age lilac-purple from spring to mid-summer; *C. semperflorens* (Morocco) is cast in a similar mould but has white flowers with purple or lilac sepals. 'Constant Cheer' is reputedly a hybrid with *Erysimum* X *allionii* and forms compact mounds of dark foliage set with 60 cm racemes of dusky red to purple flowers in summer.

Chelone (Turtlehead) (*Scrophulariaceae*)

All four species in this genus are native to E. USA and all have garden value. They are eventually widely clump-forming with bushy, leafy, erect stems and in late summer and autumn, terminal spikes of two-lipped, horizontally borne flowers which fancifully resemble the head of a turtle. Moisture-retentive fertile soil and a site in partial shade or sun are required. They thrive well in the bog garden. Planting is best autumn or spring. Propagation is by division at planting time, or by sowing seeds in spring. *C. barbata* — see *Penstemon barbatus*. *C. glabra* grows 60-90 cm tall, with lance-shaped, toothed leaves and white, purple or deep rose-flushed flowers. *C. lyonii* is similar to the next species, but the upper hooded petal of each flower is sharply ridged. *C. obliqua* is the best known and most handsome, with stems to 1 m, and rose-purple, yellow-bearded flowers well into autumn.

Chionochloa (Tussock Grass) (*Gramineae*)

Of the 19 species in this genus, all but one are New Zealanders and several are decorative and deserving to be grown more often. They are clump-forming, each plant developing into a dense tussock of gracefully arching leaves over-topped by feathery flowerheads. Moisture-retentive but well-drained, preferably neutral to acid soil is required and a site in full sun. Propagation is by seeds, ideally when ripe, or in spring. Division can also be tried in spring just as the young growth commences. *C. conspicua* is the hanangamoho of the Maoris and the most widespread in the wild. It is among the largest, attaining 1.5-2 m when adorned with its arching flowering plumes. The mountain form is best for British gardens. *C. flavescens* (snow grass) forms brownish-green tussocks and achieves 1.5 m or more in bloom. *C. rubra* (red tussock) has a brownish-red gleam to its abundant arched leaves and reaches 1-1.5 m in bloom.

Chrysanthemum (*Compositae*)

About 200 species of annuals, perennials and shrubs comprise this north temperate genus. Despite the great popularity of the so-called florists' chrysanths (derived from several Chinese and Japanese species, notably *C. indicum* and *C. vestitum* (*morifolium*)), few of these are suitable for the hardy perennial garden. Those described here thrive in ordinary but not dry soil, preferably laced with humus, and are best in a sunny site although light shade is tolerated. Planting is best in autumn or spring. Propagation is by division at planting time, but preferably in spring. *C. coccineum* (*Pyrethrum roseum*) (SW Asia) will, in spite of the botanical reclassification, long remain as pyrethrum, more especially as it is so well known and frequently planted. Its clumps of frothy, bright green, carrot-like foliage make a fine foil for the large, early summer daisies in shades of pink, red and white, single and double. *C. maximum* (Pyrenees) is the name used for the giant ox-eye or shasta daisy, which is represented in gardens by single and double, largely white daisies, to 90 cm tall. It is now suggested that most of the cultivars are of hybrid origin with the similar, but 1-2 m tall, *C. lacustre* (true *C. maximum* is only 60 cm) and should be designated *C.* X *superbum*. Well-tried cultivars include 'Everest', 'Mayfield Giant', 'Cobham Gold', 'Fiona Coghill', 'Esther Read', the last two fully double, tall and short growing respectively. *C. nipponicum* (Japan) is sub-shrubby, to 60 cm; a useful plant for late autumn when it opens white daisies with green-tinted yellow discs. *C. parthenium* (feverfew), (SE Europe to Caucasus) has been included in the genera *Pyrethrum* and *Tanacetum* and is still regularly sold by seedsmen as *Matricaria eximia*. Bushy and somewhat woody based, with bright-green lobed leaves and stems 60-90 cm, it produces abundant small white daisies over a long period from summer onwards. Double- and single-flowered selections are available, also those with yellow-flushed leaves, e.g . *C. p.* 'Aurea'. Dwarf cultivars under 30 cm are also available. *C. rubellum* and *C. erubescens* (of gardens) should now be correctly assigned to *C. zawadskii latilobum* (Japan). It resembles a 60 cm single-flowered florists' chrysanth but is rhizomatous and has beautiful pink daisies in autumn. There are several hybrid cultivars in shades of apricot, yellow and coppery-red. Crossed with *C. vestitum* (*C. morifolium*), it has given rise to the Korean chrysanthemums, bushy plants with a profusion of coloured daisies. *C. uliginosum* (*Tanacetum serotinum*) (E. Europe) is a typical clump-forming hardy perennial to 2 m tall, producing charming sprays of white daisies in autumn; a fine back-of-the-border plant which usually does not need supporting. In addition to the above, some of the hardier small-flowered florists' chrysanths make good border perennials. The Koreans have been mentioned, and several of the Pompon and Garden Spray cultivars are very hardy. Names to look out for include: 'Anastasia' (pink), 'Dr Tom Parr' (bronze), 'Emperor of China' (silvery pink), 'Mei-Kyo' (carmine), all of long standing. Some of the modern chrysanths are equally hardy however, and many could be selected by a process of trial and error.

Cichorium intybus (Chicory) (*Compositae*)

This plant is probably better known in the vegetable garden, but is well worth growing for its spikes of sky-blue dandelions on 1 m-tall branched stems. (Endive (*C. endivia*) is similar, with purple-blue flowers.) Any well-drained, preferably alkaline soil is suitable, and a site in the sun. Propagation is by seeds in spring, the young plants being set out in permanent sites once they have three or four true leaves.

Cimicifuga (Bugbane) (*Ranunculaceae*)

All 15 species in this genus come from the north temperate zone. They have affinities with baneberry (*Actaea*) but the tiny, many-stamened flowers form fluffy spikes and spires which are their main attraction. They require moisture-retentive, ideally humus-rich soil and a site in partial shade or sun. Planting can be done from autumn to spring. Propagate by division at planting time, or by seeds when ripe or in spring. *C. americana* (E. USA) is an imposing plant, 1.2-2 m tall with long spires of cream flowers in late summer. It is sometimes wrongly listed as "*C. cordifolia*". *C. foetida* (NE Asia) can attain 1.5 m in height, each stem bearing several bottle-brush-like flower spikes of greenish-white to deep cream flowers which together create an astilbe-like effect. *C. f. intermedia* − see *C. simplex*. *C. racemosa*, black snakeroot, black cohosh (E. North America) has the stance of *C. americana* and can reach 2.5 m, with white flowers in summer. *C. r. cordifolia* (*C. cordifolia*) has its leaves composed of up to nine large leaflets (*C. racemosa* has 11-27, at least the terminal one being deeply cordate). The flowers are sometimes green tinted. In British gardens it is sometimes confused with *C. americana* but that species never has cordate leaflets. *C. simplex* (*C. intermedia* of gardens) (USSR to Japan), is smaller and neater than *C. foetida* with well-spaced, arching bottle-brushes of pure white in autumn. *C. s. ramosa* (*C. ramosa* of catalogues) is a robust version of 2 m, with larger leaves. *C. s.* 'Elstead' has purplish flower spikes, while 'White Pearl' has more slender purple-white spikes and a very graceful habit.

Cirsium (Thistle) (*Compositae*)

Although many of the 150 species of thistle are handsome plants, their spiny and sometimes invasive nature deters most gardeners. The two mentioned here are well worth a place in the herbaceous garden. They require moisture-retentive but otherwise ordinary soil and a place in the sun. Planting can take place from autumn to spring. Propagation is by division at planting time, or by seeds in spring or when ripe. *C. japonicum* (*Cnicus japonicus*) has handsome basal leaves to 30 cm long, deeply lobed and spiny, and stems 1 m or more tall, with 5 cm-wide pink to rose-purple flowers in summer. Some forms have densely downy and cobwebby stems and leaves. *C. rivulare* (C. Europe to W. USSR) forms clumps or colonies of stems 60-90 cm tall which carry weakly spiny, dark-green leaves at the base and handsome purple thistle blooms in summer. A pink form is recorded. Commonest in gardens is *C. r.* 'Atropurpureum' (*Cnicus atropurpureus*) with glowing crimson flowers.

Clematis (*Ranunculaceae*)

Of cosmopolitan distribution, most of the 250 species of clematis are woody-stemmed or sub-shrubby climbers. Among the few non-climbers are several species well worth trying in the perennial garden. They grow in ordinary well-drained soil, preferably well laced with humus, and are best in a sunny site. What appear to be petals are, as in anemone, coloured sepals, and are often very thick textured. All the plants mentioned need the support of twiggy sticks if used in beds and borders. Planting should take place in autumn or spring. Propagate by careful division in late winter, by cuttings of basal shoots in spring or by seeds when ripe or in spring. *C. douglasii* (*C. hirsutissima* (NW USA) is a woody-based clump-former to 60 cm, with leaves dissected in the manner of a pasque-flower, and solitary, nodding 4-5 cm-long urn-shaped, smoky-purple flowers in summer. Attractive feathery seed heads follow. This is not an easy plant to please, needing moisture until after flowering, then a gentle baking. *C. d. scottii* (C. North USA) has much coarser, somewhat glaucous leaves and is easier to grow. It is now classified as a species in its own right. *C.* X *eriostemon* 'Hendersonii' (*C. integrifolia* X *viticella*) is much like a superior *C. integrifolia* with soft, darkish-blue flowers and is often listed as a cultivar of that species. *C. heracleifolia* (China) grows to 90 cm tall from a sub-shrubby base. The large leaves are trifoliate and the fragrant blue flowers appear in clusters during late summer and autumn. It is usually represented in gardens by *C. h. davidiana*, a richer blue form, with more widely expanded flowers. See also *C.* X *jouiniana*. *C. integrifolia* (C. Europe to C. Asia) has slender stems, simple oval leaves and solitary nodding bells of soft violet-blue in summer. It is a quietly attractive plant — some might say dull — which nevertheless can excite quite a lot of comment. *C. i. olgae* has the sepals strongly re-curved, and 'Rosea' is lavender-pink: for 'Hendersonii' — see *C.* X *eriostemon*. *C.* X *jouiniana* (*C. heracleifolia davidiana* X *C. vitalba*) reaches 2-3 m, sometimes more in mild climates, and only really looks at home among the shrubs of a mixed border. In such a situation its large trusses of opal to pale-lilac-blue flowers can be seen to advantage. Seedlings from this hybrid favour the former parent and are often listed as cultivars of it, e.g. 'Côte d'Azur' and 'Campanile' have darker blooms; 'Wyvale' has larger hyacinth flowers. *C. recta* (Europe) can attain 1 m or more if securely supported. Above the pinnate foliage it bears clouds of small, white, fragrant flowers in summer. More effective as a garden plant is *C. r.* 'Purpurea' or 'Foliis Purpureis', with purple-flushed foliage — but beware inferior forms with muddy green leaves.

Codonopsis (*Campanulaceae*)

Among the 30 or more species in this genus are annuals and perennials, some of the latter being twining climbers which can be very effective when scrambling through the shrubs in a mixed border. They need well-drained, but not dry fertile soil and thrive in sun or partial shade. Planting is best in autumn or spring. Propagation is by seeds, basal cuttings or careful division in spring. *C. clematidea* (Asian Mountains) has somewhat reclining to almost scrambling stems 50-90 cm or more long, bearing in summer milky-blue, deep bells, with intriguing brown patterning within. It needs a site where the flowers can be looked into with ease, e.g. on the top of a bank. Sometimes this plant is confused with *C. ovata*, q.v. *C. convolvulacea* (Himalayas to W. China) is a slender twiner to 2 m or more with small oval leaves and wide-open blue flowers. It is best in a sheltered site and is apt to be short lived. *C. ovata* (Himalayas) has a spreading, branched habit to 30 cm or more tall, with small grey-hairy leaves and in summer, pale-blue bells with flared lobes. *C. tangshen* (W. China) is a vigorous climber to 3 m, bearing pale-green bells charmingly patterned purple within. *C. vinciflora* (Tibet) also climbs, its slender stems reaching about 1.5 m, clad with small, toothed leaves and periwinkle-like purple to lilac-blue flowers in summer. It is not reliably hardy, needing a sheltered site; best beneath a shrub or protected with a cloche in winter.

Coreopsis (*Calliopsis*) (Tickseed) (*Compositae*)

Only a few of the 120 species in this genus are sufficiently perennial, hardy or decorative for inclusion here. These are showy, N. American plants with largely yellow daisy flowers throughout the summer and early autumn. Any well-drained soil is suitable, and a sunny site. Planting is best in autumn or spring, propagation is by careful division or by sowing seeds in spring. *C. auriculata* is a clump-former 60-80 cm tall, with the yellow notched florets bearing a basal maroon blotch. *C. a.* 'Superba' is the usual form in gardens, having larger, longer-stemmed flowers; 'Astolats' is much the same. *C. grandiflora* rarely exceeds 45-50 cm, with the bright-yellow florets deeply lobed at the tips and bearing a small basal crimson spot. *C. g.* 'Baden-gold' grows to 90 cm with larger flowers; 'Mayfield Giant' is of similar size, but orange-yellow; 'Sunburst' is double. *C. lanceolata* is much like *C. grandiflora* and is probably confused with it in cultivation. It has very narrow, unlobed leaves, whereas those of *grandiflora* are lance-shaped and often three to five lobed. The plant labelled *C. grandiflora* 'Sunburst' may belong here. *C. rosea* departs from the norm and produces flowers of deep to pale rose-pink on 60 cm stems from creeping rhizomes; a white form is known; best in moist, humus-rich soil. *C. verticillata* eventually forms wide clumps of erect, wiry stems bearing finely dissected leaves and bright chrome-tinted, yellow flowers; *C. v.* 'Grandiflora' ('Golden Shower') has a more robust habit and florets of mellower, richer hue.

Cortaderia (Pampas Grass) (*Gramineae*)

About 15 species comprise this genus of grasses from S. America and New Zealand. The larger species are statuesque plants of great garden merit but they need plenty of room to develop fully and look their best. Well-drained soil is essential and a site in the sun. Planting and propagation by division should be carried out in spring. Seeds can also be sown at the same time. *C. richardii* (*C. conspicua* and *Arundo conspicua* of gardens) (New Zealand) has the Maori name toe-toe, and forms clumps 2-3 m high when in bloom. In summer it produces arching, feathery panicles of tiny white florets which remain attractive for several months. *C. selloana* (*C. argentea*, *Gynerium argenteum*) (temperate S. America) is the pampas grass beloved by British gardeners. It forms bold and dense arching tufts of narrow, saw-toothed leaves which can cut a finger if carelessly handled. From early autumn onwards each plant rapidly produces a sheaf of eye-catching, silvery-white floral plumes. *C. s.* 'Gold Band' has yellow variegated leaves; 'Monstrosa' is the largest form, attaining 3 m or more; 'Pumila' is the smallest, forming neat, compact clumps to 1.5 m; 'Rendatleri' has arching, pink-tinted plumes, while 'Sunningdale Silver' grows to 2.5 m and has the brightest, most densely borne plumes.

Corydalis (*Fumariaceae*)

Few of the 320 species in this genus seem to have proved useful for the perennial garden, though many yet await trial. Many have prettily cut or dissected leaves and all have slender, spurred flowers in short to long racemes. Those mentioned here generally self-sow freely. Ordinary soil and sun or shade are acceptable. Planting can take place from autumn to spring. Propagation is by careful division in spring or by seeds, preferably when ripe, or in spring. *C. cheilanthifolia* (China) seldom exceeds 30 cm and is usually less, forming arching mounds of bronze-tinted leaves that rival the ferns in elegance. The pale-yellow flowers which appear from spring to autumn, are a bonus. *C. lutea* (Europe) is the best known of all the species, a cottage-garden plant that soon takes over shaded or neglected corners with its lacy mounds of glaucous leaves and non-stop display of yellow flowers. *C. l.* 'Alba' has white flowers. *C. ochroleuca* (Italy, W. Balkans) is rather like *C. lutea* but has more richly glaucous leaves and somewhat pendulous cream and yellow flowers.

Crambe (Seakale) (*Cruciferae*)

Only two of the 25 species of crambe ever seem to be cultivated, and one of these is best known as the vegetable seakale — albeit a very decorative plant. They need well-drained, at least moderately limy soil and a site in sun. Planting is best in spring with propagation by division or seeds at the same time. Root cuttings in late winter also provide a ready means of increase. *C. cordifolia* (Caucasus) is a massively handsome plant to 2 m tall with bold basal leaves and intricately branched flowering stems creating, in early summer, scented clouds of tiny white flowers of gypsophila-like effect. *C. maritima* (European coasts) reaches only 60 cm in height, with more solid domes of white flowers and intensely glaucous foliage.

Crepis incana (Hawksbeard) (*Compositae*)

A native of Greece, but hardy in Britain, this is the only one of the 200 species which is suitable for the perennial garden. It is in effect, a refined dandelion with somewhat hoary leaves and branched stems 30-40 cm tall bearing a profusion of clear-pink flowers from mid to late summer. It needs well-drained soil and a sunny, preferably sheltered, site. Planting and propagation by division or seeds is best in spring.

Cynara (*Cardunculus*) (*Compositae*)

Better known to many gardeners as cardoon (the young leaves when blanched are a nice accompaniment to salads) this plant is also highly ornamental in the best thistle tradition. Reaching 1.5-2 m in height, it has deeply lobed grey leaves and branched stems which carry large purple thistle flowers in summer. It needs fertile well-drained soil and a sunny, sheltered site. Planting and propagation by division, suckers or seeds, is best in spring.

Cynoglossum nervosum (*Boraginaceae*)

Although at least 50 species comprise this genus, only *C. nervosum* from the Himalayas is widely grown in the perennial garden. It is a clump-former to 60 cm tall with long, narrow, rough-textured leaves and an abundance of large forget-me-not-like flowers of intense blue, in the summer. Ordinary soil and a sunny site are its modest requirements. Planting and propagation by division can take place from autumn to spring. Seeds also can be sown in spring or when ripe.

Cyperus (*Cyperaceae*)

No less than 550 species of grass-like plants form this genus which is closely related to the sedges (*Carex*). Most species are tropical or otherwise too tender for outside culture, but those described

Figure 5: *Cynara cardunculus*

here survive all but the worst winters. Moisture-retentive soil and a sunny sheltered site are required. Planting and propagation by division or by seeds is best in spring. *C. eragrostis* (*C. vegetus*) (temperate S. America) is a clump-former with short, thick rhizomes and arching leaves to 60 cm long. The green to buff flowering spikelets are carried in compact heads surrounded by radiating leaf-like bracts much like those of the greenhouse umbrella grass (*C. alternifolius*). *C. longus*, galingale (Europe, Mediterranean) forms dense colonies to 1 m or more tall with dark glossy leaves that are sharply keeled, and have rough, cutting edges. The flowering spikelets are reddish-brown and green, in loose umbel-like clusters. It is best in wet soil.

Dactylorrhiza (*Orchidaceae*)

Of all the hardy orchid ground genera, this one has the most to offer the hardy planter. About 30 species are now recognised (formerly included in the genus *Orchis*), those described being the most garden worthy, both for attractiveness and for ease of cultivation. They need well-drained, but not dry, humus-rich soil and will thrive in sun or partial shade. The tubers, which should never be allowed to dry out for long, should be planted out in late summer or autumn. Propagation is by separating the tubers at planting time. *D. elata* (Algeria) can attain 60 cm or more in height, with strap-shaped leaves and dense tapered racemes of rose-purple flowers in early summer. A white-flowered form is known. *D. foliosa* (*Orchis maderensis*) (Madeira) is similar to the previous species but is generally less robust, 40-60 cm tall with, at least in the best forms, more richly hued flowers.

Deinanthe (*Hydrangeaceae*)

The two Asiatic species that comprise this genus are not only unqiue in bridging the gap between hydrangeas and saxifrages, but they have that touch of class which commends them to the connoisseur. Despite this they are not difficult if grown in humus-rich soil in partial shade and sheltered from strong winds. They can be planted from autumn to spring and propagated by division, preferably in early spring. Divisions may take a year to settle down. Seeds can be sown in spring but are slow to reach maturity. *D. caerulea* (China) is clump-forming, 30-45 cm tall, with handsome, oval, corrugated, toothed, glossy-green leaves in pairs. The mid to late summer-borne flowers are a curiously attractive shade of slaty violet-blue. They are of two forms, the fertile ones, nodding and bowl-shaped, to 4 cm wide and composed of five petals, and the sterile ones, much flatter and of two to three petal-like lobes. The rarely seen *D. bifida* (Japan) has smaller, white blooms.

Delphinium (*Ranunculaceae*)

No hardy planter's garden would be complete without at least a few of the 250 species in this genus. All do best in a humus-rich soil in sun and should be planted in autumn or early spring. Propagation is by division or basal cuttings in spring. Seeds may also be sown, preferably as soon as ripe, or in spring. *D.* X *belladonna* is the name given to a group of cultivars derived from *D. elatum* and *D. grandiflorum* and possibly *D. formosum* (of gardens). They are elegant, branched, wind-firm plants 90-150 cm tall in shades of light to deep violet-blue; e.g. 'Blue Bees', 'Lamartine', 'Wendy'. See also *D.* X *ruysii*. *D. elatum* (Pyrenees to Mongolia) is seldom grown in its wild form. Crossed with *D. exaltatum* and *D. formosum* (of gardens) it has given rise to the many majestic florists' cultivars many to 2.5 m or more tall, in shades of purple, blue and white. By using such species as *D. cardinale* and *D. zalil* together with these Elatum Hybrids, Dr R. A. Legro of Holland has raised many potential cultivars with red, orange and yellow flowers. At present however, these are proving difficult to propagate and have yet to make their impact among delphinium growers. *D. grandiflorum* (*chinense*) (China, Siberia) is well branched and graceful, usually about 45-60 cm tall with loose racemes of usually rich-blue flowers; 'Blue Butterfly' rarely exceeds 30 cm and makes a splendid front of border plant, but regrettably is short-lived. It is easily raised from seed and flowers the first year if sown early. *D. nudicaule* (California, Oregon) can vary from 30-50 cm according to soil, situation and age of plant. It has somewhat fleshy, three to five lobed leaves and loose racemes of deep-red cornucopia-shaped flowers from early summer onwards. It is short lived and is best raised from seeds which will flower the year sown. *D.* X *ruysii* 'Pink Sensation' (*D. elatum* X *D. nudicaule*) resembles a *D.* X. *belladonna* cultivar but has pink blooms. *D. tatsienense* (China) is much like *D. grandiflorum* but the plant is roughly hairy, the leaf lobes are pinnately cut and the floral spurs are twice as long as the sepals. *D. zalil* (*D. sulphureum* of gardens) (Iran) can reach 60 cm with spires of pure-yellow flowers. Unfortunately it is usually short lived and doubtfully hardy. Sharply drained soil and a sunny site are essential.

Dentaria (Toothwort) (*Cruciferae*)

The 20 species of toothwort are closely allied to *Cardamine* and were formerly included in that genus. They differ primarily in lacking basal leaves and having rhizomes that are intriguingly covered with fleshy — fancifully tooth-like — scales. The species described deserve greater popularity, being shade lovers that provide spring interest and colour. Moisture-retentive but well-drained soil is preferred and planting is best in late summer or autumn, though it can be done later. Propagation is by division at planting time, or by seeds when ripe or in spring. *D. enneaphylla* (W. Carpathians, E. Alps to Macedonia) barely reaches 30 cm tall, each stem bearing a terminal whorl of trifoliate leaves centred by a nodding cluster of white or pale-yellow blooms. *D. heptaphylla* (*D. pinnata*) (Pyrenees to Apennines) varies from 30 cm to 60 cm in height though usually 40-50 cm. It has pinnate leaves and arching racemes of white flowers. *D. pentaphylla* (*D. digitata*) (European mountains) is the most robust and showiest species, with stems 30-50 cm tall, pinnate leaves (but with a very short axis and appearing digitate) and erect racemes of pale-purple flowers from late spring to early summer; pinkish and white-flowered forms occur.

Deschampsia (*Aira*) (Hair-grasses) (*Gramineae*)

This genus of 35 species is strangely neglected in gardens, perhaps because two of the more decorative species are British natives and not uncommon. They are densely tufted grasses with arching leaves and erect wiry stems topped by airy panicles of tiny shining spikelets. Ordinary soil in sun or partial shade is satisfactory, though *D. cespitosa* grows best where it is always moist. Planting should be carried out in early autumn or spring. Propagation is by division or by sowing seeds in spring. *D. cespitosa* (*D. caespitosa*), tufted hair grass (Europe, Asia, N. America, New Zealand) forms fountain-like clumps to 1.2 m with silvery or purplish spikelets that age to a strawy tint. *D. flexuosa*, wavy hair grass (Europe, Asia, N. America) is usually about 45 cm tall, more erect than *D. cespitosa* with the combined floral panicles forming a large cloud-like mass.

Dianthus (Pinks) (*Caryophyllaceae*)

Comparatively few of the 300 species in this genus are suitable for the herbaceous garden, being either too small or not sound perennials. Those described here can be used effectively as front-of-border subjects. They need well-drained, preferably limy soil and full sun. Planting is best in autumn or spring. Propagation is by cuttings from spring to early autumn, or by seeds in spring. *D.* X *allwoodii* (*D. caryophyllus* (carnation) cultivars X *D. plumarius*) is the group name of the cultivars of the modern Garden Pink. They are tufted to mat-forming vigorous plants to 60 cm tall with greyish leaves and single or double flowers, often zoned or patterned, to 5 cm wide. The many cultivars can be classified into four groups according to the patterning of the petals: 1. Selfs, one colour only. 2. Bicolours, mainly single coloured but with a basal blotch of a contrasting shade. 3. Laced, like (2) but the petals also edged with a thick or thin band of another colour or shade. 4. Fancies, irregularly patterned. *D. carthusianorum* (Europe) presents an image of *Dianthus* different from the accepted one. The slender green leaves are borne in grassy tufts from which emerge wiry stems to 60 cm which carry aloft compact clusters of small pink to magenta flowers surrounded by purple-brown bracts. It needs to be planted fairly thickly to achieve any sort of effect. *D. knappii* (W. Yugoslavia) has something of the stance of *D. carthusianorum* but has pale to greyish leaves and stems about 30 cm with larger clusters of sulphur-yellow flowers. *D. plumarius*, common pink (E. and C. Europe) can reach 40 cm in height but is often less. In the wild forms the pink flowers are about 3 cm wide and each petal has a fringe equal to about half its length. The common pink is the primary ancester of the Old Garden Pink cultivars (see also *D. X allwoodii*). *D. superbus* (Europe, Asia) is rather woody-based and of tufted habit with usually green leaves and stems 40-60 cm tall. The lilac to rose-purple flowers have a long hanging fringe which gives them a rather shaggy look. Crossed with *D. X allwoodii* it has given rise to 'Loveliness', a more compact, but less fully perennial race with flowers in shades of red, pink and purple.

Dicentra (Dutchman's Breeches) (*Fumariaceae*)

Sometimes still erroneously listed as *Dielytra*, the 20 species in this genus are typified by their pendent, locket or heart-shaped flowers. All the species mentioned have the added attraction of dissected, fern-like foliage. They thrive best in humus-rich soil and partial shade. Planting can take place from autumn to spring. Propagation is by division at planting time or by root cuttings in late winter. Seeds may be sown, ideally when ripe, or in spring, but are slow to reach flowering size. *D. eximia* (E. USA) is rhizomatous and forms colonies. From late spring to autumn it bears compact, nodding clusters of narrow heart-shaped flowers on 30 cm stems. *D. e.* 'Alba' is pure white. *D. formosa* (mountains of California) is much like *D. eximia* and is confused with it in gardens, but is a little more robust with larger, looser, red to pink flower clusters. *D. f. oregana* (*D. oregana*) has the leaves glaucous on both surfaces, and paler flowers. The following cultivars are sometimes listed under *D. eximia*: 'Adrian Bloom' (crimson), 'Bountiful' (glaucous leaves, rich-red flowers), 'Spring Morning' (light pink, glaucous foliage). *D. spectabilis* (bleeding heart) (China, Korea, Japan) is a clump-former to 60 cm tall with coarser foliage than the preceding species, but with a more spectacular showing of larger, rose-crimson, white-tipped flowers in spring and early summer. *D. s.* 'Alba' is pure white and most desirable.

Dictamnus albus (Burning Bush) (*Rutaceae*)

Formerly known as *D. fraxinella*, the burning bush is the only one of this six-species genus to be cultivated. It is a long-lived, woody-based clump-former to about 80 cm tall, with lustrous, pinnate leaves. The plant is glandular and aromatic, the developing seed pods in particular giving off a volatile oil which, during still, hot weather can be ignited − without harm to the plant. The white flowers which appear in terminal spikes in early summer have an orchid-like quality and this is particularly apparent in the purple-pink, darker veined *D. a. purpureus*. Burning bush requires fertile soil in a sunny site, though partial shade is tolerated. Planting is best in early autumn or spring. Propagation is by careful division, but a full growing season is required for the divisions to establish. Seeds can be sown, ideally as soon as ripe. Dried seeds take about one year to germinate. If the weather is warm and dry when the seed pods are ripe they explode violently. Enclosing them in a piece of nylon stocking or a small paper bag may be necessary to save them.

Digitalis (Foxglove) (*Scrophulariaceae*)

There are about 26 different kinds of foxgloves, some biennials and shrubs. All are typified by summer-borne, one-sided spires of flattened, thimble-shaped flowers, though the latter vary very much in size, degree of lobing and colour. They grow in ordinary but not dry soil and thrive in partial shade or sun. Planting can take place autumn to spring. Propagation for all species is best by sowing seeds in late spring, though clump-formers can also be divided. *D. ferruginea* (SE Europe) is usually 80-90 cm tall with yellowish to reddish-brown, darker-veined flowers 2.5-3.5 cm long. *D. grandiflora* (*D. ambigua*) attains 60 cm or more in height with lustrous leaves and 4-5 cm-long soft-yellow flowers, brown netted within; often short lived but easily seed raised. Sometimes confused with the next species. *D. lutea* (West and W. Central Europe) is similar to *D. grandiflora* in growth but has paler-yellow flowers only 2-2.5 cm long, a free-seeding species that can become almost a weed. *D.* X *mertonensis* (*D. purpurea* X *D. grandiflora*) is a true-breeding tetraploid hybrid raised at the John Innes Institute *c.* 1925 (then at Merton, Surrey). It most resembles the first parent but is more compact, 60-90 cm tall and bears flowers of an unique crushed-strawberry shade. *D. purpurea*, common foxglove (SW Europe) should not really be included as it is primarily a biennial. However, in any batch of plants some will persist as short-lived perennials and it also freely regenerates *in situ* from seeds. It is the most handsome member of its genus, often reaching 1.5 m or more with long racemes of 5 cm-long deep rose-purple, maroon-spotted flowers. *D. p.* 'Alba' is white with or without spots. 'Shirley' is a strain with a wider colour range, while 'Excelsior' has the same variety of colours but the flowers are evenly arranged all round the stem.

Diphylleia cymosa (Umbrella Leaf) (*Podophyllaceae*)

The only member of its genus, this is one of those plants which, while not spectacular, has a touch of class and connoisseur appeal. Its vernacular name is apt, each 60 cm stem being topped by a pair of large, rounded leaves which are handsome enough, without embellishment. In summer a cluster of small white flowers arises between each leaf pair which, under ideal conditions, give way to deep-blue berries. It is not difficult to grow in humus-rich, moisture-retentive soil in partial shade and can be planted from autumn to spring. Propagation is by careful division in spring or by seeds when ripe. Seedlings are slow to reach maturity.

Disporum (Fairy Bells) (*Liliaceae*)

About 20 species comprise this genus which seems to blend the characters of Solomon's seal *Polygonatum* and *Uvularia*. They are woodlanders needing humus-rich soil and partial shade to flourish. Planting can take place from autumn to spring, and propagation by division at planting time. *D. pullum* (E. Asia) is clump-forming with purplish stems to 90 cm and in early summer, tubular bells variable in colour but usually a shade of green flushed with purple. *D. sessile* 'Variegatum' (*Oakesiella variegata* of gardens) (Japan) is grown primarily for its white-striped leaves and the wild green-leaved species is seldom cultivated. It grows to 60 cm, forming wide colonies when happily situated. The creamy-white flowers are narrowly bell shaped and open in spring. *D. smithii* (*D. oreganum, Prosartes oregana, P. menziesii*) (California to British Columbia) barely reaches 30 cm and forms bushy clumps and colonies. The wiry, branched stems bear greenish-white to cream tubular bells in spring and early summer, later followed by pale-orange berries.

Dodecatheon (Shooting Stars) (*Primulaceae*)

Depending on the botanical authority, there are 14-52 species of shooting stars, all but one from N. America. The flowers have the form and charm of a cyclamen, but several are carried in terminal clusters above rosettes of generally narrow leaves. The nomenclature of cultivated plants, in Britain at least, is confused and all names are suspect. Whatever the name and source most plants are referable to the two species described below. Shooting stars grow in ordinary, preferably humus-enriched soil that does not dry out too rapidly and in partial shade or sun. Planting can take place from late summer to spring. Propagate by seeds when ripe or in spring, or by careful division of multiple-crowned plants at planting time. *D. meadia* (*D. pauci- florum* and *D. paucifolium* of catalogues) (E. USA) is usually about 45 cm in bloom, with flowers to 2.5 cm long, in shades of pink to lilac or white, from late spring to mid-summer. The oval seed pods that follow are tough and leathery. *D. pulchellum* (W. USA) is very similar in effect but the flowers vary from red and magenta to lavender and the seed capsules are thin and papery. *D. p.* 'Red Wings' is a good crimson selection.

Doronicum (Leopard's Bane) (*Compositae*)

The 35 species that comprise this genus have close affinities with each other and there is a deal of confusion over their naming. Those described are among the best, providing very welcome displays of bright-yellow daisies in spring. They grow in ordinary soil and flourish in partial shade or sun. Planting can be done from late summer to late winter. Propagation is by division at planting time. Seeds may be sown in spring but the results are likely to be inferior to reliably named species or cultivars. *D. austriacum* (C. and S. European mountains) has somewhat heart-shaped basal leaves, branched stems to 45 cm and more and 6 cm-wide flowers. *D. columnae* (*D. cordatum* of gardens) (mountains of E. Europe) rather resembles a neat, small *D. austriacum* to about 30 cm tall. *D.* 'Miss Mason' is one of the best doronicums, being reliable, vigorous and showy – in fact, a superior *D. austriacum* and probably a hybrid of that species with the next. *D. orientale* (*D. caucasicum*) (SE Europe) is similar to *D. columnae* but taller; 'Spring Beauty' is a double-flowered version, perhaps of hybrid origin. *D. pardalianches* (great leopards bane) (Europe) is mentioned only because its name is sometimes used for other, finer plants. The true plant reaches 90 cm and has smallish flowers. It is inclined to be invasive and is now seldom offered by nurserymen. *D. plantagineum*, plantain-leaved leopards bane (W. Europe) has oval to elliptic basal leaves, stems to 80 cm and flowers 5 cm or more wide. It is mainly represented in gardens by the more robust, larger-flowered 'Harpur Crewe' ('Excelsum').

Dracocephalum (*Labiatae*)

This genus of 45 species of annual and perennials is rather neglected by gardeners. The species here are all deserving of more frequent planting. They are allies of the dead nettle and catmint, having opposite pairs of leaves and whorled spikes of tubular two-lipped flowers fancifully like gaping mouths. Ordinary fertile soil is all that is required, and a sunny site. Planting can take place from autumn to spring. Propagation is by careful division at planting time, by basal cuttings or by seeds in spring. *D. grandiflorum* (Siberia) is a clump-former about 30 cm tall and makes an eye-catching front-of-the-border subject with its long, violet-blue flowers erupting from reddish calyces in summer. *D. prattii* (of gardens) is included under *D. sibiricum*. *D. ruyschianum* (Pyrenees to USSR) produces its 50-60 cm-tall stems in clumps and bears dense spires of violet, pink or white flowers in summer. *D. r. speciosum* (*D. argunense*) (NE Asia) has longer leaves and larger flowers. *D. sibiricum* (*D. pratii, Nepeta macrantha, N. sibirica*) can reach 1 m in height and resembles a giant, erect catmint with lavender-blue flowers in late summer.

Dryopteris (Buckler Fern) (*Aspidiaceae*)

About 150 species of deciduous and evergreen ferns comprise this world-wide genus. Those described here are fully hardy, forming clumps of handsome shuttlecock-shaped rosettes. They grow in ordinary, preferably moist, humus-rich soil in full sun or partial shade and look well beneath trees. They can be planted any time from autumn to spring. Propagation is by division at planting time or spores in spring. For *D. borreri* — see *D. pseudomas*. *D. carthusiana* (*D. lanceolatocristata, D. spinulosa*), narrow buckler (north temperate zone) will stand a lot of sun if planted in moist soil and is an ideal fern for bog and waterside, where it can reach 1 m. In drier sites it may be only half this height. The deciduous fronds are bright to yellow-green and bipinnate. *D. cristata*, crested buckler (Europe to C. USSR) is a deciduous species 60-90 cm tall with shorter, sterile outer fronds. It grows and looks well by the waterside. *D. dilatata* (*D. austriaca*) broad buckler (Europe and temperate Asia) has dark-green, almost triangular fronds to about 60 cm, each one neatly and tripinnately dissected; 'Lepidota Cristata' has narrower leaflets and the frond tips crested. *D. erythrosora* (China, Japan) is evergreen in sheltered sites. It is similar to a smaller spreading male fern (*D. filix-mas*) but easily identified by its coppery-red young fronds and bright-red immature spore cases (sori). *D. filix-mas*, male fern (north temperate zone and southern hemisphere mountains) is the most commonly cultivated species, with firm shuttlecocks of rich-green foliage; semi-evergreen in sheltered sites. There are several mutant forms with narrow leaflets and crests. *D. pseudo-mas* (*D. borreri*) is much like a bolder male fern with thicker textured, more reliably evergreen fronds.

Echinacea purpurea (Purple Cone Flower) (*Compositae*)

E

Of the three species that form this genus, the purple cone flower is the finest and most generally grown. A native of E. North America it is a clump-former 90-120 cm tall with rough-textured, rich-green oval leaves. Rudbeckia-like flowerheads with orange-brown discs and red-purple ray florets open in late summer and autumn. *E. p.* 'Robert Bloom' has spreading ray florets of cerise-crimson with a hint of mauve; 'The King' has drooping crimson-pink rays and 'White Lustre' is warm white. Fertile moisture-retentive soil and a sunny site are required. Planting and propagation by division are best in spring.

Echinops (Globe Thistle) (*Compositae*)

Comparatively few of the 100 species of globe thistle have ever been cultivated; some are annuals, others are fiercely spiny and difficult to handle. The genus is typified by ball-like flower clusters of unique structure being composed of many small, slender flowerheads each with a solitary floret and a circle of bracts. The lobed leaves are usually spiny or prickly. Any well-drained soil in sun is suitable and planting can take place from autumn to spring. Propagation is by division at planting time, or by seeds in spring. The following flower from late summer onwards and are clump-forming. *E. bannaticus* (SE Europe) is a fine robust species to 1.5 m or more with the arching leaves white-downy beneath and grey-blue flowers in heads to 5 cm wide. *E. exaltatus* (*E. commutatus*) is similar but with larger heads of white to palest grey-blue *E. humilis* (Asia) is confused in gardens with *E. ritro*, but is taller, to 1.2 m and has wavy-margined, almost spineless, leaves. *E. h.* 'Taplow Blue' achieves 1.5 m or more and has bright-blue flowers. For *E. nivalis* and *E. niveus* of catalogues – see under *E. sphaerocephalus*. *E. ritro* (E. Europe, W. Asia) is seldom seen as the true species, being confused with *E. humilis* and hybrids. It is a slender plant to 60 cm with slender leaf lobes (about 4 mm wide) and metallic-blue flowerheads. *E. r.* 'Veitch's Blue' is more robust with richer blue heads, and may be of hybrid origin. *E. r. ruthenicus* (*E. ruthenicus*) has the leaf lobes even narrower (2 mm). The plant under this name in gardens is probably of hybrid origin; it grows 1-1.2 m with rich-green leaves and bright-blue heads and is one of the most handsome and garden worthy. *E. sphaerocephalus* (C. Europe, W. Asia) resembles *E. exaltatus* but the leaves clasp the stems (those of *E. exaltatus* are stalked) and have rolled margins. It is often listed under the invalid names *E. nivalis* and *E. niveus*.

Elymus arenarius (Lyme Grass) (*Gramineae*)

Curiously enough this is the only one of the 70 known species to be cultivated and then not commonly. Although rhizomatous and capable of forming extensive colonies it is very handsome and well worth a site where it will not intrude on choicer plants. It has broad, bright-blue-grey arching leaves to 60 cm long which in late summer are over-topped by grey wheat-like flower spikes. Ordinary soil is suitable, ideally sandy and it must be well drained with a site in full sun. Planting and propagation by division is best in spring.

Eomecon chionanthum (Snow or Dawn Poppy) (*Papaveraceae*)

The only member of its genus, the snow poppy is native to E. China where its slender rhizomes wander through the humusy soil of woods and thickets. In the garden too it is a coloniser, emitting at invervals tufts of long-stalked, kidney-shaped, somewhat glaucous leaves and stems to 30 cm or more tall bearing one to several white poppy flowers. It is best in humus-rich well-drained soil in partial shade and can be planted from autumn to spring. Propagation is by division of the rhizomes in spring.

Epilobium (Willow Herb) (*Onagraceae*)

Among the 215 species of willow herb there is very little of value to the hardy planter, most of the really attractive species being too small or weedy. Those described here however are worthy of trial. They grow in ordinary soil and are best in sun. Planting can take place from autumn to spring with propagation by division during the latter season. *E. chloraefolium* (New Zealand) is a variable plant and only the more robust forms should be obtained, in particular *E. c. kaikour-ense* (sometimes listed as "*E. kaikoense*"). This usually reaches 30 cm or more, with oval, often pinkish-brown-flushed leaves and comparatively large cream flowers in summer. Pinkish-flushed forms are known. *E. dodonaei* (S. France to W. Ukraine) can best be described as a more refined form of the rosebay willow herb, forming wide dense clumps of slender stems 70-90 cm tall with tapered spires of bright-pink flowers and narrow grey leaves. *E. glabellum* (New Zealand) can reach 30 cm in height in fertile soils, forming mats of fresh green leaves and white to cream flowers. Pink forms are known in the wild and *E. g.* 'Sulphureum' has soft-yellow flowers. It makes an interesting front-of-the-border subject.

Epimedium (Barrenwort) (*Berberidaceae*)

Barely half of the 21 speices in this genus are cultivated but a number of hybrids greatly increases their variety and usefulness. All are first-rate front-of-the-border plants especially for shaded sites, providing pleasing to highly decorative dissected foliage and spring-borne spurred flowers. The evergreen species are particularly desirable. They grow in ordinary, ideally humus-enriched soil that does not dry out, in partial shade or sun. Planting can take place from autumn to spring. Propagation is by division at planting time or after flowering. Seeds may also be used, but if not sown as soon as ripe (in summer) usually take one and a half years to germinate. *E. alpinum* is the common barrenwort from N. and C. Italy to Albania. It spreads by rhizomes and can form extensive colonies to 30 cm tall. The deciduous leaves are composed of several heart-shaped leaflets which are prettily pale veined and copper-red flushed when young. The small dark-red flowers have bright-yellow spurs. For *E. colchicum* – see under *E. pinnatum*. *E. grandiflorum* (*E. macranthum*) (Japan) is tightly clump-forming with neat, deciduous foliage and flowers that vary from white to rose-red and violet. The latter are the largest in the genus and exquisitely shaped, with slender spurs 1 cm or more long; *E. g.* 'Rose Queen' (crimson pink), 'White Queen' (pure white) and 'Violaceum' (deep lilac) can all be recommended. *E.* X *perralchicum* is a name covering the hybrids between *E. pinnatum colchicum* and *E. perralderanum* and which blend the parental characters in various ways. *E. perralderanum* (Algeria) is the finest of the evergreen species forming wide clumps of very durable, lustrous, trifoliate leaves just overtopped by bright-yellow flowers with small brown spurs. *E. pinnatum* (Iran) is evergreen in all but the hardest winters and is akin to *E. perralderanum* but has more variable leaves composed of three to nine leaflets. The yellow flowers tend to be hidden by the previous year's leaves and if a floral display is wanted these should be cut away in early spring. *E. p. colchicum* is somewhat larger, usually more than 30 cm tall, each leaf being composed of three to five large leaflets. *E. pubigerum* (Caucasus to Balkan peninsula) is clump-forming, with lustrous leaves of three to five heart-shaped leaflets. It is the tallest in bloom (to 45 cm) with airy sprays of small pink to cream or white blooms. *E.* X *rubrum* (*E. alpinum* X *E. grandiflorum*) is much like the first parent but more robust and with strongly red-tinted young leaves. The flowers are red with white spurs. It is sometimes listed as *E. alpinum rubrum*. *E.* X *versicolor* is a deciduous hybrid between *E. grandiflorum* and *E. pinnatum colchicum* which blends parental characters in various ways. The leaves are coppery tinted and the flowers are similar in form to those of *E. grandiflorum* but are smaller, in shades of yellow and pink with red-tinted spurs; 'Sulphureum' is pale yellow. *E.* X *warleyense* is probably *E. alpinum* X *E. pinnatum colchicum* with spreading rhizomes and 30 cm-tall leaves of five to nine leaflets. The flowers are coppery-red and yellow. *E.* X *youngianum* (*E. diphyllum* X *E. grandiflorum*) is deciduous and clump-forming with pale leaves of nine leaflets, and white and green flowers. *E.* X *y.* 'Niveum' has good, pure-white flowers but is only 15 cm tall.

Eremurus (Foxtail Lily) (*Liliaceae*)

About 50 species of these statuesque plants are known, many of them inhabiting the dry steppe countries of W. and C. Asia. Although often offered in bulb catalogues they are in every way herbaceous perennials arising annually from crowns of long roots rather like those of asparagus but more fleshy. They require well-drained, fertile soil in full sun, but preferably sheltered from early morning sun, as the young leaves are frost tender. Planting is best in autumn. Propagation is by careful division at planting time, or by seeds in spring. The latter method is slow, five years or more being required to reach flowering size. For *E. bungei* – see *E. stenophyllus*, and for *E. elwesii* – see under *E. robustus*. *E. himalaicus* (NW Himalayas to Nuristan) is one of the easiest to grow but is the least spectacular of those described here. It varies from 90 cm to 150 cm in height with spires of white flowers in late spring. *E. olgae* (Iran, Afghanistan) is in effect, a finer version of *E. himalaicus* but with much narrower leaves (to 1.5 cm only, whereas those of *himalaicus* are 4 cm); the white, rarely pink, flowers open in summer. *E. robustus* (Turkestan) grows 2-3 m tall, with broad bluish-green foliage and long spires of peach-pink flowers in summer. *E. r. elwesii* has purer pink flowers which open earlier; it is sometimes offered as *E. aitchisonii*. *E.* X Shelford (*E. olgae* X *E. stenophyllus*) comprises a range of hybrid cultivars and their unnamed seedlings. They attractively combine their parental characters with flowers in shades of yellow to orange-buff, pink and white. *E. stenophyllus* (Iran and adjacent USSR) varies from 1-1.5 m in height with dense spires of bright-yellow flowers in summer.

Erigeron (Fleabane) (*Compositae*)

Among the 200 species of fleabane are worthless annual weeds and first-rate border plants. The latter have typically daisy-like flowers but are highly distinctive by reason of the multiplicity of very slender ray florets. Ordinary soil, ideally enriched with humus, and a sunny site are all that is required. Planting can take place from autumn to spring, with propagation by careful division or by basal cuttings in spring. *E. aurantiacus* (Turkestan) is the only true orange-flowered species in cultivation, and being only about 30 cm makes a fine splash of colour in summer at the front of the border. *E. a. sulphureus* is yellow. *E. glaucus*, seaside daisy (California, Oregon) forms broad mats or low hummocks of evergreen, glaucous, spoon-shaped leaves and a succession of mauve daisies to 8 cm wide in summer and autumn. It is a maritime plant in its home country and is excellent for seaside gardens. *E. g.* 'Elstead Pink' is lavender pink and 'Rose Purple' is a deep mauve-purple. *E. grandiflorus* is a name sometimes used for the hybrids derived from the next species. *E. speciosus macranthus* (*E. macranthus* and *E. mesa-grandis*) (W. North America) forms clumps to about 60 cm tall, each stem clad with narrow leaves and topped by three to five daisies with purple to blue rays in the summer. Crossed with *E. glaucus* and *E. aurantiacus* and possibly allied species, it has given rise to many fine cultivars, the modern ones with extra rays and in shades of deep violet to pink.

Erodium (Stork's Bill) (*Geraniaceae*)

Most of the garden-worthy members of this 90-species genus are rock plants, but a few are larger and those mentioned provide both attractive summer flowers and long-term foliage for the front of the bed. They need well-drained, ordinary soil and a sunny site, though partial shade is tolerated. Planting is best in autumn or spring with propagation by division at the same time. Seeds can also be sown in spring. *E. carvifolium* (C. Spain) rarely exceeds 25 cm but is substantial enough for the perennial garden with its feathery bipinnate leaves. The flowers are purple, the two larger upper petals of which have almost black basal blotches. *E.* X *hybridum* (*E. daucoides* X *E. manescavii*) is similar to the latter parent but with more deeply dissected leaves and paler, rosy flowers. This name must be treated with caution in catalogues as it is sometimes erroneously used for the tiny *E. reichardii* 'Roseum'. *E. manescavii* (W. and C. Pyrenees) eventually forms loose mats of lush fern-like foliage overtopped by 30-50 cm-tall stems bearing purple to carmine-purple flowers 3 cm wide.

Eryngium (Sea Holly) (*Umbelliferae*)

The 230 different species of sea holly have an almost world-wide distribution in temperate and sub-tropical countries. They vary much in foliage and habit but all have flowerheads composed of cone-shaped clusters of tiny florets surrounded by often coloured, somewhat petal-like bracts. No herbaceous bed or border is complete without at least one or two of these distinctive plants. They require well-drained but otherwise ordinary soil and a sunny site. Early autumn or spring are the best planting times. Propagation is by careful division in spring, root cuttings in late winter or seeds when ripe or spring. The following are all summer flowering. *E. agavifolium* (Argentina) has bold, evergreen, spiny-toothed, sword-shaped leaves in rosettes and robust stems to 1.5 m tall with disappointingly small whitish-green flowerheads. *E. alpinum* (European mountains) is the queen of the hardy species with handsome, broadly oval basal leaves and stems to 70 cm tall bearing the largest blue cones surrounded by an elegant ruff of slender, almost feathery metallic-blue bracts. *E. amethystinum* (Italy, Sicily, Balkan Peninsula) is rarely encountered in gardens, its hybrids masquerading under its name. It grows up to 60 cm with slender, much-branched stems and small blue flowerheads surrounded by amethyst bracts; in overall appearance it resembles the more frequently grown *E. tripartitum*. *E. bourgatii* (Pyrenees) would be worth growing for its grey-green leaves alone. These are basically trifoliate but with each leaflet deeply cleft into narrow, waved and angled, white-veined lobes. The stems rise to 60 cm and bear blue-green heads. *E. decaisneana* (S. America) is usually grown under its former name *E. pandanifolium*. At 2.4 m or more it is one of the tallest species with slender sword-shaped evergreeen leaves and massive panicles of purplish-brown heads barely larger than peas. Regrettably it is not as hardy as it might be and needs a sheltered site. *E. eburneum* (temperate S. America) is frequently grown as *E. bromeliifolium* and is also synonymous with *E. paniculatum* and *E. balansae*. It is an ever-green clump-former with rich green, arching, almost grassy foliage and stems 60-90 cm tall bearing pale-greenish heads with white stamens. (True *E. bromeliifolium* is a stiffer, half-hardy Mexican.) *E. giganteum* (Caucasus) should strictly not be mentioned as it is only a biennial. However, as it regularly self-sows, it behaves as a perennial though changing its site from year to year. It has distinctive long-stalked oval leaves and large heads with blue-tinted bracts. In gardens it is fre-quently represented by 'Miss Willmott's Ghost', a form with ivory bracts which gleam in the dusk. *E. maritimum* (Europe) is the only species that truly merits the name sea holly, being native to mari-time sand dunes and beaches. Though seldom cultivated it is a most striking plant with intense grey holly-like leaves and blue flower-heads. *E.* X *oliveranum* has an uncertain ancestry but reputedly arose as a seedling of *E. alpinum* perhaps with *E. amethystinum* or *E. planum* as the other parent. It is not unlike a smaller flowered ver-sion of *E. alpinum* with broader bracts of rich steely blue. *E. planum* (C. and SE Europe) can reach 90 cm in height with persistent oblong to oval leaves and light-blue flowerheads surrounded by greenish-blue, spine-toothed bracts. *E. p.* 'Blue Dwarf' is short and compact. For *E. pandanifolium* of gardens – see *E. decaisneana*. *E. protei-florum* (Mexico) has sword-shaped evergreen leaves with marginal spines that are sometimes three pronged. Robust stems arise to 90 cm and produce quite large, cone-shaped greenish heads surrounded by numerous shining steely-white bracts. It is inclined to be short lived and not easy to please and sometimes tries unsuccessfully to flower in winter. Some catalogues erroneously list it as Delaroux, the name of the French botanist who first described the species. *E. serra* (Brazil) resembles a shorter *E. agavifolium* with smaller, rounded flowerheads and doubly toothed leaves. *E. tripartitum* (of gardens) is fairly cer-tainly a hybrid, perhaps from *E. planum* which it most resembles, It grows to 75 cm tall with slender much-branched stems and numerous deep-blue bracted heads. *E. variifolium* (Moroccan moun-tains) has glossy, conspicuously white-veined leaves which are attractive all the year round. The stiff flowering stems bear dull greenish heads enlivened by narrow, long-spiny, white bracts. *E.* X *zabelii* should strictly cover hybrids between *E. alpinum* and *E. bour-gatii* but is also used for hybrid cultivars of similar but more uncertain parentage. Several very garden-worthy large-flowered cultivars belong here, notably 'Jewel' (deep violet), 'Spring Hills' (deep blue) and 'Violetta' (metallic blue), all about 1 m tall.

Erysimum – see under *Cheiranthus*.

Eupatorium (Hemp Agrimony, Boneset) (*Compositae*)

This huge genus of 1,200 species provides very few herbaceous perennials of note, though several species are surprisingly negelected. Those described here respond best to fertile, moisture-retentive soil in sun or light shade. Planting can take place from autumn to spring. Propagation is by division at planting time or by sowing seeds in spring. *E. cannabinum* (Europe to C. Asia and N. Africa) is the common hemp agrimony of Britain, with erect bristly stems to 1.2 m clad with opposite pairs of trifoliate leaves and topped by fluffy clusters of tiny pale-purple to whitish flowers in summer. It is seldom cultivated, but the double 'Plenum' is worth looking out for. *E. purpureum* joe-pye weed (E. USA) is a statuesque clump-former like a grand version of *E. cannabinum* 2-3 m tall with much larger trusses of rose-purple to magenta-crimson flowers on purple stems in early autumn. A white form is known and the richer coloured clones are often listed as 'Atropurpureum' and 'Purpurascens'. *E. rugosum* (E. North America) has the curious vernacular name of white snakeroot and is considered synonymous with *E. ageratoides*, *E. fraseri* and *E. urticifolium*. It grows to 1.5 m in height with large, nettle-shaped leaves and flattish heads of white flowers in early autumn. The plant grown as *E. ageratoides* in Britain is usually about 90 cm tall, and slenderer.

Euphorbia (Spurge) (*Euphorbiaceae*)

Among the 2,000 species of spurge are annuals, perennials, shrubs and succulents, some of the latter of tree size. Although of widely differing habits and forms, the flowers are immediately recognisable. What appears to be an individual flower is technically a cyathium, a tiny cup-shaped whorl of fused bracts containing several male flowers, reduced to one stamen each, and a single female reduced to a three-lobed stalked ovary. The cyathia are often arranged in clusters (technically cymes) and these are again grouped in umbels. At the bases of the cyathia, cymes and umbels are leafy bracts which may be coloured. The seed capsules are explosive. The species mentioned grow in ordinary soil and in sun or partial shade; see individual descriptions below for more definite cultural preferences. Planting can take place from autumn to spring. Propagation is by division, or by seeds in early spring or cuttings of basal shoots in late spring. *E. amygdaloides*, wood spurge (Europe to SW Asia and N. Africa) forms colonies of unbranched, erect biennial stems 30-60 cm or more tall, springing from creeping roots. The bright yellow-green floral bracts form short terminal columns, especially dense and effective on the richer, limy soils. *E. a.* 'Purpurea' has the narrow leaves and stems suffused purple. A variegated form is sometimes available.

E. characias (Mediterranean and Portugal) is sub-shrubby, with erect stems to 1 m or more in height clad with narrow, greyish-green leaves. The flowers have reddish-brown glands and are surrounded by yellow-green bracts, many being densely arranged in columnar trusses. *E. c. wulfenii* (*E. veneta* and *E. sibthorpii*) from the eastern Mediterranean is taller and more robust with greyer-green leaves and bright yellow-green bracts and glands. *E. corallioides* (C. and S. Italy, Sicily) forms loose colonies of slender stems 40-60 cm long clad with oblong leaves that can take on red tints in autumn. The best forms have the floral bracts red-flushed. *E. cyparissias*, Cypress spurge (Europe) is disarmingly graceful and attractive with slender stems and grassy grey leaves that turn red in autumn. On light soils however, it can soon become an ineradicable weed and it should always be planted with this caution in mind. *E. dulcis* (W. and C. Europe) has a creeping knobbly rhizome and slender stems 25-40 cm tall bearing elliptic leaves that colour in autumn, and greenish-yellow bracts surrounding dark purple cyathial glands. *E. epithymoides* (C. and S. Europe) is still better known under its earlier *E. polychroma* name. It forms dense hummocks to about 30 cm at flowering time and becomes smothered in spring with chrome-yellow bracts, a real must for early colour in the perennial garden. *E. griffithii* (Himalayas) forms clumps and colonies to 1 m tall with narrow red-veined leaves and terminal clusters of light-red floral bracts. *E. g.* 'Fireglow' is bright brick-red and the clone most commonly grown. *E. hyberna*, Irish spurge (W. Europe) has a stout rhizome and stems 40-60 cm tall bearing oblong leaves that eventually turn reddish, and with long-lasting yellow-green bracts. *E. myrsinites* (S. Europe) is prostrate and should not be included but looks splendid as a frontage piece or spilling over a raised border edging. It has intense grey leaves like fish scales which overlap along the stems, and chrome-yellow bracts in spring. For *E. niciciana* – see under *E. seguierana*. *E. palustris* (Europe) can be conveniently described as a robust *E. epithymoides* to 1 m or more tall and flowering a little later. The leaves often colour well in autumn. It thrives well in wet soils. *E. pilosa* 'Major' (*E. villosa*) (Europe) is related to *E. corallioides* but is taller and more robust, with larger clusters of greenish-yellow bracts creating the effect of an inferior *E. palustris*. *E. rigida* (*E. biglandulosa*) (S. Europe) is in effect an erect growing and less hardy *E. myrsinites*, with stems to 45 cm. *E. robbiae* (NW Turkey) produces plantlets from its far-questing roots and soon forms wide colonies even in dryish, heavily shaded sites. Each 30 cm-tall stem is topped by a rosette of obovate, lustrous deep-green leaves which make a fine foil for spring-borne, bright yellow-green flowers that hover above. *E. seguierana* (Europe to SW Asia) has a tufted habit, with ascending stems about 45 cm tall clad with slender blue-grey leaves and topped by loose clusters of lime-green bracts in the summer. *E. s. niciciana* is somewhat more robust and the sub-species generally met with in gardens. *E. sikkimensis* (E. Himalayas) needs moisture-retentive, fertile soil to do well, and then attains 1.2 m or more and looks really handsome with its pale-veined leaves, red stems and greenish-yellow bracts from mid to late summer. As a bonus it provides glossy bright-red young shoots in spring. For *E. veneta* and *E. wulfenii* – see under *E. characias*.

Festuca (Fescue) (*Gramineae*)

Although most of the 80 fescue grasses are either small or lacking in charm, a few are decidedly garden worthy and provide distinctive foliage for frontal positions. The species mentioned are densely tufted with rolled, thread-fine foliage in shades of deep to pale blue and grey-green. The generally narrow, erect panicles of flowering spikelets are of no great attraction. Any well-drained soil is suitable and a site in full sun. Planting is best early autumn or spring with propagation by division or by seeds in spring. *F. amethystina* (C. Europe, Balkan peninsula) reaches 45 cm or more in flower. It is a variable grass but in the best forms the grey-green leaves are shot with violet or lilac. *F. eskia* (*F. crinum-ursi*) (Pyrenees) eventually forms carpets of rich-green foliage rarely above 30 cm in height in flower. *F. glacialis* (*F. ovina frigida*) (Pyrenees) is like a smaller, more congested *F. ovina*. *F. glauca* (*F. ovina glauca*) (S. France) resembles *F. ovina* but is more robust with bright blue-grey leaves 15-25 cm long. Flowering stems rise to 40 cm or so. *F. ovina*, sheep's fescue (north temperate zone) is densely tufted with 15-25 cm-long leaves that can be green or glaucous, and stems to 30 cm or more with violet-tinted spikelets. *F. punctoria* (*F. acerosa*) (W. Turkey) has glistening grey-green, prickly-tipped leaves to 10 cm long and flowering stems to 30 cm with greyish spikelets. *F. scoparia* (*F. gautieri*) (France, NE Spain) is sometimes called bear grass and forms dense, wide clumps of bright-green foliage and stems 30-50 cm tall with yellow-green spikelets.

Filipendula (Meadowsweet) (*Rosaceae*)

Ten species form this decorative genus of mainly tall, often statuesque plants. They are allied to spiraea and have good pinnate foliage and minute flowers in large, frothy panicles in summer. All but *F. vulgaris* need moisture-retentive, fertile soil, and are fine by the waterside in sun or partial shade. *F. vulgaris* needs well-drained soil and full sun. Planting can take place from autumn to spring with propagation by division at the same time. *F. kamtschatica* (N. Japan, Kamchatka) is the giant of the genus usually exceeding 2 m when happily situated, with broad panicles of white or pinkish flowers.

It is occasionally listed as *Spiraea gigantea*. *F. k.* 'Elegantissima' is a pink-tinted selection and 'Rosea' is blush pink throughout. *F. palmata* (Japan) should now be known as *F. multijuga* but this name is not as yet used by nurserymen. It grows to 1 m or more with clouds of clear pink blossom. *F. p.* 'Nana' (*Spiraea digitata nana*) is a miniature, 30-45 cm tall and ideal for the small garden. *F. purpurea* also comes from Japan but is not known in the wild and is probably a hybrid of *F. palmata*. It reaches 1.5 m and has leaves with few or no lateral leaflets. The cerise flowers are carried in large flattened heads. *F. rubra* (*Spiraea venusta*), queen of the prairie (E. USA) attains 1.5-2 m in height, with large leaves and rich peach-pink flowers. *F. r.* 'Venusta' has larger clusters of deep-pink blossoms and is probably the most desirable and garden-worthy member of its genus. *F. ulmaria* (Europe, W. Asia) is the familiar common meadow-sweet of wet meadows and ditches, and though a lovely plant is seldom cultivated. Rising 90-120 cm in moist rich soil, its creamy-white flowers are heavily fragrant. *F. u.* 'Aurea' has yellow leaves when young which age to bright pale-green, and the flower stems are shorter; 'Variegata' is more of a curiosity having yellow-blotched and striped leaves. *F. vulgaris* (*F. hexapetala*, *Spiraea filipendula*) dropwort (Europe to Siberia) grows in dry situations usually on limy soils. It attains a modest 60 cm or so in height with dense clusters of pinkish buds and creamy-white flowers. For the garden, the larger selection 'Grandiflora' is recommended. *F. v.* 'Plena' ('Flora Plena') has double, longer lasting flowers, but they get heavy in wet weather and the plant usually needs support.

Foeniculum vulgare (Fennel) (*Umbelliferae*)

Although two to five species have been credited to this genus, only *F. vulgare* appears to be cultivated and then generally as a herb and vegetable. A native of S. Europe, it is a long-lived, clump-forming plant 1.2-2 m tall with erect stems that branch above and produce numerous umbels of small yellow flowers in the summer. Its main charm however, is in the incredibly finely dissected leaves which create an almost smoky effect from a distance. The whole plant has a curious but pleasantly aromatic smell. Forms with bronze to blackish-purple leaves occur, the darker sorts being listed as *F. v.* 'Purpureum'. They combine well with yellow, daisy-like flowers such as coreopsis and helenium. Ordinary well-drained soil and a sunny site are the fennel's modest requirements. Planting can take place from autumn to spring. Propagation is by careful division in spring, or by seeds when ripe or in spring.

Francoa (Bridal Wreath) (*Francoaceae*)

One variable species forms this genus of evergreen perennials from Chile. It is not reliably hardy in the colder areas of Britian but is so easily raised from seed and long lasting in flower it is worth the gamble of occasional loss. *F. appendiculata* (*F. ramosa*, *F. sonchifolia*) is clump-forming, with mostly basal pinnate leaves that have an extra large, lobed and waved, terminal leaflet. The wand-like flowering stems reach 60-90 cm in height and bear in summer numerous, somewhat bell-shaped, five-petalled, white, pink or red flowers, generally darker spotted within. *F. a. ramosa* has branched racemes of white flowers; *F. a. sonchifolia* has simple racemes of pink blossom. Humus-rich, well-drained soil and a sheltered, sunny or partially shaded site are recommended. It is an ideal candidate for the border against a south or south-west wall. Propagation is by seeds under glass or basal cuttings in spring.

Funkia — see *Hosta*.

G

Gaillardia (Blanket Flower) (*Compositae*)

Although 28 species are known, only two, and hybrids between them, represent the genus in gardens. They are usually not long lived, but are showy and easily raised from seeds and are a must for all hardy planters. Ordinary soil and sun are their modest requirements. Propagation is by careful division, cuttings or seeds sown in spring, the latter either *in situ* or in nursery rows. Sown early under glass it will flower the first year. *G. aristata* (NC and NW North America) usually reaches 60 cm or more in height with greyish downy, lobed leaves. The daisy flowers are 6-7 cm wide with broad three-lobed ray florets of rich yellow, sometimes stained red-purple at the bases; the disc florets are brownish-purple. *G. X grandiflora* is the name used for hybrids between the previous and the next species, though not all cultivars so listed may in fact be of hybrid origin. 'Dazzler' is probably a selection from *G. aristata* and has bright orange-yellow flowers; the same may be true of 'Croftway Yellow'. Other cultivars of merit are 'Ipswich Beauty', deep red with yellow tips; 'Mandarin', rich yellowish-orange, and 'Wirral Flame', mahogany red with small yellow tips. *G. pulchella* (C. and S. USA and Mexico) is much like *G. aristata* but rarely above 45 cm, having purple-red florets with or without small yellow tips.

Galax urceolata (Galaxy or Wand Flower) (*Diapensiaceae*)

Better known under its former name of *G. aphylla*, this eastern N. American plant is the only member of its genus. It is a plant of real quality, quietly handsome with its long-stalked, circular to heart-shaped polished leaves and slender 60 cm spires of small white flowers in summer. There is a bonus in autumn when the evergreen leaves take on tints of bronze, purple or red. Flower arrangers find the leaves irresistible. Forming dense clumps and colonies, galaxy makes fine ground cover. Like all things of quality, it is not for everyone; it must have an acid or peaty soil to thrive, and partial or full shade. Planting is best in autumn or spring and propagation is by division at the same time, or by seeds when ripe.

Galega (Goats' Rue) (*Leguminosae*)

Two species and their variants form this indispensable and decorative genus. They form clumps or colonies of fresh green pinnate leaves and bear abundant spike-like racemes of small pea flowers in summer. Ordinary soil and sun are their requirements but light shade is tolerated. Planting can take place from autumn to spring. Propagation is by division at planting time or by seeds in spring. *G. officinalis* (C. Europe to SW Asia) is clump-forming to 1.5 m tall with purple-blue, pink or white flowers. Forms with bicoloured blooms of deep purple-blue and bluish-white have been described as *G. bicolor* and *G. patula*. Hybrids between *patula* and true *officinalis* (formerly called *G. hartlandii*) have provided the finest cultivars, e.g. 'Lady Wilson' (mauve-pink) and 'Her Majesty' (clear lilac). *G. orientalis* (Caucasus) differs from *G. officinalis* primarily in its rhizomatous spreading habit; it can be mildly invasive in some soils. The flowers are violet-blue on stems to 1.2 m.

Gaura (*Onagraceae*)

This genus of 18 species is allied to the evening primroses and there are strong resemblances in all but the small woody seed capsules. Only one species is generally grown in Britain, *G. lindheimeri* from Louisiana, Texas and Mexico. It is a tufted plant with branched, wiry stems 90-120 cm tall, lance-shaped leaves and airy panicles of 3-4 cm-wide white flowers which age to pink. Flowering time extends from summer well into autumn. It is a short-lived perennial but easily raised from seeds which, if sown early under glass, will flower the same year. Ordinary well-drained soil and a sunny, preferably sheltered site are preferred.

Gentiana (Gentian) (*Gentianaceae*)

Most of the 350-400 species of gentians are rock-garden plants but a few attain sufficient height and robustness to merit inclusion in beds and borders. Those described need fertile, moisture-retentive soil and thrive in partial shade or full sun. Planting is best in spring or early autumn. Propagation is by seeds when ripe or in spring, or by careful division at planting time. *G. asclepiadea*, willow gentian

(Alps, N. Apennines) has clumps of slender stems which arch gracefully to 60 cm or more in height. Typical deep-blue, paler striped gentian blossoms erupt from the upper leaf axils from late summer to autumn. *G. a. alba* is white, and deeper and paler blue forms occur regularly in batches of seedlings. *G. lutea*, great yellow gentian (C. and S. European mountains) has erect, robust, unbranched stems to 1.2 m or more arising from large basal leaves not unlike those of veratrum. The yellow flowers are most un-gentian like with short tubes and long spreading petal lobes. They form imposing tiered spikes in summer.

Geranium (Crane's Bill) (*Geraniaceae*)

Of cosmopolitan distribution there are an estimated 300-400 different sorts of crane's bill, including annuals, biennials and perennials. Among the latter are plants to please all tastes, choice and easy alpines and herbaceous perennials for attractive blossom and ground cover. They must not be confused with the florists' geraniums so popular as pot plants, which are members of the closely allied genus *Pelargonium*. The name crane's bill refers to the beaked fruit (seed head) with its five basal seeds which are flung off balista fashion when ripe and ready for dispersal. All the geraniums mentioned here thrive in ordinary soil and a site in sun or partial shade. Planting can take place from autumn to spring and propagation is easy by division at the same time. Seeds may be sown when ripe or in spring. Some species may take several weeks or months to germinate. For *G. armenum* – see *G. psilostemon*. *G. atlanticum* is probably not, or very rarely cultivated, *G. malviflorum* (q.v.) masquerading in its place. *G. candicans* and *candidum* are names misapplied to *G. lambertii* (q.v.). *G.* X 'Claridge Druce' (*G. endressii* X *G. versicolor*) is a vigorous hybrid forming dense ground-covering mats and bearing abundant pink-purple flowers on 40-60 cm-tall stems in summer and autumn. It is a fertile plant and somewhat inferior seedlings sometimes stand in for the original. *G. delavayi* of gardens is *G. sinense* (q.v.). *G. endressii* (SW France, Spain) is rhizomatous forming wide clumps 30-50 cm tall with five-lobed leaves and pink flowers in summer and autumn. It is a fine dual-purpose ground-cover and flowering plant, especially in its selected forms 'A. T. Johnson' (silvery pink), 'Rose Clair' (white-feathered purple) and 'Wargrave Pink' (bright salmon). *G. himalayense* is better known as *G. grandiflorum* and is sometimes listed as *G. meeboldii*. It spreads underground to form wide colonies 30-45 cm tall of long-stalked seven-lobed leaves and 5 cm-wide saucer-shaped flowers of deep violet-blue with red veins, in early summer. *G. h.* 'Alpinum' ('Gravetye') is more compact and 'Plenum' has double flowers. *G. ibericum* is seldom cultivated – see *G.* X *magnificum*. *G. lambertii* (*G. candicans* and *G. candidum* of gardens) (Himalayas) has trailing stems 60-90 cm long with side branches to 30 cm tall that bear beautifully formed, nodding 3.5 cm-wide, bowl-shaped, white flowers with light-crimson centres during late summer and autumn. It is seen to best advantage when trailing over and between low shrubs. *G. macrorrhizum* (mountains of S. Europe) forms wide, weed-smothering mats of stout overground, and slender underground rhizomes. The deeply five to seven lobed, aromatic leaves often turn red in autumn, and the pink to red flowers are carried in clusters from late spring to summer. *G. m.* 'Album' has white petals and red calyces; 'Bevan's' is crimson-purple; 'Ingwersen's', pink; 'Variegatum' has leaves splashed creamy-white. *G. maculatum* (E. North America) forms clumps 45-60 cm tall with five-lobed leaves and an abundance of rose-purple to lilac-pink flowers late spring to early summer. *G.* X *magnificum* (*G. ibericum* X *G. platypetalum*) is generally listed under the names of its parents. It resembles a robust *G. platypetalum* to 60 cm tall, with larger, more handsome leaves and flowers. It is sterile, failing to produce viable seeds. *G. malviflorum* (W. Mediterranean) usually masquerades as *G. atlanticum*. It has tuber-like rhizomes in dense clumps and freely borne rich bluish-lilac, darker-veined flowers in late spring. The plant dies back to ground level in July resuming growth about six to eight weeks later. *G. nodosum* (Pyrenees to Yugoslavia) has erect to reclining stems up to 50 cm tall, three to five lobed, somewhat lustrous, leaves and lilac to pink flowers form late spring to autumn. *G. phaeum*, mourning widow (Europe to W. USSR) is more curious than beautiful in its commonly seen brownish to blackish-purple flowered forms. The pure white is beautiful, and the wild lilac-purple sort very pleasing in late spring. Densely clump-forming and useful as ground cover it can attain 60 cm or more in height. *G. pogonanthum* was for long grown as KW22796, then erroneously identified as *G. yunnanense*. It is a clump-former 45 cm or more tall with cyclamen-shaped rosy-mauve flowers in summer. *G. platypetalum* (Caucasus, Turkey) seldom occurs in gardens, *G.* X *magnificum* almost invariably taking its place. It is worth seeking out however, being a compact plant to 45 cm with softly hairy leaves that may turn red in autumn, and violet-blue, darker-veined flowers in summer. *G. pratense*, meadow crane's bill (Europe to Asia) is a handsome clump-former 50-90 cm tall with long-stalked five to nine lobed leaves, and 3 cm-wide violet-blue flowers in summer. Long grown in our gardens it has given rise to several distinct forms or cultivars: *G. p.* 'Album' has white flowers and 'Album Plenum' is double though individual blooms are small; 'Plenum Caeruleum' has double lavender-blue flowers; 'Plenum Violaceum' larger and attractively rosetted deep violet-blue ones; 'Roseum' is pink with darker veins; 'Striatum' ('Bicolor') has erratically white-striped or sectioned petals. 'Johnson's Blue' is rarely

79

above 30 cm tall with large lavender-blue, darker-veined flowers and is probably of hybrid origin with *G. himalayense*. *G. procurrens* (Himalayas) is sometimes listed incorrectly as *G. collinum*. It is a high-speed ground coverer capable of producing stems up to 2 m long in one season, clad with deeply cleft leaves that are almost pentagonal in outline. The upward-facing, wide-open 2-3 cm-wide flowers are a rich rosy-mauve with a maroon eye and an almost bluish satiny lustre. They open from late summer to late autumn and can be delightful even in November. *G. procurrens* is a rampant coloniser and must be planted with caution. In the smaller garden it should be restricted to dry shady sites or where the soil is poor. *G. "rectum album"* of catalogues is a form of *pratense* from Kashmir, with a running root stock and large white flowers with dark veins and has now been christened 'Kashmir White'. Similar but a deep purplish-lilac is 'Kashmir Purple', often still listed as *G. bergianum*. *G. psilostemon* (*G. armenum*) (USSR-Armenia) is not unlike a robust *G. pratense* with coarser foliage and black-eyed crimson-magenta flowers. *G. punctatum* (of gardens) is confused with *G. maculatum*, but much like *G. phaeum* with leaves having purple-brown blotches and mauve flowers. *G. reflexum* (S. Europe) in habit rather resembles *G. phaeum* but the rosy-mauve petals reflex back in cyclamen fashion. It is at its best in early summer. *G. renardii* (Caucasus) rarely reaches 30 cm in height even in flower, but its foliage is so good it merits a place at the front of a bed or border. The leaves are grey-green, sage-like in texture, finely wrinkled above and felted beneath and form dense, neat mounds about 15 cm tall. Borne in summer, the largish flowers have widely spaced white petals with a bold purple veining. *G. X 'Russell Prichard'* (*G. endressii* X *G. traversii*) is generally thought of as a rock plant being about 20 cm tall in bloom. Its spreading habit, silvery leaves and rose-magenta flowers from early summer to autumn make it ideal for the border edge. *G. sanguineum* (Europe to W. Asia) has the improbable name of bloody crane's bill though the early to late summer-borne flowers are red-purple. Tufted in habit it produces spreading mats of slender stems neatly clad with smallish, deeply and sharply lobed leaves. *G. s.* 'Album' has white flowers; 'Prostratum' is lower and flatter growing, while *G. s. lancastrense* is prostrate with pale-pink red-veined flowers. *G. sinense* (*G. delavayi* of gardens) (W. China) has good clumps of dark-green leaves and small but intriguing maroon flowers with sharply reflexed petals borne from late summer to autumn. *G. sylvaticum*, wood crane's bill (Europe to Siberia) resembles *G. pratense*, but seldom exceeds 60 cm. It has more broadly fingered leaves and somewhat cupped, bluish-purple flowers. *G. s.* 'Album' is white and 'Mayflower' rich violet-blue, while 'Roseum' and 'Wanneri' come in shades of pink. *G. tuberosum* (S. Europe) has a rounded, tuber-like rhizome and slender erect stems to 40 cm or so.

Figure 6: *Geranium procurrens*

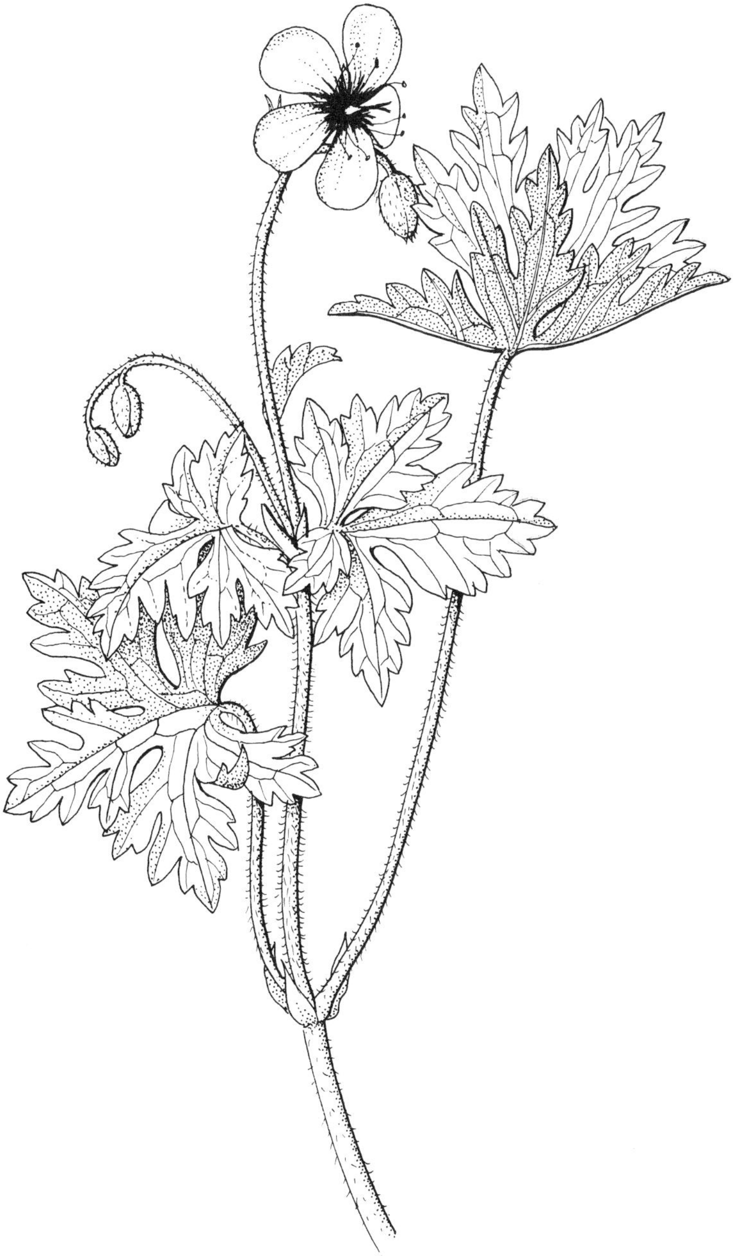

The leaf lobes are jaggedly toothed and the early summer flowers have rosy-purple, notched petals. The plant dies down about mid-summer, leafing again in autumn. *G. wallichianum* (Himalayas) resembles *G. lambertii* in habit but has upturned flatter flowers of mauve to blue-violet with pale to white centres; 'Buxton's Blue' is the finest selection having almost true blue flowers with clear white eyes; a fine plant for late summer to autumn colour. *G. wlassovianum* (China to Siberia) forms clumps of rich-green, almost velvety leaves with stems 50-60 cm tall bearing deep-violet flowers in early summer. For *G. yunnanense* of catalogues — see *G. pogonanthum*.

Geum (Avens) (*Rosaceae*)

The 40 species in this genus are distributed in the temperate zones of both hemispheres. The taller sorts mentioned here have bold pinnate leaves with extra large terminal leaflets and five-petalled flowers like those of potentilla. They thrive in any moderately fertile soil that does not dry out. Planting can take place from autumn to spring. Propagation is by division at planting time, or by seeds when ripe or in spring. *G.* X *borisii* is reputedly *G. reptans* X *G. bulgaricum*, but evidence suggests that the true red-flowered *G. coccineum* from the Balkan peninsula is the second parent. It grows to 30 cm or so tall with 2.5 cm-wide flowers of bright, clear orange in early summer. 'Georgenberg' is a similar hybrid with pale-toned flowers. *G. chiloense* (*G. coccineum* of gardens) (Chile, Chiloé) grows to 60 cm in height with scarlet flowers from early summer to autumn. This species is mainly represented in gardens by larger, semi-double flowered cultivars, notably 'Fire Opal' (rich bronze-scarlet), 'Lady Stratheden' (soft rich yellow), 'Mrs Bradshaw' (bright brick-red). The name *G. chiloense* is now stated to have no botanical standing, the correct name being *G. quellyon*. *G. rivale*, water avens (northern hemisphere) can form wide clumps in moist soil, the 30-40 cm-tall stems bearing nodding orange and pink flowers with purplish, bell-shaped calyces. The overall effect is quite unlike that of most other members of the genus. *G. r.* 'Album' has pale-green calyces and white petals; a plant for the connoisseur. More showy are the named hybrids with the wood avens (*G. urbanum*). These should be listed under *G.* X *intermedium*, and 'Leonard's Variety' with larger, coppery-pink petals is the most eye-catching; 'Lionel Cox' is yellow.

Gillenia trifoliata (Indian Physic) (*Rosaceae*)

This E. North American genus contains two species, *G. trifoliata* being the most garden worthy and generally available in Britain. It is a graceful clump-former to 1 m or more in height with slender red stems and trifoliate leaves formed of slender-pointed, sharply toothed, ovate leaflets. The starry-white flowers vary from 2.5-4 cm wide and are carried in airy terminal clusters in summer. After the petals fall the red calyces enlarge and remain in a decorative state until the seeds ripen. Ordinary soil that does not dry out is all that is required, with a site in partial shade, though full sun is tolerated. Planting and propagation by divison can take place from autumn to spring. Seeds can be sown in spring.

Glaucidium palmatum (*Glaucidiaceae*)

This is the only member of its genus, and is a plant of beauty and refinement. Regrettably it needs shelter from wind, cool, moist shade and a soil largely of humus to thrive; it is native to the high mountain forests of northern Japan. It produces long-stalked, large maple-shaped leaves from among which rise sturdy 30-60 cm-tall stems bearing a few smaller leaves and 5-8 cm wide lavender poppy-like flowers in late spring. Planting is best in early autumn or spring. Propagation is by careful division of mature clumps at planting time or by sowing seeds when ripe. Seedlings take several years to reach flowering size.

Glaucium flavum (Horned poppy) (*Papaveraceae*)

The common horned poppy of W. and S. European sea coasts, this is the only one of 25 species that is reasonably perennial and commercially available. It has pinnately lobed, crinkly, grey leaves in basal rosettes and yellow poppy-like flowers on stems to 45 cm or more from summer to autumn. The intriguing horn-like pods that follow are 15-30 cm long. Root disturbance is resented and plants are best grown from seeds sown *in situ* in spring. Sharply drained soil and full sun are the ingredients for success but this is always a short-lived perennial.

Glyceria maxima (Reed Sweet Grass) (*Gramineae*)

Also known as reed meadow grass this is the most handsome and largest member of 20 wetland species from the temperate regions of both hemispheres. Rhizomatous and soon forming colonies it has wide, ribbon-like leaves and stems to 2 m topped by graceful plumes of tiny, often purple-tinted spikelets. *G. m.* 'Variegata' was formerly misidentified as a variegated form of *G. aquatica* (*Poa aquatica*) hence the use of these names in catalogues. It is one of the most appealing of coloured-leaved grasses, the boldly cream-striped leaves being pink flushed when young. To thrive at its best this grass needs moist to wet soil and a sunny site. Planting should be done in spring with propagation by division at the same time.

Gunnera (*Gunneraceae*)

Only the two hardiest and most massive members of this 50 species genus are generally cultivated though the rock gardener will know of several other improbably tiny species. Those described are water-side plants needing perpetually moist humus-rich soil in partial shade or sun with shelter from strong cold winds. They should be planted in spring and propagated by division at the same time. *G. manicata* (Brazil, Colombia) is the most commonly seen in Britain and the largest, with great lobed leaves 2 m or more wide and high. The tiny greenish to pinkish flowers are densely carried in conical clusters to 1 m high in summer. It is not totally hardy and it is wise to pile the dead leaves over the crowns in late autumn. *G. tinctoria* (*G. chilensis*) (temperate S. America) much resembles *G. manicata* and is confused with it. The leaves are somewhat smaller however and the plant more tightly clump-forming. The flower clusters also are shorter and stiffer, often strongly red-flushed with side branches up to 10 cm long (those of *manicata* are usually 15 cm).

Gypsophila (Chalk Plant) (*Caryophyllaceae*)

This varied genus of 125 species of annuals, rock garden and border perennials provides the indispensable baby's breath, *G. paniculata* (C. Europe to C. Asia). This is a plant so useful for providing contrast to more boldly fashioned subjects and as an accompaniment for cut-flower arrangements and bouquets. It is a tap-rooted plant forming dense tufts of intricately branched erect stems 90-120 cm tall, with small narrow leaves and dense clouds of tiny white flowers in summer. Cultivars usually represent it in gardens, best loved being the double white 'Bristol Fairy'; 'Flamingo' is a less vigorous, pale-pink version of it. *G. p.* 'Rosy Veil' ('Rosenschleier') is dwarf to 40 cm tall with rose-pink double flowers.

Hacquetia epipactis (*Umbelliferae*)

At only 15-25 cm tall, this little clump-forming plant from C. Europe should not be included. However, as it provides colour and interest early in the year it makes a very worthwhile front-of-the-border plant for the more discerning gardener. It has fresh green trifoliate foliage, the leaflets of which are deeply cleft and toothed. From late winter to spring a succession of button-shaped heads of tiny yellow flowers appear, each head surrounded by a ruff of yellow-green bracts in the manner of a winter aconite. Planting is best in early autumn or late winter. Propagation is by seeds when ripe or by careful division at planting time.

Hakonechloa macra (*Graminaeae*)

The only species of its genus, this rhizomatous Japanese grass is grown as a foliage plant providing colour and interest at the border front. Of dense and spreading to semi-erect habit, it has stems 30-50 cm long with slender leaves and nodding oval panicles of tiny green spikelets. These are not commonly produced on the cultivars that represent it in Britain: 'Albo Aurea', leaves white and yellow striped, often with an overall bronze hue; 'Albo-Variegata', green and white striped; 'Aureola', leaves mainly yellow with faint green lines. Ordinary but not dry soil is suitable and ideally, a site in partial shade. Planting should take place in spring with propagation by division at the same time.

Helenium (Sneezeweed) (*Compositae*)

Although only one species and its cultivars is grown out of the 40 listed, this is an indispensable border perennial providing colour in late summer and autumn in the best daisy-flower tradition. Clump-forming and soundly perennial it needs ordinary fertile soil that does not dry out, and a sunny site. Planting can take place from autumn to spring with propagation by division at the same time. *H. autumnale* (E. USA) is 1 m tall, the erect leafy stems bearing branched clusters of 5 cm-wide yellow flowers with almost globular discs and wedge-shaped florets which partially reflex with age. Most of the following cultivars are of hybrid origin mainly with the similar *H. bigelovii* from W. USA which has darker yellow rays and sometimes, purple-brown discs: 'Bruno', mahogany red, 1 m; 'Butterpat', rich yellow, 90-100 cm; 'Coppelia', coppery-orange, 90 cm; 'Pumilum Magnificum', clear yellow; 'Riverton Beauty', yellow and maroon, 1.5 m; 'Wyndley', yellow, flecked orange-brown, to 90 cm.

Helianthella quinquenervis (*Compositae*)

This is the only member of a ten-species genus from W. USA and Mexico likely to be seen in British gardens. In cultural requirements and general appearance it resembles the familiar *Helianthus*, but the long-stalked primrose flowers nod elegantly from 1.5-1.8 m-tall stems in late summer.

Helianthus (Sunflower) (*Compositae*)

North and South America are the homes of the many sorts of sunflower variously estimated at between 110 and 150 species. The perennial species are mainly tall and rather coarse growing, sometimes invasive but nevertheless are indispensable border plants for their showy yellow flowers in late summer and autumn. Ordinary fertile soil and sun are the basic requirements and planting can take place from autumn to spring. Propagation is by division at planting time. *H. atrorubens* (*H. sparsifolius*) (E. USA) has rough, hairy leaves to 18 cm long and erect stems 1.5-2 m tall bearing rich-yellow flowers with purple-black discs; 'Monarch' is the most commonly grown, having larger semi-double flowers. *H. decapetalus* (E. USA) is similar to the preceding species but with pale-yellow flowers. It is seldom cultivated but the name is sometimes used in catalogues for its hybrids with *H. annuus* (*H. X multiflorus*) and *H. tuberosus* (*H. laetiflorus*). The cultivars are robust, showy plants; 'Loddon Gold' reaches 1.8 m with golden-yellow double flowers; 'Capenoch Star' attains 1.2 m and is lemon-yellow. 'Soleil d'Or' reaches 1.5 m with double rich yellow flowers, and 'Triumph de Gand' varies from 1.2-1.5 m with clear yellow semi-double blooms. *H. salicifolius* (*H. orgyalis*) willow-leaved sunflower (SE USA) is the neatest and most graceful of the hardy perennial sunflowers with willow-like, rich green foliage and stems up to 2 m tall bearing in early autumn smallish lemon-yellow flowers with purple-brown centres. For *H. sparsifolius* — see under *H. atrorubens*.

Helichrysum 'Sulphur Light' (*Compositae*)

Cast in the mould of an *Anaphalis* and having the same cultural preferences, this newish plant to the nursery trade must surely have a bright future. It is clump-forming to 45 cm with slim white, woolly leaves and clusters of glowing sulphur-yellow flowers in late summer.

Helictotrichon (*Gramineae*)

About 90 species comprise this genus of grasses from Europe, Africa and Asia, but only *H. sempervirens* (SW Europe) has found favour as a garden plant. Still frequently listed as *Avena candida* or *A. sempervirens*, it forms dense tufts of narrow, arching, grey-green leaves to 45 cm long. In summer slender stems soar 1-1.2 m bearing nodding panicles of small purple-tinted spikelets. Ordinary well-drained soil in sun are its simple requirements. Planting time and propagation is best in spring.

Heliopsis (Ox-eye) (*Compositae*)

This genus of twelve species is much like *Helianthus* and requires the same culture. The species described are showy and are among the mainstays of the herbaceous garden for late summer and autumn colour. *H. helianthoides scabra* (*H. scabra*) (E. North America) forms clumps to 1.5 m tall with toothed leaves in pairs (those of *Helianthus* are mostly alternate) and 6-7 cm-wide yellow daisy flowers. Most of the cultivars are dwarfer with larger flowers: 'Gigantea' is deep yellow; 'Gold Greenheart' has double chrome-yellow heads with a green centre, 90 cm; 'Golden Plume' is double orange-yellow, 1 m; 'Incomparabilis' has orange, almost fully double heads, 1 m; whilst 'Patula' has chrome-yellow frilled blooms on 1.3 m stems.

Helleborus (Hellebore) (*Ranunculaceae*)

Although none of the 20 species of hellebore are bright showy plants they have a certain air about them and appeal strongly to many

Doronicum caucasicum

Iris kaempferi

Stipa calamagrostis

Actaea rubra

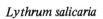

Lythrum salicaria

Ligularia clivorum

Euphorbia wulfenii

Euphorbia palustris

Astilbe 'Spinell'

Veronica exaltata

Lysimachia ephemerum

Asplenium scolopendrium
'Undulatum'

Ranunculus
gramineus

Penstemon
'Pennington Gem'

Rheum palmatum
'Purpureum'

Eupatorium
purpureum

Geranium pratense 'Kashmir White'

Helenium 'Golden Youth'

Monarda didyma 'Croftway Pink'

Meconopsis grandis

hardy planters. A decided attraction is their winter-to-early-spring flowering period. Most have good foliage particularly the fully ever-green species. Ordinary, preferably humus-rich soil that does not dry out, and partial shade provide ideal conditions, though full sun is tolerated. Planting is best in autumn or after flowering. Propagation is by division at planting time or by seeds when ripe. Dried seeds may take 18 months or more to germinate, seedlings flower at two to three years old. Hellebores divide into two groups on growth-form characters: Group 1: Clump-forming, all the main leaves arising at ground level. Group 2: Shrub-like, with tufts of biennial leafy stems. In both groups the apparent petals are coloured sepals, the true petals being transformed into nectaries (honey leaves). For *H. abs-chasicus* (of gardens) — see under *H. orientalis*. *H. atrorubens* (of gardens) (Group 1) has deciduous, long-stalked leaves divided into about nine narrow leaflets, and 30 cm-tall stems bearing nodding, bowl-shaped green flowers, shaded with red-purple in winter. It is probably a hybrid allied to the *H. orientalis* group. For *H. corsicus* — see under *H. lividus*. *H. cyclophyllus* (Balkan peninsula) (Group 1) is like *H. orientalis* but with palest-green flowers with a glaucous hue. *H. foetidus*, stinking hellebore (Group 2) (W. Europe) has deepest-green, many-fingered evergreen foliage which is attractive in itself and combines well with the pale green of *Alchemilla mollis* and other pale or silvery plants. It is also the perfect foil for its own winter-to-spring-borne pale-green cup-shaped flowers. This is a very shade-tolerant plant and will stand spells of drought well. The vernac-ular name is libellous and the alternative setterwort is to be prefer-red. *H. kochii* (of gardens) is rather like a shorter *H. orientalis* with large, coarsely toothed foliage and yellow-green budded, pale-yellow flowers. It may be a form of the true *H. orientalis* and was named 'Bowles Yellow' (after its introducer, E. A. Bowles) by Graham Thomas. There is also a mystery plant akin to *H. multifidus* which has been distributed as *H. kochii*. *H. lividus* (Group 2) (Majorca) grows 30 cm or more, with trifoliate leaves having a marbled pattern of pale veins and reddish stalks. The spring-borne yellow-green flowers are flushed with purple. It is regrettably less than hardy and not easily obtained but worth seeking and giving a sheltered corner. *H. l. corsicus* (*H. corsicus*) is much hardier and more robust, to 60 cm tall, having clear glossy-green leaflets margined with prominent teeth (those of *H. lividus* itself are smooth edged). The larger flowers are bright yellow-green and open earlier. *H. l. sternii* covers all the hybrids between *lividus* and *corsicus* most of which tend to resemble the latter parent in vigour and hardiness. *H. multifidus* (Group 1) (Yugoslavia, Albania) is rare but most desirable. Each erect leaf stalk is topped by a ruff of deeply dissected leaflets creating the effect of a diminutive palm tree. The nodding yellow-green flowers open in early spring. *H. m. istriacus* is less rare and has coarser leaves divided to about halfway (those of *H. multifidus* are divided to the base). *H. niger* (Group 1) (E. Alps, Apennines) is the familiar Christmas rose though its lovely bowl-shaped white flowers seldom open in time for Christmas. There are several selected clones with more sumptuously formed flowers, 'Potters Wheel' being noteworthy. *H. orientalis* (Group 1) (Greece, Turkey) forms large clumps of dark-green palmate leaves and stems 40-60 cm tall bearing bowl-shaped creamy-green, sometimes pink-tinted flowers from late winter onwards. Most of the plants in gardens under this name are hybrids with such allied species as *H. abschasicus* (deep red-purple), *H. cyclophyllus* (see above), *H. guttatus* (like *orientalis* but red-purple spotted within), *H. purpurascens* (deep purple with glaucous sheen) and *H. atrorubens* (see above). Several cultivars and unnamed seedlings are available in shades of white, pink to red-purple and almost black. Names to look out for are: 'Georgina Nightingale', 'Hazy Dawn', 'Maroon', 'Petsamo', 'Snow White', 'Winter Cheer' and 'Wood Nymph'. *H. viridis*, green hellebore (Group 1) (W. and NW Europe) has coarsely toothed palmate leaves to 23 cm wide and stems to 30 cm topped by nodding 4-5 cm-wide bowls of rich green with a greyish sheen in winter. *H. v. occidentalis* has larger leaves and smaller pure-green flowers and stands deep shade.

Hemerocallis (Day Lily) (*Liliaceae*)

Although about 15 species of the day lily are recorded, less than half have contributed to the wide range of cultivars now available. They are clump-forming plants with arching grassy leaves and large six-petalled flowers of lily-like form. The species and older hybrids have a short season of flowering with each bloom lasting no more than a day or two. Since early this century and especially during the past 30 years, many hundreds of cultivars have been raised in Britain and particularly in the USA by crossing together most of the species mentioned below, with *H. fulva*, *H. lilioasphodelus* and the now rarely seen *H. citrina* as the main parents. They are generally tall with large flowers of good substance in shades of orange, red, yellow, pink, ivory and white. There are also smaller cultivars and those with larger clusters of small wide-open flowers. Choice of the many cultivars available is a matter of personal taste and the catalogues of specialists should be consulted. The most exciting development of recent years has been the bud-building mutation. Instead of each inflorescence having a limited number of flowers, buds continue to form at the tips thus greatly prolonging the blooming period. A range of cultivars with this characteristic will be something to look forward to. Day lilies thrive in ordinary fertile, moisture-retentive soil and sun, though light shade is tolerated. Planting can take place from autumn to

Figure 7: *Helleborus orientalis* hybrid

spring. Propagation is by division at planting time or by sowing seeds in spring. Only the species will come true to type from seeds. *H. dumortieri* (Japan) is 45 cm tall with grassy leaves and compact clusters of fragrant orange flowers in late spring. *H. fulva* (Europe to Siberia) grows 80-100 cm in height with buff-orange, 10 cm-long flowers in summer; *H. f.* 'Kwanso' (*H. disticha* 'Flore Pleno') has semi-double blooms tinted red and copper, while 'Rosea' is a pink mutant from China. *H. lilioasphodelus* (*H. flava*) (SE Europe to Siberia) has long been a denizen of our gardens, forming colonies of broad foliage and stems 60-75 cm tall set with clear yellow flowers in spring. *H. middendorffii* (Siberia to Japan) forms dense clumps to 60 cm and bears fragrant yellow-orange blooms in early summer. *H. minor* (E. Asia) is about 45 cm tall and in late spring produces brown-tinted buds which open to clear yellow flowers. *H. multiflora* (China) is valued for its late-summer-to-autumn-borne small and fragrant orange-yellow flowers charmingly set on 1 m-tall stems. *H. nana* (China) has strongly recurved foliage and fragrant 7 cm-long orange flowers in summer.

Heracleum mantegazzianum (*Umbelliferae*)

Aptly known as giant hogweed, this is the only member of a 70-strong genus to be generally cultivated. A native of the Caucasus and naturalised elsewhere, it is at the most a short-lived perennial and often dies after flowering. It sets seeds prolifically however and self-sows in most gardens. The deeply cut basal leaves which can be 1 m tall are handsome by themselves but when overtopped by 2-4 m-tall ribbed and red-spotted stems and huge white floral cartwheels the effect is splendid and a talking point for every passer by. A group at the edge of a large lawn can make a very telling focal point. It is not for the small garden. The sap of the giant hogweed contains a substance which can neutralise the skin's resistance to sunlight and severe and rapid sunburn results. This effect is often spoken of as an allergy, but it is essentially a chemical reaction and anyone can suffer who handles the plant during sunny weather. It needs moisture-retentive fertile soil and partial shade if it is to get really big. Propagation is from seeds when ripe, ideally sown *in situ* and thinned later.

Hesperis matronalis (Dame's Violet) (*Cruciferae*)

Also known as sweet rocket this once popular cottage-garden plant is the only one of about 30 species to have acquired garden favour. A native of Europe and temperate Asia it is a somewhat woody-based plant with large basal lance-shaped leaves and erect branched stems of fragrant stock-like flowers from early to late summer. Pale lilac-purple is the usual colour but darker shades and white ('Candidissima') are available. Less common are the old double forms which, though not easy to please, are worth seeking. Ordinary well-drained, preferably limy soil and sun or partial shade suit dame's violet. Propagation is best by seeds when ripe or in spring; the doubles are propagated by basal cuttings or by careful division in spring.

Heuchera (Alum Root) (*Saxifragaceae*)

Depending on the botanical authority, 30-50 species are recognised in this largely N. American genus. The cultivated species are tufted at first, spreading later as the thick rhizomes elongate. They are evergreen with rather maple-like, long-stalked leaves and wand-like spikes of tiny flowers. Well-drained, ordinary soil, ideally humus enriched and partial shade are required though full sun is tolerated. Planting can take place either immediately after flowering, or from autumn to spring. Propagation is by division at planting time or seeds in spring. *H. americana* has large leaves that are flushed and veined coppery brown when young, maturing to deep lustrous green. The greenish or red-tinged flowers appear in early summer on 45 cm stems and are not very noteworthy, a good ground-cover species. *H.* X *brizoides* is used for hybrids between *H. sanguinea*, *H. micrantha* and perhaps *H. americana*. They basically resemble the first parent, with elegant panicles of bell-shaped flowers in summer. Noteworthy cultivars are: 'Bressingham Hybrids' (dark red to pale pink), 'Coral Cloud' (light crimson), 'Pearl Drops' (soft white), 'Scintillation' (bright purple-red) and 'Splendour' (salmon-scarlet, bronzy foliage). Others are available and all can be found under *H. sanguinea* in some catalogues. *H. cylindrica* (NW North America) has lobed and scalloped foliage and wiry stems to 75 cm tall bearing dense spikes of cream to greenish yellow in summer; 'Greenfinch' is a greenish-sulphur and has great appeal for flower arrangers. *H. maxima* (California) forms mounds of robust, erect rhizomes and seven to nine lobed leaves with prominently pointed teeth. Bell-shaped white flowers appear in 70-90 cm-tall narrow panicles in the summer. *H. micrantha* (Oregon, California) much resembles the previous species but has smaller leaves (to 8 cm long), often greyish marbled, and smaller flowers often with purple-flushed calyces. *H. richardsonii* (NW North America to Indiana) is rather like a green-flowered version of the next species. *H. sanguinea*, coral bells (SW USA and Mexico mountains) is the showiest member of its genus, with marbled leaves and 40-45 cm-tall panicles of bell-shaped crimson to scarlet flowers in early summer. Good selected colour forms include 'Bressingham Blaze' and 'Shere' (intense scarlet). *H. villosa* (E. North America) produces its white to cream, often pinkish-tinted flowers on 60 cm stems during late summer. The large, hairy, bright-green leaves make good ground cover.

X *Heucherella* (*Heuchera* **X** *Tiarella*) (*Saxifragaceae*)

This name covers two bigeneric hybrids which blend the characters of their parents and have the same cultural requirements as *Heuchera*. They are especially valuable for shady sites. X *H. alba* 'Bridget Bloom' (*H.* X *brizoides* X *T. wherryi*) favours the *Tiarella* parent but with dainty panicles of light-pink flowers on wiry stems to 45 cm in early summer. X *H. tiarelloides* (*H.* X *brizoides* X *T. cordifolia*) is a spreading plant but less vigorous than the *Tiarella* parent and with salmon-pink bells.

Hieracium (Hawkweed) (*Compositae*)

Very few of the 700-1,000 different sorts of hawkweed have caught the gardener's fancy but those that have are worthy of a place in any garden. They are easy going, thriving in poor, dryish soil and in full sun or partial shade. Planting can take place from autumn to spring. Propagation is by division, or seeds in spring or basal cuttings in late summer. *H. aurantiacum*, grim-the-collier, fox and cubs (N. and E. European mountains, naturalised elsewhere) should be planted with caution as its mats of underground stolons can be invasive. It has lance-shaped leaves to 15 cm long, and from summer to autumn has erect stems to 50 cm tall topped by clusters of orange to reddish flowers, the surrounding bracts of which bear long, dark hairs. *H. a. carpathicola* (*H. brunneocroceum*) has many above-ground, often leafy stolons, and smaller flowerheads. *H. lanatum* (C. South Europe) is the correct name for plants sometimes wrongly offered as *H. waldsteinii* and *H. welwitschii*. It is a choice member of its genus, forming clumps of large silvery-grey felted, ovate leaves and branched stems to 60 cm bearing bright-yellow dandelion-like flowers in summer. *H. maculatum* (W. and C. Europe) has a tufted habit, with leafy stems 50-80 cm tall and is best considered as a foliage plant, each 5-15 cm-long leaf being blotched with brownish-purple. The small dandelion-like yellow flowers are carried in branched clusters during summer and autumn. *H. villosum* (European mountains) is a plant of distinction with tufts of oval, densely silky, white-woolly leaves and in summer, 4-5 cm-wide rich yellow flowers on stems to 30 cm tall.

Holcus mollis 'Variegata' (*Gramineae*)

This form of the common creeping soft grass is the only representative of its genus likely to be seen in gardens, though several of the other species have ornamental possibilities. It is a tufted grass capable of creeping extensively underground in light, rich soils. The slender, softly hairy leaves are white-striped and up to 15 cm or more long. Flowering is not so profuse as on its green-leaved progenitor, and the narrow panicles of whitish spikelets do not add greatly to the foliage effect. Any well-drained soil is suitable and sun or partial shade is tolerated. Planting and propagation are best in spring.

Hosta (*Funkia*) (Plantain Lily) (*Liliaceae*)

Truly herbaceous, and providing both attractive foliage and pleasing flowers, the plantain lilies typify splendidly that group of hardy plant genera rightly claimed as indispensables. Most of the 40 species have been cultivated, though not all are superlative or large enough for inclusion here. They grow best in a fertile, moisture-retentive soil in partial shade and can be planted from autumn to spring. Propagation is by division at planting time, or by seeds in spring. Seedlings from garden sources are seldom true to type and take several years to make sizeable plants. With one exception, the species which follow are native to Japan. They are all tightly clump-forming with long-stalked, prominently ribbed leaves and spires of trumpet-shaped flowers. *H. albomarginata* has mostly elliptic leaves to 15 cm long usually with a white border, but plain green clones are available. Pale-violet flowers appear on 60 cm-tall stems in late summer. Some botanists have renamed this *H. sieboldii*, but as there is likely to be confusion with the popular *H. sieboldiana* the better-known name has been retained here. *H. crispula* produces ovate-lanceolate, broadly white-banded, waved leaves to 20 cm long. In late summer they are overtopped by 50-80 cm-tall stems and lavender flowers. It is sometimes confused with the previous species but the waved leaves are diagnostic. *H. decorata* has rich green rounded leaves to 15 cm long with broad white margins and dark-lilac flowers on 60 cm stems in early summer. This is a rhizomatous species and can spread widely in rich soils. *H. elata* is sometimes wrongly grown as *H. sieboldiana* but the somewhat wavy, glossy deep-green leaves and 5-6 cm-long bluish-violet flowers clearly distinguish it. *H. fortunei* has leaves of ovate-cordate outline to 13 cm long and dense racemes of lilac to violet flowers on 90 cm-tall stems in summer. *H. f.* 'Albopicta' produces leaves which are yellow with green borders when young; 'Aurea' ('Aureo-marginata') has the young leaves entirely yellow. *H. f. hyacinthina* has glaucous leaves and reddish-violet tinted flowers. *H. f.* 'Marginato-alba' ('Albomarginata') has broadly white-margined sage-green leaves of substantial texture and must not be confused with 'Obscura Marginata' which has cream-margined, clear green foliage; 'Obscura' itself is plain green. For *H. glauca* – see *H. sieboldiana*. *H.* 'Honeybells' (reputedly *H. plantaginea* X *H. lancifolia*) much resembles the first parent but is more robust with racemes to 1 m tall and fragrant white flowers with purple lines. *H. lancifolia* has slender-pointed, lustrous-green leaves that arch strongly outwards. In late summer they are embellished by deep-purple flowers on 40-60 cm

tall stems. *H. l.* 'Albo-marginata' equals *H. albomarginata* (q.v.)
H. plantaginea comes from China and has bright-green lustrous leaves
to 25 cm long and elegant, pure-white, fragrant flowers in autumn.
H. p. 'Grandiflora' has longer petals and leaves and is the form most
frequently grown in British gardens. *H. rectifolia* (*H. longipes* of
gardens) produces dark-green leaves to 15 cm long, and 60-90 cm-
tall spires of violet flowers with darker lines, in late summer. It is
not one of the best species for ground cover with its erect leaves in
less than dense clumps; 'Tall Boy' is a superior hybrid of it, having
better clumps of broader leaves and deep-lilac flowers on taller stems.
H. X 'Royal Standard' arose at the Wayside Gardens, USA and has
close affinities with its main parent *H. plantaginea*. The white flowers
have a hint of lilac, are fragrant and held 60-80 cm above the heart-
shaped, boldly veined leaves. *H. sieboldiana* (*H. fortunei robusta*,
H. glauca) without doubt is the most imposing species, having broad,
thick-textured glaucous leaves up to 38 cm long which form imposing
and luxurious mounds. The pale-lilac flowers are less satisfactory,
being borne in congested racemes often half hidden by the leaves.
H. s. elegans has more intensely glaucous leaves which are prominently veined and corrugated; a real eye-catcher. The summer-borne
flowers just overtop the foliage; 'Frances Williams' ('Gold Edge')
has strikingly yellow-margined leaves. *H. tardiflora* (*H. sparsa*) is
almost a miniature (there are much smaller species) with lustrous
deep-green, lance-shaped leaves 10-15 cm long and 30 cm-tall bronze-
mottled stems bearing lily-like flowers in autumn. Respected authorities describe these as 'deep lilac' or 'deep mauve', but the Award
of Merit description in the RHS Journal of 1948 states 'silvery-lilac'
and one wonders if there are two distinct clones in cultivation. *H.
tardiflora* itself is not known in the wild and may be of Japanese
garden origin, perhaps derived from *H. lancifolia*. *H.* 'Thomas Hogg'
may be of hybrid origin. It is often confused with *H. albomarginata*
and *H. crispula* but it flowers in early summer and has pointed-tipped
foliage which is smooth surfaced and less wavy. *H. tokudama* can
best be described as a small version of *H. sieboldiana* with somewhat cupped leaves and has been aptly known as *H. s. condensata*.
H. tokudama 'Variegata' has stripy yellow-green patterning. *H. undu-
lata* has strongly waved elliptic leaves to 15 cm long, each with a
central splash of white of varying size; in 'Univittata' it is a broad
stripe only. The flowers are pale violet to lavender and open in late
summer. *H. u. erromena* has pure green, less waved leaves and is more
robust with flower stems 60 cm or more tall; presumably the original
plant, but not known wild. *H. u.* 'Albomarginata' has green, narrowly
white-margined leaves, while 'Mediovariegata' is an unnecessary name
for the original plant described above. *H. ventricosa* makes a handsome pile of heart-shaped lustrous dark foliage overtopped by 1 m-tall

stems and deep-violet flowers with an intriguing vein pattern, in late summer. *H. v.* 'Aureomaculata' has the leaves centrally splashed and irregularly striped with cream, while those of 'Variegata' are boldly margined creamy-yellow. If only one hosta with cream/yellow-margined leaves is required, this latter should be chosen.

Houttuynia cordata (*Saururaceae*)

The only member of its genus, this native of the Himalayas and Japan has several unique characteristics and not a little charm, but it creeps underground at speed and can be very invasive. About 30 cm tall, it has heart-shaped, thick-textured leaves which are red-flushed when young, take on purplish or bronze hues in full sun and can colour brightly in autumn. When bruised they give off a smell of Seville oranges. What appears to be a flower is in fact a cylindrical cluster of tiny petal-less florets surrounded by four white, petal-like bracts. In the most desirable double form, 'Plena', smaller white bracts occur on the flower spike, each 'flower' then looking like a small, untidy pagoda. Any ordinary moist to wet soil is suitable in sun or shade. Planting can take place from autumn to spring with propagation by division at the same time.

Incarvillea (*Bignoniaceae*)

This variable genus of 108 species provides a touch of tropical beauty to the hardy plant scene with its funnel-shaped, broadly lobed, bright flowers. (Most members of the *Bignoniaceae* are natives of warm countries and are often woody climbers.) The following are hardy, requiring well-drained fertile soil and a sunny site. Planting is best in autumn or spring. Propagation is by seeds under glass, or by careful division where possible in spring or by basal cuttings in early summer. *I. delavayi* (China) has a thick tuber-like root, lustrous, arching, pinnate leaves and 40-60 cm spikes of 7 cm-wide bright purple-rose flowers with yellow throats in early to late summer. *I. mairei* (*I. grandiflora brevipes*) (Nepal to China) is like a condensed *I. delavayi* with 30 cm spikes of wider, richer coloured flowers and leaves with a large terminal leaflet. *I. m.* 'Frank Ludlow' is crimson-pink; 'Nyoto Sama' is bright pure pink, both rarely above 20 cm tall.

Inula (Elecampane) (*Compositae*)

Depending on the botanical authority there are 100-200 species in this genus. They vary greatly in stature and effect, but most have yellow, daisy-like flowers with numerous, very slender ray florets. Ordinary, moisture-retentive soil and a site in sun are suitable, though some are bog plants, and most will tolerate some shade. Planting can take place from autumn to spring, propagation is by division, or by seeds in spring. *I. ensifolia* (E. Europe to Caucasus) bears a remarkable resemblance to a smaller, narrower-leaved *Buphthalmum salicifolium* with stems 30 cm tall, more numerous, narrower leaves and richer yellow flowers from mid to late summer. *I. helenium* (probably C. Asia to SE Europe but much naturalised elsewhere) would be an imposing plant were its 1.5-2 m height balanced by proportionately large flowers. The latter are bright yellow, 7-8 cm wide and the ovate basal leaves can be 60 cm or more long. The roots were formerly used for coughs and lung complaints. *I. hookeri* (Himalayas) at 60-75 cm tall is perhaps the most useful and appealing species, with its 7-9 cm-wide light-yellow daisies and sturdy clump-forming habit. In moist rich soil it can form extensive colonies. *I. magnifica* (*I. afghanica* of gardens) is the most majestic species, an elecampane in stature — about 2 m tall — with 13-15 cm-wide deep bright-yellow flowers. *I. orientalis* (*I. glandulosa*) (Caucasus) grows to 50 cm with oblong leaves and woolly-budded, orange-yellow flowers to 7 cm wide; a good, bright, front-of-the-border plant. *I. royleana* (Himalayas) has fine, 10 cm-wide, orange-yellow flowers on 60 cm leafy stems. In full bloom it makes an arresting sight and should be grown more often.

Iris (*Iridaceae*)

About 300 species comprise this familiar genus of bulbous and rhizo-matous species. All have flowers of easily recognisable form though there are many variations on the theme. Each flower has its parts in threes; three petal-like sepals with stalk or haft-like bases which may arch outwards or hang down (the falls) and three true petals which may stand erect or arch inwards (the standards). Alternating with the standards are three winged styles (the style arms) each sheltering a stamen and pressed close to the base of the falls. The hardy rhizomatous, mainly early-summer-blooming species described here are mostly satisfied with ordinary soil and a sunny site. Some need more moisture and others tolerate shade and this will be mentioned in the species entries below. Planting can take place from autumn to spring or immediately after flowering. Propagation is by division at planting time or by seeds in spring. For the *I. albicans* of gardens — see *I. X germanica florentina*. *I. bulleyana* (W. China) forms clumps to 45 cm tall with cream and pale blue-purple flowers. *I. chrysographes* (W. China) is clump-forming, producing slender stems to 45 cm bearing velvety violet-purple flowers with golden veins. *I. c.* 'Rubella' has self-coloured, wine-red petals; 'Black Night' is velvety black-purple and there are several clones with tones of varying intensity between this and the wild species. *I. clarkei* (Himalayas) is not unlike the previous species but grows taller and has violet-purple flowers marked yellow and white. *I. delavayi* (W. China) resembles *I. clarkei* but has purple and white flowers on 90 cm stems and prefers a moist soil. There are plants under this name with yellow areas on the falls, which may be of hybrid origin. *I. douglasiana* (California, Oregon) has lilac flowers in late spring, against a background of deeply hued evergreen foliage. It is a primary parent — with the dwarf vari-coloured *I. innominata* and others — of the very garden-worthy Pacific Coast hybrids available in a wide range of purple, yellow and white shades. *I. foetidissima* gladwin (W. Europe, N. Africa) forms clumps of dark, tough, evergreen leaves to 60 cm long and will thrive in quite deep shade. The smallish purple-grey to yellowish flowers are followed by large capsules which gape open to display bright orange-coated seeds. *I. f.* 'Citrina' is more robust, with larger pale-yellow flowers, while 'Variegata' has its foliage white-striped. *I. forrestii* (W. China) forms clumps to 45 cm tall with purple-brown-veined yellow flowers. *I.* X *germanica* is a hybrid of unknown origin but perhaps derived partly from *I. pallida* which it much resembles, though the flowers are deep purple and the leaves are greener. *I.* X *g. florentina* is the orris root, with fragrant rhizomes and almost white flowers; not to be confused with the true *I.* X *albicans*. See also the entry Bearded Hybrids below. *I. graminea* (Europe) forms dense clumps of arching leaves 50-90 cm long among which are par-tially hidden intriguing blue-violet, pinkish-purple and yellow flowers with a fragrance of ripe plums; *I. hoogiana* (Turkestan) is a species of quality, bearing tall domed flowers of lavender blue on stems to 60 cm. It requires well-drained soil and a sunny sheltered site. White and rich purple forms are known. *I. japonica* (Japan, China) spreads underground by stolons and forms wide colonies of broad, glossy evergreen leaves. The smallish white, orange and purple flowers have prettily crimped petals and the appeal of an orchid. Shade, shelter and humus-rich soil provide the best condition for this woodland species. The reputedly hardier 'Ledgers' is the form generally avail-able in Britain. *I. kaempferi* (Japan) in reality covers all the large-flowered cultivars of the rarely grown species, *I. ensata*. It is the water iris *par excellence* but also thrives in lime-free moist soil. Of regal appearance it has stems 60-90 cm tall with flowers up to 15 cm wide with the falls and standards similar and borne together, creating an almost clematis-like appearance. There are several culti-vars, mainly of Japanese origin, in shades of blue, lavender, red-purple, pink and white, sometimes with an appealing darker vein pattern. *I. laevigata* (Japan) is akin to *I. kaempferi* but the blue flowers have erect standards. It needs moist soil, or will grow in shallow water. It tolerates lime. 'Rose Queen' is a charming hybrid with *I. kaempferi*, and has pink flowers. *I.* X 'Margot Holmes' is probably *I. chrysographes* X *I. douglasiana* and resembles the former parent, growing to 60 cm with wine-red and yellow flowers. *I. mis-souriensis* (C. and W. North America) has attractive grey foliage and

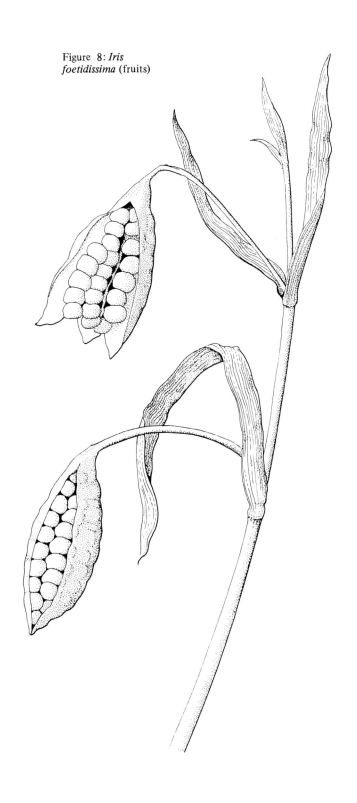

Figure 8: *Iris foetidissima* (fruits)

purple-veined white to pale-lilac flowers in the summer. *I. monnieri* (Crete) is like a robust *I. spuria* with lemon-yellow flowers on stems to 1 m tall. *I. ochrolenuca* (W. Turkey) is now rather confusingly named *I. orientalis* (see also under *I. sanguinea*). It is a statuesque species 1.2 m tall with *spuria*-type flowers of white and yellow. *I. pallida dalmatica* (SE Europe) can best be considered as the proto-type of the bearded hybrids (see below) with fine grey leaves and 90 cm-tall stems bearing large lavender flowers which as buds are sheathed in papery spathes. *I. p. d.* 'Variegata' ('Argenteo-variegata') and 'Aurea-variegata' have the leaves respectively striped white and yellow. *I. pseudacorus*, yellow flag (Europe, W. Asia) is a marsh plant but will grow in moist soil. In rich soil it can achieve 1.2 m in height, with stiff leaves and bright-yellow flowers in summer. *I. p.* 'Bastardii' has creamy-yellow flowers, and 'Variegata' bears yellow stripes on its leaves. *I. sanguinea* (*I. sibirica orientalis*) (Japan, Manchuria) can be likened to a dwarf (45 cm) version of *I. sibirica* with larger, purple-blue and white flowers. *I. setosa* (Alaska, NE Asia) forms com-pact clumps of pale-green foliage overtopped by stems to 60 cm and deep blue-purple and white flowers in summer. It is often repre-sented in gardens by the less compact, smaller *I. s. canadensis*. *I. sibirica* (C. Europe to Russia) is an excellent border species forming upstanding clumps of grassy foliage over-topped by stems to 1 m or more. The neat blue-purple flowers have rounded falls with a purple-netted white, basal patch. Several cultivars are available notably: 'Blue Mere', 'Cambridge' (turquoise-blue), 'Caesar' and 'Emperor' (deep violet-purple), 'Heavenly Blue', 'Helen Astor' (light plum-red), 'Mrs Rowe' (pearly grey), 'Perry's Blue' (sky-blue, large), 'Snow Queen' and 'Anniversary' (white). *I. spuria*, butterfly iris (C. Europe to Iran) is probably the most variable of all the species in overall height, flower size and colour. It has somewhat glaucous leaves and firm, neat flowers with rounded falls, typically in shades of blue-purple to lilac on stems 60-90 cm tall. Plants of this type are best considered as *I. s. halophila*; 'A.W. Tait' is pale lavender-blue and yellow. Plant breeders are now crossing the various species in the *Spuria* group and producing some charming cultivars including shades of yellow and white. *I. tectorum*, Japanese roof iris (China, long cultivated in Japan) has wide glossy leaves and lilac to blue-purple flowers, often blotched or veined darker, the rounded falls with a white crest; 'Alba' is white. *I tenax* (N. California to Washington State) is akin to *I. douglasiana*, but is hardier and has pale-green leaves and smaller flowers in shades of lavender, blue or purple and yellow, rarely white. *I. unguicularis* (*I. stylosa*), winter iris (Greece and Algeria east to Syria) forms dense evergreen clumps of grassy, leathery leaves to 60 cm high. The fragrant, solitary, deep bright-lilac flowers lurk among the leaves but are nevertheless very welcome, opening as they do from autumn to spring — depending on the clone and the season. It is best planted at the foot of a sunny wall in poorish soil. *I. u.* 'Alba' is off-white and rather small — 'Bowles White' is superior but hard to come by. *I. u. speciosa* has larger, richer-hued flowers, often represented in gardens by 'Mary Barnard', while 'Walter Butt' is pale lilac. *I. versicolor* (E. North America) is clump-forming, about 60 cm tall, with lavender to blue-violet flowers, the falls often with a greenish basal spot. Superior as a garden plant is *I. v.* 'Kermesina' with wine-magenta flowers — a fine waterside iris but thriving also in ordinary moist soil. *I. wilsonii* (China) is rather like a 45-60 cm-tall *sibirica* with flowers in shades of pale yellow veined reddish-brown.

Bearded Hybrids. This heading covers all the popular large-flowered so-called 'flag' irises. It has arisen from the crossing of several related species, all typified by having a beard-like crest of short fleshy hairs along the top of the basal half of the falls. The many cultivars can be grouped into three divisions: tall, with stems 85 cm or more tall; intermediate or median, having stems 25-65 cm; and dwarf with stems up to 23 cm. The tall-bearded group has *I. pallida, mesopotamica, trojana* and *variegata* among its progenitors and resembles mainly the first. The dwarf-bearded division derives from *I. chamaeiris, pumila* and *flavescens*, and the intermediates have arisen from crossing members of the two. These bearded hybrids have been further divided by colour: Amoena has white standards and coloured falls; Bicolor has flowers of one colour but with the standards a lighter hue; Blend has several colours in one flower overlying a basal yellow ground colour; Plicata has a white or yellow ground colour stippled, speckled or feathered around the petal margins with other colours; Self has the whole flower of one colour; Variegata has standards yellow or orange with falls of a contrasting colour either pure or veined, generally a shade of brown or red. Very many good cultivars are available and choice is a personal one, ideally from a specialist's catalogue.

Kirengeshoma palmata (*Hydrangeaceae*)

This is another of those Asiatic woodland plants with that extra something that gives it quality and appeal. Formerly classified in the *Saxifragaceae*, current botanical thought now leans towards a family of its own, the *Kirengeshomaceae*. It is clump-forming with stems 60-120 cm tall clad in decorative maple-shaped leaves to 20 cm long. In autumn the stem tips branch and bear pendent clusters of bell-shaped flowers formed of five fleshy yellow petals. *K. p. koreana* (*K. p. erecta*) has sometimes been considered a separate species but differs only in its somewhat taller stems and wider-open semi-erect flowers. It is not difficult to please, requiring moisture-retentive, humus-rich soil and partial shade. Planting is best in spring, or autumn just as the plant dies down. Propagation is by careful division, or by sowing seeds in spring.

Knautia (Scabiosa) (*Dipsacaceae*)

The 40 species in this genus differ only in small botanical characters from *Scabiosa*, have the same garden uses and require the same culture. The common and undeniably attractive field scabious *K. arvensis* is seldom cultivated but is well worth considering. Superior in garden impact is *K. macedonica* (*Scabiosa rumelica*) from the Balkan peninsula and Romania with 5 cm-wide rich crimson flowers on 60 cm stems above hairy dissected leaves.

Kniphofia (Redhot Poker, Torch Lily) (*Liliaceae*)

About 70 species of redhot poker have been described, most from South Africa, and in recent years many hybrids and cultivars have been created. Mainly grassy leaved with their narrowly bell-shaped or tubular flowers in dense spikes, the many species yet contrive to be very different, some large and stalwart, others small and graceful. They need fertile, reasonably moisture-retentive soil and a sunny site though some shade is tolerated. Planting is best in spring and propagation is by division at the same time. Seed raising in spring is easy, but the cultivars do not come true to type and the species often vary. For *K. alooides* – see under *K. uvaria*. *K. caulescens* has a trunk-like stem which reclines with age and bears tufts of grey-hued leaves, and in autumn 1-1.5 m-tall flowering stems topped by light salmon-red florets that age yellow. *K. galpinii* (of gardens) is one of the most graceful and charming torch lilies with slender stems to 75 cm and well-spaced florets of bright reddish-orange well into autumn. Similar plants are called *K. macowanii* and *K. nelsonii* and all three appear to be clones of *K. triangularis*, a name seldom encountered in catalogues. For *K. modesta* (of gardens) – see *K. sparsa*. *K. northiae* resembles an aloe with its broad glaucous leaves carried on a short, thick stem. As a foliage plant it is outstanding in its genus, imparting a touch of the tropics to the temperate garden scene. The flowers are rather ordinary, red, ageing pale yellow, on stems to 1.2 m tall. It needs a sheltered site and moist soil. *K. pumila* is neat and desirable with grassy glaucous leaves and orange-red flowers on 45-60 cm stems in late summer. *K. sparsa* (*K. modesta*) reaches 60 cm in height and has eye-catching spikes of rose-red buds that open ivory-white. *K. tuckii* (of gardens) is much like *K. uvaria* but has pinkish-red flower buds that open sulphur-yellow. *K. uvaria* (*K. alooides*) is the best-known and first torch lily to be introduced (in 1705) with its rather floppy evergreen leaves and fine upstanding 1.5 m-tall torches of scarlet and yellow in late summer and early autumn. *K. u.* 'Nobilis' (*K. u.* 'Grandiflora', *K. alooides* 'Maxima') is some-what taller and earlier flowering with longer spikes of more orange-tinted flowers. Some botanists make it a separate species as *K. prae-cox.*

Hybrids. Many fine cultivars of hybrid origin are now available and the catalogues of specialists should be consulted. Particularly garden worthy are: 'Atlanta', which is very valuable as it opens its *uvaria*-like spikes in early summer; 'Royal Standard' follows on with a similar display in bright shades of red and yellow; both are 1.2 m tall. In the 60-90 cm height range are 'Buttercup' and 'Yellow Hammer' in shades of yellow, and the ivory-white 'Maid of Orleans'. 'Springtime' is creamy buff and red, while 'Timothy' is a charming shade of pink.

Lamiastrum galeobdolon (Yellow Archangel) (*Labiatae*)

Still listed as *Lamium galeobdolon* and *Galeobdolon luteum*, this is the only species of its present genus. Native to Europe it is represented in cultivation by its silvery-patterned leaf form 'Variegata' ('Floren-tina') a plant of undeniable attraction but excessive vigour. Evergreen and particularly fine as a foliage plant in winter, it also produces erect 30-60 cm-tall stems of bright-yellow dead-nettle flowers in early summer. Its rampant nature makes it unsuitable for the small garden and elsewhere it is best kept as ground cover beneath trees or large shrubs. Any soil and sun or shade are suitable. Propagation is by division or by cuttings of the creeping stems.

Lamium (Dead Nettle) (*Labiatae*)

About 40-50 species form this genus, several being familiar weeds. Those described here are useful and decorative plants either as ground cover or for the flower border. Any not too dry soil and a sunny or partially shaded site is suitable. Planting can take place from autumn to spring. Propagation is by division at planting time or by seeds in spring. *L. garganicum*, large red dead nettle (S. Europe) forms clumps 30-40 cm tall with rounded toothed, cordate leaves and 2.5-4 cm-long hooded pink or red flowers in spike-like clusters from late spring. *L. maculatum*, spotted dead nettle (Europe) forms wide-spreading clumps of triangular-ovate leaves each with a central silvery-white stripe above which are carried purple-red flowers on 20-40 cm-tall stems. The colour forms 'Album' (white) and 'Roseum' (soft clear pink) are particularly desirable, as is 'Beacon Silver', a comparatively new mutation with the entire upper leaf surface bearing a bright silvery-white patina. Interestingly enough this fine plant comes partially true from seeds. Another foliage form 'Aureum' has yellow-flushed leaves but it is of rather weak growth needing richer soil and shade to look good. With the exception of the latter, all forms of *maculatum* make good ground cover. *L. orvala* (Austria to N. Italy and Yugoslavia) is the giant of its genus and the most striking in bloom, resembling a more robust *L. garganicum* up to 60 cm or more in height with smooth stems and rich green leaves and 4-5 cm-long red-purple flowers in summer. To do its best however, it must have a rich, moist soil.

Lathyrus (Everlasting Pea) (*Leguminosae*)

Very few of the 100-150 species in this genus are hardy perennials of distinction, but those mentioned are well deserving of cultivation in suitable sites. They grow in ordinary soil in sun or partial shade and are generally long lived. Some sort of support is needed for the climbing species. Planting can take place from autumn to spring, and propagation by seeds or by division in spring. For *L. cyaneus* of catalogues — see *L. vernus*. *L. latifolius*, everlasting pea (Europe, naturalised in Britain and elsewhere) is a climber to 3 m or more, with winged stems and leaves formed of two narrowly oval or lance-shaped leaflets and a central branched tendril. The typical pea flowers are rose-purple in axillary racemes of 5-15 from summer to early autumn. *L. l.* 'White Pearl' ('Albus' or 'Albiflorus') has white flowers; 'Rose Queen' is pink and white. *L. rotundifolius*, Persian everlasting pea (W. Asia to C. USSR) is a climber to 80-150 cm tall and not unlike a smaller version of *L. latifolius* with rounded leaflets and racemes of fewer but larger rose-pink flowers in summer. *L. vernus* (*Orobus vernus*), spring vetch (Europe) forms dense clumps of erect, branched stems bearing pinnate leaves of four to eight lanceolate leaflets and racemes of three to ten red-purple and blue flowers in spring. *L. v.* 'Albo Roseus' has pink and white flowers and is sometimes confused with *L. cyaneus* (*L. digitatus*) an allied species with grassy leaflets.

Lavatera (Tree Mallow) (*Malvaceae*)

This genus covers 20-25 species of annuals, biennials, perennials and shrubs, all with the typical mallow flowers. The perennials grow in ordinary soil and sun and are best planted in spring. Propagation is easily effected by division, basal cuttings or seeds in spring. *L. cache-miriana* (*L. kashmiriana*) (Kashmir) is a clump-former from an almost woody crown, the wind-resistant stems attaining 1.5-2.4 m in height. The downy leaves are palmate and get progressively smaller up the stem. In the axils of the upper leaves, 6.5-7.5 cm-wide pink flowers with well-spaced notched-tipped flowers expand in summer and early autumn. See also comment under *L. thuringiaca*. *L. olbia* (W. Mediterranean, Portugal) is rather like a small, shrubby hollyhock with branched stems to 2 m tall and reddish-purple notched petals. It is seldom cultivated, being represented in gardens by *L.* X 'Rosea', a hybrid probably with *L. cachemiriana* or *thuringiaca* as the other parent and bearing larger, bright lilac-pink flowers. Both are really shrubs and not fully hardy in severe winters. They are however, best cut back to near ground level each spring, when they then behave as herbaceous perennials. *L. thuringiaca* (SE Europe) is much like *L. cachemiriana* though a little less elegant in habit and with broader less, deeply notched petals. From time to time it parades under the *cachemiriana* name.

Lespedeza thunbergii (*Leguminosae*)

This is the only member of a 100-species genus to be generally culti-vated. Strictly, it is a sub-shrub but usually dies back to ground level each winter and behaves as a herbaceous perennial. Formerly known as *L. sieboldii, Desmodium thunbergii* and *D. penduliflorum* it is sur-prisingly neglected, providing as it does a wonderful show of deep rose-purple pea flowers in early autumn. Of graceful arching habit it grows up to 2 m in height with silky-hairy trifoliate leaves and 1-1.5 cm-long pea flowers in laburnum-like clusters. Any moder-ately fertile, well-drained soil and a sunny, preferably sheltered site is required. Planting is best in spring; propagation is by division or seeds in spring.

Liatris (Button Snake Root, Kansas Gay Feather) (*Compositae*)

Although this genus of 40 N. American species has a tuberous root, it is so much the typical herbaceous perennial that it must be included here. All the species have narrow, almost grassy leaves and spikes of big, rather fluffy groundsel-like flowerheads which open from the top downwards. They grow best in ordinary, well-drained but not dry soil in sun. Planting can take place from autumn to early spring. Propagate by division at planting time or by sowing seeds in spring. *L. pycnostachya* grows 1-1.5 m tall and is the most imposing species in cultivation with its long spikes of rose-purple flowers from summer into autumn. *L. scariosa* has a similar impact to the preceding species and can reach 90 cm. The flowers are purple, but 'Snowflake' is white. *L. spicata* (*L. callilepis*) is the best known, bearing dense spikes of rose-purple flowers in summer and autumn. The wild type can reach 1 m or more, but the shorter *L. s. montana* mainly repre-sents it in gardens, and *L. s. m.* 'Kobold' ('Gnome') which is also commonly seen is less than 60 cm.

Libertia formosa (*Iridaceae*)

This Chilean plant is the only reasonably hardy member of a genus of about twelve species of iris-like plants from the southern hemisphere. It forms dense tufts of bright-green sword-shaped leaves, and in early summer bears 60-90 cm-tall dense panicles of pure-white, three-petalled flowers. It looks delightful by the waterside and combines well with blue flowers. *L. grandiflora* from New Zealand is similar, but has diffuse panicles and lacks the floral impact. Similar comment could be levelled at *L. ixioides*, also a New Zealander, but it has intriguing, slender leaves, usually with a pale mid-rib and orange-brown basal margins. Ordinary well-drained but not dry soil and a sheltered site in sun or part shade are required. Planting and propagation by division or seeds should be done in spring.

Ligularia *(Senecio)* *(Compositae)*

Depending on the botanical authority, there are 80-150 species in this genus of mainly robustly handsome perennials. Those described have bold foliage and either broad clusters or stout spires of yellow daisy-like flowers. They make imposing specimen plants or groups and look especially well by the waterside. Moist but not wet, preferably humus-enriched soil in sun produces the best results. Planting can take place from autumn to spring. Propagation is by division at planting time or by sowing seeds in spring. *L. dentata* (*L. clivorum*) (China) is the best-known species, with kidney-shaped leaves to 30 cm long and broad clusters of bright orange-yellow daisies on 90-120 cm-tall stems in summer. *L. d.* 'Desdemona' and 'Othello' have leaves and stems suffused rich red-purple and they are more compact. 'Golden Queen' has richer-hued flowers, while 'Orange Princess' and 'Orange Queen' have orange flowers. *L.* X *hessei* (*L. dentata* X. *L. veitchiana* X *L. wilsoniana*) nicely blends the characters of its parents, producing broad spikes of yellow-orange flowers on stems 1.5-2 m tall; a vigorous and very garden-worthy plant. 'Gregynog Gold' is a hybrid between the first two species, and is a similar plant with orange flowers. *L. hodgsonii* (Japan) is best likened to a smaller version of *L. dentata*, with stems from 60-90 cm tall and yellow-orange flowers. 'Golden Queen' is most probably a good form of this plant rather than of *L. dentata*. *L. japonica* (Japan, China, Korea, Taiwan) has rounded leaves to 30 cm long which are ornately cleft, fingered and toothed. The orange flowers are relatively large but only two to eight are carried on each 1.2-1.5 m tall stem in early summer. *L.* X *palmatiloba* is its hybrid with *L. dentata*, and is a much more satisfactory garden plant having the cut leaves combined with a *dentata* floral display. *L. przewalskii* (N. China) also has deeply cut, rounded leaves but they are smaller and on longer, dark stalks. The small, bright-yellow summer-borne flowers are carried in long, wand-like spikes to 1.5 m or more. 'The Rocket' is usually ascribed to this species, sometimes to the next. On leaf character alone it could well be a hybrid between the two. It is a vigorous plant with black-purple stems. *L. stenocephala* (China, Japan, Taiwan) has a similar impact to *L. przewalskii*, but the leaves are more triangular in outline and sharply toothed — not lobed. *L. veitchiana* (China) has orbicular leaves to 30 cm wide and 1.5 m-tall slender spikes of yellow florets, each in the axil of a broad bract. It makes an imposing waterside plant for a late summer display. *L. wilsoniana* (China) is much like it, but the spikes are a little broader, the floral bracts narrow and the leaf-stalks hollow (those of *veitchiana* are solid).

Limonium latifolium (Sea Lavender) (*Plumbaginaceae*)

This is the only readily available statice suitable for the perennial garden. Still often catalogued as *Statice latifolium* and a native of SE Europe and USSR, it forms clumps of oblong, dark evergreen basal leaves 15-25 cm long which are satisfying in themselves. In late summer numerous, elaborately branched wiry stems rise up 30-50 cm, bearing clouds of tiny lavender flowers with the impact of a gypsophila. Several clones of rich colouring, i.e. 'Blue Cloud', 'Blue Gown', 'Grandiflora', 'True Blue' and 'Violetta' are available. Ordinary well-drained soil and a sunny site are required. Planting is best in autumn or spring and propagation is by division, or seeds in spring or root cuttings in late winter. Other taller members of this 150-300-species genus are sometimes available and worth trying, e.g. the not too hardy white-flowered *L. mouretii* from Morocco.

Linaria (Toadflax) (*Scrophulariaceae*)

The 100 species of toadflax are allied to *Antirrhinum* and have flowers that are almost identical but for the rear-pointing spur. They grow in ordinary soil and need a sunny site. Planting is best in autumn or spring. Propagation is by careful division, or seeds in early spring or root cuttings in late winter. *L. genistifolia dalmatica* (*L. dalmatica*) (E. South and C. Europe) has shallow, horizontal roots which at intervals emit tufts of more or less erect, branched stems up to 90 cm tall. These are clad in oval, grey-blue tinted leaves terminating in wands of primrose-yellow flowers 4-5 cm long, in summer and autumn. It is an ideal plant for the mixed border where its reclining stems can gain support from low shrubs. *L. purpurea*, purple toadflax (C. and S. Italy, Sicily, but widely naturalised elsewhere) forms small clumps of slender, very erect, wiry stems 60-120 cm tall bearing very narrow, glaucous leaves in whorls. The small violet-blue and white flowers are carried in slender spires during summer and autumn. *L. p.* 'Canon Went' is pink and comes true from seeds if grown apart from the type.

Lindelofia longiflora (*Boraginaceae*)

Pure gentian-blue is a comparatively rare colour among hardy perennials so this species should be sought out and grown more often. It is one of ten species all of which have been classified as *Cynoglossum* in the past. Formerly known as *C. longiflorum* and *Lindelofia spectabilis*, this Himalayan plant has a superficial resemblance to *Cynoglossum nervosum* but with anchusa-like flowers on stems to 45 cm. Culture as for *Cynoglossum*.

Linum (Flax) (*Linaceae*)

Annuals, perennials and shrubs of cosmopolitan distribution are numbered among the 200-230 species of flax. The hardy perennial members are rather few in number but all those described here are worthy of cultivation with their wiry stems and summer-borne satiny-textured five-petalled flowers. They require well-drained soil and sun. Planting is best in early autumn or spring; propagation is by seeds in spring or by cuttings in summer. *L. flavum*, yellow flax (C. and SE Europe) is a woody-based species forming mounds of spoon-shaped leaves in rosettes above which rise 40-60 cm-tall stems bearing clusters of yellow flowers. It varies in the depth of the flower colour and tint of foliage, some clones having almost glaucous foliage. Plants offered as *L. paniculatum* are usually forms of this species. There is a dwarf, 'Compactum' cultivar. *L. monogynum* (New Zealand) is not fully hardy and rather short lived, but is mentioned as it is the only tallish white species. It has 30-40 cm stems in tufts from a woody base, narrow, somewhat glaucous leaves and flowers 2-3 cm wide; there are bluish-tinted forms. *L. narbonense*, beautiful flax (C. and W. Mediterranean) must be accorded the accolade for blue flaxes. It is like a robust *L. perenne* with wider leaves and rich azure flowers 3 cm wide. *L. perenne* (*L. sibiricum*) (Europe) covers many forms, some of which are inferior. At its best it is a splendid plant forming clumps to 60 cm tall with glaucous-tinted, very narrow leaves and sky-blue flowers about 2.5 cm wide carried in well-branched panicles over a long period. *L. p. alpinum* and *extraaxillare* are decumbent to ascending dwarf plants suitable for the front of a narrow border or bed.

Liriope (Lily Turf) (*Liliaceae*)

About six species of grassy-leaved perennials with spikes of grape-hyacinth flowers form this Asiatic genus. They grow in ordinary soil but need shaded, sheltered sites to thrive and are excellent beneath trees. Planting is best in spring and propagation is by division at the same time. *L. graminifolia* (China, Vietnam) spreads underground and forms colonies of grassy, arching tufts to 20 cm tall. Racemes of small, pale-violet, bell-shaped flowers just rise above the leaves but are not particularly noteworthy. It makes an interesting ground cover. *L. muscari* (*L. platyphylla*, *L. graminifolia densiflora*) (China, Japan, Taiwan) is undoubtedly the finest species, forming dense clumps of arching, somewhat lustrous dark-green leaves 30 cm or more long, and taller, dense racemes of violet-purple bells in autumn. It is excellent for dryish shade but must have a sheltered site.

Lobelia (*Campanulaceae*)

Of cosmopolitan distribution, the 375 species in this genus cover annuals, perennials, shrubs and (rarely) trees. Most are tender, but a few hardy or almost hardy perennials of distinction are available. All are clump-forming with spires of fan-shaped flowers. They thrive best in humus-rich soil that does not dry out, and look well by the waterside. Planting is best in spring with propagation by division or by seeds at the same time. *L. cardinalis*, cardinal flower (E. North America) grows 60-90 cm tall with rich scarlet flowers in late summer. The basal leaves are evergreen. It is sometimes confused with the similar but winter-tender *L. splendens* (*L. fulgens*) from S. USA and Mexico. Although fully hardy, rotting may occur during mild, wet winters. *L. c.* 'Alba' has white blossoms, 'Rosea' is pink and 'Queen Victoria' has beetroot-coloured leaves. *L.* X *gerardii* is better known as *L.* X *vedrariensis* and nicely combines *L. cardinalis* with *L. siphilitica*. *L.* X *hybrida* is considered a synonym though it has been used for triple hybrids including *L. splendens*. Several cultivars are sometimes available in shades of pinkish-violet to royal purple. *L. siphilitica* (*syphilitica*), blue cardinal flower (E. USA) has broader, mat-green leaves and stems to 80 cm or more with good blue flowers. It thrives best in damp soils. *L. s.* 'Blue Peter' is a superior and soundly perennial selection. *L. tupa* (Chile) should not be mentioned here being somewhat less than hardy. However, it strikes such an individual note in the garden that it is well worthy of the sheltered sunny nook it requires. This it embellishes with clumps of erect stems 1.5-2 m tall, clad with large, pointed, palish-green leaves and quaintly shaped flowers like crimson, winged fish-hooks from late summer to autumn. For *L.* X *vedrariensis* – see under *L.* X *gerardii* above.

Lunaria (Honesty) (*Cruciferae*)

Of the three known species of honesty the best known is *L. annua* (which generally behaves as a biennial). It is grown for its spring-borne red-purple or white flowers and flat, oval seed pods. These are much used for dried-flower arrangements when stripped of their outer valves and seeds to disclose the silvery membrane. Strangely neglected is *L. rediviva* (Europe), a true clump-forming perennial to 60 cm, with white to lilac flowers and smaller, narrowly elliptic pods. It grows in ordinary soil in sun or partial shade and can be planted from autumn to spring. Propagation is by division or by sowing seeds in spring.

Lupinus (Lupin) (*Leguminosae*)

Among the 200 different sorts of lupins are shrubs, annuals and perennials. Very few members of the latter are cultivated and those only by collectors. Curiously enough, all the many cultivars of lupin grown today are derived from forms of one shrubby species, *L. arboreus* and the herbaceous *L. polyphyllus*, both from W. North America. As the result of many years of breeding and selection work, the famous Russell strain emerged, sturdy plants to 90 cm tall, with dense spires of pea flowers in all colours of the rainbow, many strikingly bicoloured. They may be bought as named cultivars or raised from seeds which can be mixed, or bought in more restricted colour selections, e.g. shades of yellow, rose and white, or blue and white. The Monarch Dwarf Lulu Strain is very sturdy and wind resistant to 60 cm tall. Although very tolerant of soil and situation, a humus-rich, well-drained but moisture-retentive soil in sun gives the best results. Planting can take place from autumn to spring, propagation by division at planting time, cuttings of basal shoots in a cold frame and seeds in spring.

Luzula (Woodrush) (*Juncaceae*)

This genus contains 80 species of grassy-leaved perennials of cosmopolitan distribution. Very few of the larger species are cultivated though it is likely that other garden-worthy species await trial. They grow in ordinary soil in sun or shade and are best planted in spring. Propagation is by division or by sowing seeds in spring. *L. nivea* (mountains of C. and W. Europe) is known as snowy woodrush, though the clustered flowering spikelets on their wiry 50-80 cm tall stems are too creamy a tint to suggest real snow. It is a tufted plant with an unassuming elegance and deserves to be seen more often. *L. sylvatica* (*L. maxima*), greater woodrush (Europe including Britain) forms robust mats of glossy deep-green leaves dense enough to provide serviceable ground cover even in quite deep shade. The clustered flowering spikelets are chestnut-brown and rise on stems 40-60 cm tall in early summer. Greater woodrush is almost entirely represented in cultivation by *L. s.* 'Marginata' having a narrow, creamy border to each leaf.

Lychnis (Catchfly) (*Caryophyllaceae*)

Depending on the classifier there are 12-35 species in this genus and among them are several fine border perennials. Closely allied to *Silene* they have typical campion-like flowers with tubular, sometimes inflated calyces, and five petals held flat. They grow well in ordinary fertile soil in sun. Planting can take place from autumn to spring with propagation by division at the same time or by seeds in spring.

L. X *arkwrightii* (*L. chalcedonica* X *L.* X *haageana*) favours the *L.* X *haageana* parent, being about 30 cm tall with dark, pointed leaves and small clusters of large, intensely red flowers in summer. It tends to be short lived but makes a vivid splash of colour at the front of the border. *L. chalcedonica*, Maltese or Jerusalem cross (N. USSR) is a clump-former to 90 cm or more, with rough-textured ovate leaves and dense, flattened terminal clusters of up to 50 small bright-scarlet flowers the petals of which are deeply cleft. It is perhaps the finest border species though the intense colour does not please all gardeners. *L. coronaria* (*Agrostemma coronaria*), rose campion (SE Europe) makes clumps of charming white-woolly leaves and would be worth growing for these alone. In summer, branched stems rise to 60 cm and bear a long succession of purple-cerise or pure-white campion flowers. *L. flos-jovis*, flower of Jove (Alps) has white-woolly leaves of similar impact to those of the previous species followed by less branched stems of similar height. The red-purple or white flowers are smaller however, and borne in rounded clusters from early summer. More frequently seen is 'Hort's Variety' with rose-pink blossoms. *L.* X *haageana* grows to about 30 cm tall and forms small clumps of dark-green ovate to lanceolate leaves that are often purple-flushed. In summer each stem tip bears small clusters of 5 cm-wide flowers in shades of orange, scarlet or white. Although coming true from seeds it is reputedly a cross between *L. fulgens* (similar to *L. chalcedonica*) and *L. coronata* (a dwarf, large-flowered Asiatic plant). It is short lived and rather weak stemmed, but a striking front of the border plant. *L. viscaria* (*L. vulgaris, Viscaria vulgaris, V. viscosa*), German catchfly (Europe) forms tufts or small clumps to 50 cm tall. Between each pair of narrow leaves there is a sticky zone on the stem – hence the catchfly name, though only occasionally does one see a tiny fly caught. The clustered, red-purple to pink or white flowers are carried in spike-like clusters in summer. *L. v.* 'Splendens Plena' has double purple-red flowers.

Lysichiton (*Lysichitum*) (*Araceae*)

The two species that form this genus are large perennials with impressive foliage all the summer, and arum-like flowering spathes with the unfolding leaves in early spring. They are essentially plants for the waterside and do best in a bog bed, but will grow in ordinary moist soil well watered during hot, dry weather. Planting should take place in autumn or spring with propagation by division in the latter season. *L. americanum*, yellow skunk cabbage (California to Alaska and Montana) is the largest species, with paddle-shaped leaves 60-150 cm long, and yellow spathes. *L. camtschatcense* (N. Japan to Kamchatka) has somewhat smaller, sea-green leaves and white spathes which open a few weeks later.

Lysimachia (Yellow Loosestrife) (*Primulaceae*)

About 165 species form this cosmopolitan genus of annuals, perennials and shrubs. Very few are hardy perennials of note and even the attractive ones described here can be invasive. In informal sites or by the waterside however, they can be satisfying and long-lived plants. Moist soil and a sunny site are best though light shade is tolerated. Planting can take place from autumn to spring with propagation by division at the same time. *L. ciliata* (*Steironema ciliata*) (N. America) is sometimes called fringed loosestrife on account of the hair-fringed (ciliate) leaf stalks. It is a strangely neglected plant considering its slim and elegant appearance, with willow-like leaves and light-yellow flowers held in airy terminal panicles during the summer. *L. clethroides*, gooseneck loosestrife (China, Japan) forms colonies to 90 cm tall with oval leaves and terminal, tapered white flower spikes that arch over with the tips inclined upwards. It makes a distinctive and elegant show in the late summer. *L. ephemerum* (SW Europe) is distinct on several counts, being tightly clump-forming and non-invasive, the possessor of appealing grey foliage and departing from the norm with its slender spires of small, pearly to grey-white flowers from summer to early autumn. A quietly attractive plant that deserves to be seen more often. *L. punctata* (E. Central and S. Europe) forms extensive colonies even where the soil is not noticeably moist. The erect stems attain 60-90 cm in height and in summer are topped by whorls of bright-yellow flowers. It is best in the wild garden. In name at least sometimes confused with the seldom cultivated *L. vulgaris*, a taller plant with smaller flowers in leafy panicles.

Lythrum (Purple Loosestrife) (*Lythraceae*)

Of the 30-35 species of shrubs and perennials that form this genus only two are cultivated and one not commonly. They are unrelated to the yellow loosestrifes with much smaller flowers in dense spikes, and are non-invasive. Culture is as for *Lysimachia*; they may also be propagated by basal-stem cuttings in spring. *L. salicaria* (Europe, N. Africa, W. and N. Asia) is a woody-based herbaceous plant to 1.2 m in height with pairs of narrow leaves and long spikes of bright rose-purple to magenta flowers from summer to early autumn. Several cultivars are available some of which are probably hybrids with the next species, e.g. 'Brightness' and 'Robert' which are pink, 'The Beacon' and 'Firecandle', rose-crimson. *L. virgatum* (E. Europe, W. Asia) rarely exceeds 90 cm and is slenderer than *L. salicaria*, with purplish-rose flowers. *L. v.* 'Rose Queen' has brighter, clearer tinted flowers; 'The Rocket' is rose-red.

Macleaya (*Bocconia*) (Plume Poppy) (*Papaveraceae*)

This genus contains two species of tall perennials which combine handsome foliage with a delightful floral effect. Although they can add that extra touch at the back of a border, they are best used where the whole plant can be seen, as for example, when set by the waterside or beside an expanse of lawn. Ordinary soil is suitable with a site in sun or partial shade. Planting is best in autumn or spring; propagation is by division in spring or by root cuttings in late winter. *M. microcarpa* (C. China) attains 2.1-2.4 m in height, with deeply round-lobed leaves with white reverses, the basal ones to 25 cm long. The tiny, petal-less flowers have eight to twelve stamens and two buff-pink sepals, many together forming eye-catching, elegant plumes during the summer. *M. m.* 'Coral Plume' has pinker-tinted flowers. Of suckering habit, *M. microcarpa* can soon form extensive colonies. It is still often confused with *M. cordata*, but that Japanese and Chinese species has white flowers with 24-30 stamens and is much less invasive.

Malva (Mallow) (*Malvaceae*)

The 30-40 species of mallow are closely allied to *Lavatera* and have the same floral impact. Their culture too is much the same. *M. alcea* (Europe) produces well-branched, erect stems to 1.2 m, clad with rounded, shallow-lobed leaves and bearing a succession of 5-7 cm-wide pink to pale rose-purple flowers from summer to autumn. It is largely represented in gardens by *M. a.* 'Fastigiata' which has ascending lateral branches and a neater outline. *M. moschata*, musk mallow (Europe including Britain, N. Africa) forms dense tufts of branched stems 60-80 cm in height with prettily divided palmate leaves and short spikes of 5 cm-wide, bright rose-purple flowers in summer and autumn. *M. m.* 'Alba' is one of the loveliest of pure white flowers for the perennial garden and comes true from seeds.

Marrubium (White Horehound) (*Labiatae*)

Very few of the 35-40 species in this genus have found favour as garden plants though several have pleasing woolly foliage. In appearance they are somewhat dead-nettle-like but more woody stemmed and bushy, the species here described needing well-drained soil and a sunny site. Planting is best in autumn or spring. Propagation is by division, basal cuttings or seeds in spring. *M. cylleneum* (Greece) usually has unbranched stems to 50 cm long bearing rounded, yellowish, woolly leaves and creamy two-lipped flowers. It can sometimes be confused with the similar *M. thessalum*, also from Greece, with oblong, white-woolly leaves. *M. incanum* (Italy, Sicily, Balkan peninsula) is a similar plant but usually taller with white-felted stems and oblong, evergreen leaves that are grey-green above, whitish beneath. The flowers are white. *M. vulgare* (Europe) is the common white horehound, a branched plant 45-60 cm tall with grey-green leaves, white hairy stems and small white flowers in tight, rounded clusters. *M. v.* 'Variegata' has variegated leaves.

Matteuccia (Ostrich Fern) (*Aspidiaceae*)

The three species that form this genus are all handsome ferns well worthy of garden room. They grow best in humus-rich moist soil in partial shade but are reasonably adaptable. Planting can take place from autumn to spring. Propagation is by separating in spring the young plants which grow from underground rhizomes. *M. struthiopteris*, (*Onoclea s.*, *Struthiopteris germanica*) (NE and C. Europe) is the best-known and most readily available species, forming elegant shuttlecock-shaped rosettes of bright-green, dissected, sterile fronds 60-120 cm in height. In the centres of mature rosettes are borne the short, erect spore-bearing leaves which turn a rich brown when ripe. *M. orientalis* (*Onoclea* and *Struthiopteris orientalis*) (Himalayas, E. Asia) much resembles the previous species but has less finely dissected, somewhat shorter fronds with relatively longer stalks.

Meconopsis (Blue Poppy) (*Papaveraceae*)

About 40 species are contained in this queen of the poppy family. Regrettably, few are soundly perennial but they are such desirable hardy plants that they are well worth the trouble of regular replacement by seeds. They require humus-rich, well-drained but moisture-retentive soil and a site in partial shade, though full sun is tolerated providing the soil does not get dry. Planting of evergreen species can take place in summer or earlier, that of the deciduous species during the winter and early spring also. Propagation is by seeds when ripe or in spring under glass; fully perennial species can also be carefully divided in spring. *M. betonicifolia* (*M. baileyi*) (China, Tibet, Upper Burma) is *the* blue poppy and can behave as a biennial or a short-lived perennial. It is recommended that the first flowering stem is removed when young to promote the growth of offsets which will flower in subsequent years. This deciduous plant can reach 90 cm or more with 6 cm-wide poppy flowers that are sky blue on acid soils, lavender on alkaline ones, opening in early summer. *M. cambrica* (Welsh poppy) (W. Europe) forms perennial tufts or clumps of fresh green, pinnate leaves and slender stems to 45 cm or more, bearing yellow poppies from late spring onwards. *M. c. aurantiaca* has rich orange blooms. *M. chelidonifolia* (W. China) is a slenderly elegant perennial to 1 m or more in height with pinnately lobed, hairy leaves and panicles of pale-yellow flowers. A most distinctive plant all too seldom seen, but it must have shelter from strong, drying winds.

113

M. grandis (Himalayas) should be grown in preference to *M. betoni-cifolia* for it is a similar but superior plant in every way, being somewhat taller with larger, richer-hued flowers and is more reliably perennial. There are some fine hybrids between the two species under such names as 'Branklyn', 'Sheldonii' and 'Crewdson Hybrid'. *M. horridula* (*M. prattii*) (Nepal to W. China) can behave as a biennial, or flowers the third year from seeds. It has rosettes of bristly, elliptic leaves and spiny-bristly stems 60-90 cm tall bearing a spire of purple, blue or white flowers in summer. *M. integrifolia*, Farrer's lampshade poppy (Himalayas to W. China) is monocarpic, with softly hairy, narrow, light-green leaves in rosettes and bowl-shaped 10 cm-wide yellow flowers on stems about 30 cm tall, but sometimes up to twice this; best in sunny sites. *M. napaulensis* (*M. wallichii*) satin poppy (E. Himalayas to China) merits the title statuesque when its 1.5-2 m-tall stems expand, bearing a narrow panicle of 5-7.5 cm-wide poppies in shades of red, pink, purple and less commonly, blue or white, in the summer. It is evergreen and the large, deeply lobed, hairy leaves form ornate rosettes which stay attractive all the winter. *M. paniculata* (Himalayas) can fairly be described as a yellow-flowered version of *M. napaulensis* with even larger and more handsome winter rosettes. *M. quintuplinervia*, harebell poppy (China, Tibet) is a rhizomatous perennial forming colonies of deciduous rosettes of small, narrow, hairy leaves above which rise slender stems each bearing a solitary, nodding 6-8 cm-wide bowl-shaped flower of lavender to purple-blue. *M. regia* (Nepal) has close affinities with *M. napaulensis*, but the rosette leaves are less boldly lobed and more densely silvery – sometimes golden-hairy and very effective in winter. The flowers are yellow. *M. superba* (Bhutan, Tibet) is akin to *M. regia* but shorter and with 6-7 cm-wide white flowers. *M. villosa* (Bhutan, Nepal) has long-stalked, bipinnate, golden hairy leaves that always attract attention in winter. Bright-yellow poppies are carried several together in summer on stems 45-60 cm tall. It is perennial but usually not long lived, and is best away from overhanging trees.

Melica (Melick) (*Gramineae*)

About 70 species of grasses of almost world-wide distribution form this genus. Several are quietly attractive with neat, ovoid spikelets in nodding panicles. They grow in ordinary soil in sun or shade, particularly the latter. Planting is best in spring, with propagation by division or by seeds in spring. *M. altissima* (E. Europe) forms loose clumps of fairly broad, arching leaves and slender stems up to 1 m or more, terminating in spike-like panicles of brownish spikelets in the summer; 'Atropurpurea' ('Rubra') is deep purple, and 'Alba' is almost white. *M. uniflora* (Europe) is the familiar wood melick, a tufted, rhizomatous species with arching leaves and lax panicles

Figure 9: *Meconop-sis napaulensis*

of smooth, elliptic, purple or brownish-tinted spikelets from early to late summer. *M. u.* 'Variegata' has the leaves striped cream. There is also an albino with whitish spikelets.

Melissa officinalis (Lemon Balm) (*Labiatae*)

The common or lemon balm is the only one of the three species in this genus to be cultivated. More of a herb than an ornamental it is not worth giving it room in the ornamental garden but in wilder areas it makes compact, fresh green clumps of lemon-scented foliage about 60 cm tall. Small white two-lipped flowers open in late summer. *M. o.* 'Aurea' has the leaves blotched yellow. Any soil that is not waterlogged is suitable in sun or partial shade. Plant and propagate by division from autumn to spring.

Melittis melissophyllum (Bastard Balm) (*Labiatae*)

The only species in its genus, this clump-former grows 25-45 cm tall and has pleasantly aromatic, finely corrugated leaves in pairs. In early summer, quite large two-lipped cream and rose-purple flowers open in the upper leaf axils. It thrives best in humus-rich, well-drained soil in partial shade but will stand full sun. Planting is best in autumn or spring, with propagation by division or seeds at the latter time.

Mentha (Mint) (*Labiatae*)

Most of the 25 species of mint are culinary plants and too invasive or lacking in grace for the flower garden. The following are decorative but should be planted with circumspection. Ordinary soil, and sun or partial shade are the basic cultural requirements, with planting taking place from autumn to spring; propagation is by division at planting time. For the *M. alopecuroides* of catalogues – see under *M.* X *villosa*. *M. gentilis* 'Variegata', variegated ginger or Scotch mint (*M. arvensis* X *M. spicata*) has the spearmint smell of *M. spicata* and the rich green foliage with a yellow-vein pattern. The stems reach 45-60 cm and terminate in leafy spikes of tiny lilac flowers in summer. *M. longifolia*, long-leaved or horse mint (Europe to W. Siberia) is like a more robust version of the common spearmint (*M. spicata*) but is grey-white hairy, with longer spikes of mauve flowers; *M. l.* 'Buddleia' has intensely grey-white leaves and is a striking foliage plant. *M.* X *piperita citrata* (*M. aquatica* X *M. spicata*) is the Eau de Cologne, orange, lemon or bergamot mint. It grows to 50 cm tall with broad, often purple-tinged leaves and clusters of lilac-pink flower in interrupted spikes. It is best valued for its sharp, sweetly aromatic smell when bruised. The *M. rotundifolia* 'Variegata' of gardens should not be confused with the *M. longifolia* X *M. suaveolens* hybrid also now known as *M.* X *rotundifolia*. The proper name for this robust, hairy mint with creamy-white-margined leaves on 60 cm-tall stems is *M.* X *villosa* (*M. spicata* X *suaveolens*). Of the same parentage is *M.* X *alopecuroides*, now frequently grown in the herb garden as 'Bowles Mint' and perhaps the best mint of all for the making of mint sauce.

Mertensia (*Boraginaceae*)

An estimated 45 species of tufted to clump-forming deciduous perennials form this genus but very few are cultivated. The species mentioned here have pleasing grey to blue-green tinted leaves and nodding clusters of tubular flowers with flared mouths. They grow in ordinary, preferably humus-rich soil in sun or partial shade. Planting should take place in autumn or spring with propagation by division at planting time or by sowing seeds when ripe or in spring. *M. ciliata* (W. USA) has oval leaves to 15 cm long and stems to 60 cm tall, bearing pale-blue flowers with fringed calyces in spring and summer. *M. echioides* (Himalayas) has oblong to spoon-shaped leaves which are downy beneath, and in summer, deep violet-blue flowers. *M. sibirica* (Asia) is similar to *M. ciliata* but has deeper blue flowers and the calyces are not fringed. *M. virginica*, Virginian cowslip (Kansas to New York State, south to Alabama) is perhaps the loveliest species with glaucous leaves and 2.5 cm-long violet-blue flowers on 45 cm-tall stems in spring. It is essentially a woodland plant which dies back to a fleshy root stock around mid-summer.

Meum athamanticum (Spignel) (*Umbelliferae*)

Of the two species in this genus, spignel or bald money is the only one likely to be seen in gardens, and then rarely. It deserves to be grown more widely for its froth of rich green leaves divided into hair-fine segments provide very pleasing contrast to bolder plants. The flattish heads of its white flowers open on 45-60 cm-tall stems in summer. Ordinary soil and sun are its simple requirements. Planting can take place from autumn to spring; seeds are sown when ripe or in spring.

Milium effusum 'Aureum' (Wood Millet) (*Gramineae*)

This is the only garden representative of the six species that form this genus of northern temperate grasses. Also known as 'Bowles Golden Grass' after the plantsman E. A. Bowles, it is a tufted, short-lived perennial up to 60 cm in height. The arching leaves, stems and small millet-like flowering spikelets are a soft but bright greenish-gold and light up the shady sites it prefers. It grows in ordinary soil in partial shade or sun. It is best planted in spring, propagation is by division or seeds. The plant usually produces self-sown seedlings which come true to type.

Mimulus (Monkey Flower) (*Scrophulariaceae*)

Comparatively few of the 100-150 species in this genus are hardy perennials, but those that are provide a long season of showy flowers that seem to combine features of antirrhinum and petunia. They need moisture-retentive but otherwise ordinary soil and are best in sun though partial shade is tolerated. Planting is best in spring with propagation by divison or seeds at the same time. *M.* X *bartonianus* (*M. cardinalis* X *M. lewisii*) rather resembles the latter parent but has rose-red flowers with red-brown throats spotted yellow. *M. cardinalis* (SW USA, N. Mexico) is a clump-former to 90 cm in height with oblong, downy foliage and scarlet flowers of somewhat snap-dragon form but slimmer, from summer to autumn; 'Rose Queen' is pink. *M. cupreus* (S. Chile) is much like the well-known *M. luteus* but more compact in habit and unreliably perennial. The yellow flowers age to coppery-orange and redder forms are known. *M. guttatus* (*M. langsdorfii*) also resembles *M. luteus* but tends to be taller to 60 cm, with yellow flowers having red-spotted throats and bell-shaped calyces. *M.* X *hybridus* (*M. luteus* X *M. guttatus*) blends the parental characters in various ways. *M. lewisii* (W. North America) is often confused in cultivation with its hybrid *M.* X *bartonianus* (q.v.). The true plant has sticky-downy leaves and rose-purple blooms. *M. luteus*, monkey flower or musk (Chile) is also naturalised in Europe and elsewhere. It forms mats of creeping stems from which arise leafy racemes 30-50 cm or more tall, bearing the typical musk flowers variously spotted and blotched maroon-crimson. Several cultivars and seed strains are available including 'Red Emperor' and the mixed 'Queens Prize' some, if not all referable to *M.* X *hybridus*. *M. ringens* (N. America) is a distinctive species with slender but strong stems and elegantly poised antirrhinum-like flowers of rich clear purple with a yellow throat, borne in summer. A water plant in the wild, it will also grow in permanently moist soil.

Miscanthus (*Gramineae*)

About 20 species of perennial grasses from Asia comprise this genus. The two cultivated eventually form dense broad clumps which make good bamboo substitutes in the smaller garden. They thrive best in humus-rich soil that does not dry out and in sunny and partially shaded sites. Planting should take place in spring with propagation by division at the same time. *M. sacchariflorus*, Amur silver grass (E. Asia) produces stems to 3 m-tall, clad with arching, 2 cm-wide leaves. Feathery, grey to mauve-brown flowering spikelets make up terminal plumes in autumn but are rarely seen in Britain, requiring warmer, late-summer weather to develop. *M. s.* 'Aureus' has golden variegated leaves. *M. sinensis* (*Eulalia japonica*) can attain 3 m when happily situated and even under dryish conditions can exceed 2 m. In other respects it is like the preceding species but with narrower, 1 cm-wide leaves having a whitish midrib. It also seldom flowers, but see notes on the cultivars which follow. *M. s.* 'Gracillimus' is so unlike its robust progenitor as to appear a different species, being very slender of stem and leaf — the latter about 5 mm wide, and only 1-1.5 m in height. 'Silver Feather' is like the type species but in autumn regularly produces pinkish-brown floral plumes with a satiny sheen. 'Variegatus' ('Vittatus') has the leaves neatly striped longitudinally with white. 'Zebrinus' is the eye-catching tiger grass having each leaf broadly cross-banded with yellow; it also flowers regularly in autumn.

Molinia (Moor Grass) (*Gramineae*)

Five species of densely clump-forming grasses form this genus, two of which are ornamental and combine well with broader leaved plants. They need moisture-retentive but otherwise ordinary soil and a sunny site. Planting and propagation by division are best carried out in spring. *M. arundinacea altissima* (*M. altissima*, *M. caerulea altissima* and *M. littoralis*) (Europe and Asia) is in effect a giant form of the next species to 1.2 m or more tall. *M. caerulea*, purple moor grass (Europe, Asia) forms dense tufts of deciduous, slender, arching leaves to 20 cm long. In late summer arise wiry stems, 45-65 cm tall topped by panicles of tiny purplish spikelets. For garden decoration, *M. c.* 'Variegata' makes more impact with leaves striped creamy-white and often pink tinted when young.

Moltkia doerfleri (*Boraginaceae*)

This is the only member of a six-species genus to be considered as a hardy perennial. Formerly *Lithospermum doerfleri*, it hails from the mountains of Albania and grows 30-50 cm tall with lanceolate leaves and nodding clusters of tubular, deep-purple flowers to 2.5 cm long in summer. Ordinary well-drained soil in sun is required and planting can be carried out from autumn to spring. Propagation is by division and by sowing seeds in spring.

Monarda (Bee Balm) (*Labiatae*)

Out of the twelve species of this genus from E. USA, one is a regular and popular member of our beds and borders. One other similar species is usually available and the two are sometimes confused. Ordinary, preferably humus-rich, moisture-retentive soil in partial shade or sun is required. Planting and propagation is by division and can take place from autumn to spring. *M. didyma*, common bee balm, bergamot or Oswego tea, forms wide clumps of erect, square-sectioned stems to 90 cm tall, clad with pairs of pointed, oval leaves.

In summer the stems are topped by dense heads of out-curving, slender, two-lipped, tubular, scarlet flowers. Several cultivars are available, e.g. 'Cambridge Scarlet' (crimson-scarlet) 'Croftway Pink' (clear pink), 'Mahogany' (brownish-red) 'Snow Queen' (white) and 'Violet Queen' (violet-purple). *M. fistulosa* has narrower, hairy leaves and usually solitary clusters of lavender-purple flowers (*M. didyma* often has two clusters of flowers per stem, one above the other). Some of the *M. didyma* cultivars are probably hybrids with *fistulosa*.

Morina longifolia (*Dipsacaceae* (*Morinaceae*))

This is the only member of this 108-species genus which is generally available. Other equally attractive species still await trial. *M. longifolia,* the whorlflower, comes from the Himalayas. It forms clumps of evergreen, narrow, thistle-like foliage which arches gracefully outwards. In summer, rigid stems to 90 cm arise, the upper part bearing whorls of slender-tubed flowers which open white and age crimson. It combines well with small shrubs and needs a site where the dark-green foliage can be appreciated. Ordinary fertile soil and sun or partial shade are all that is required. Planting is best in autumn or spring. Propagation is by division or by seeds in spring.

Myrrhis odorata (*Umbelliferae*)

Best known as sweet Cicely, and the only member of its genus, this is a quietly attractive plant with aromatic foliage of fern-like delicacy, and flat umbels of white flowers on 60-90 cm-tall stems in early summer. In effect it is like a refined and superior cow parsley. The heads of large, ribbed, brownish-black seeds also have appeal. Any soil is suitable and it looks best in shade though will tolerate full sun. Propagation is by seeds when ripe, preferably *in situ*. Division in spring is also possible.

Nepeta (Catmint) (*Labiatae*)

Although a well-known name to the hardy planter, few of the 250 species in this genus are cultivated. Spreading to erect in habit they have aromatic foliage and tubular two-lipped flowers sometimes in abundance. All the species mentioned are easy going and indispensable for the front of a border or as a filler. They grow in ordinary well-drained soil and prefer a sunny site. Planting can take place from autumn to spring. Propagation is by division or by sowing seeds in spring. Most species are attractive to cats who may chew or roll on the plants – a few prickly twigs or holly leaves are the best deterrent. *N. cataria* is the common catnip or catmint from Europe and Asia. It grows 60-90 cm tall and has grey-green leaves and white purple-dotted flowers in late summer but is not particularly ornamental. *N.* X *faassenii* (*N. mussinii* X *N. nepetella*) is similar to and often confused with its *N. mussinii* parent but bears it sprays of violet-blue flowers more freely and does not produce self-sown seedlings. If cut back after its main summer flush it will flower again more profusely than if left to its own devices. For *N. macrantha* – see under *Dracocephalum sibiricum*. *N. mussinii* (Iran, Caucasus) is a tufted plant forming mats to 30 cm tall with its long, arching stems, grey-downy leaves and lavender-blue flowers. In light soils it self-sows freely and can be a nuisance. *N. m.* 'Superba' is listed as being more robust, to 90 cm tall with broader leaves and darker flowers. *N. nervosa* (Kashmir) is erect of habit, to 60 cm tall with narrow leaves to 10 cm long and dense terminal spikes of usually blue or yellow flowers in summer. For *N. sibirica* – see under *Dracocephalum sibiricum*. *N.* X 'Six Hills Giant' is also '*N. gigantea*' of catalogues and is more like a more erect version of *N.* X *faassenii* to 90 cm tall. *N.* 'Souvenir d'André Chaudron' ('Blue Beauty') is probably a hybrid with *Dracocephalum sibiricum* as the other parent and is not unlike a shorter, more compact version of it.

Oenothera (Evening Primrose) (*Onagraceae*)

About 80 species form this genus of annuals and perennials from the Americas. The taller, hardier perennial members are showy plants with bowl- or cup-shaped flowers formed of four broad petals mainly in shades of yellow. They thrive in ordinary soil in sun but tolerate partial shade. Planting can take place autumn to spring, with propagation by division at the same time or by seeds in spring. For the *O. cinaeus*, *O. fruticosa* and *O. glaber* of catalogues – see under *O. tetragona*. *O. nuttallii* (NW North America) resembles the better-known *O. speciosa* but with leaves never pinnately lobed and somewhat cupped flowers. Sometimes confused in British gardens with the dwarf yellow-flowered rock plant *O. tanacetifolia*. *O. perennis* (*O. pumila, Kneiffia perennis*), sundrops (E. North America) varies from under, to well above, 30 cm in height. Rather small in leaf and blossom it has its uses at the front of the border. The numerous wiry stems bear a succession of reddish-tinted buds and yellow flowers 1.5-2 cm wide in summer. For the *O. riparia* of catalogues – see under *O. tetragona*. *O. speciosa* (S. USA, Mexico) grows to 60 cm tall with narrow, greyish leaves that are usually pinnately lobed. The handsome 5 cm-wide flowers open white and gradually age to pink. *O. stricta* (*O. odorata, O. sulphurea* of gardens) (Chile) tends to be a short-lived perennial but usually maintains itself by self-sown seedlings. It is a slender plant, 60-90 cm tall with narrow basal leaves to 10 cm long and pale-yellow flowers ageing to red, from summer to autumn. *O. tetragona* (*O. fruticosa youngii, O. youngii* of gardens) (E. USA) grows to about 45 cm tall, the stems clad with many small lance-shaped leaves and topped by spikes of 3-5 cm-wide rich-yellow flowers in summer. *O. t. fraseri* (*O. cinaeus*, *O. fruticosa fraseri* and *O. glauca*) has broader leaves that are glaucous beneath. *O. t. f.* 'Fyrverkeri' ('Fireworks') has flower buds waxy red. *O. t.* 'Glaber' has red-purple flushed foliage. *O. t. riparia* is dwarf and bushy with well-branched stems to 23 cm tall. *O. t.* 'Yellow River' is a good yellow selection to 60 cm tall.

Onoclea sensibilis (Sensitive Fern) (*Aspidiaceae*)

The one species in this genus has a remarkable range, being found wild in the temperate regions of both hemispheres. It is a rhizomatous, deciduous fern, eventually forming extensive colonies of elegant, 40-60 cm-tall pinnate fronds. These are bright green and rendered more conspicuous by reason of their wavy-toothed segments which pick up the light in the most effective way. The vernacular name refers to the sensitivity of the fronds to the first severe frosts of autumn. Moisture-retentive but otherwise ordinary soil is suitable, preferably in light shade. Full sun is tolerated only in constantly moist soils. Planting is best in spring with propagation by division or spores at the same time.

Ophiopogon (*Liliaceae*)

The ten species in this genus are closely allied to *Liriope* (q.v.) and when not in flower can be confused with it. They are tufted, often stoloniferous plants with leathery grassy leaves and racemes of small nodding flowers followed by blue or purple berry-like fruits. Culture is as for *Liriope*. *O. jaburan* (Japan) is clump-forming with lustrous, deep-green outcurving leaves 30-60 cm long. Small, summer-borne, white to pale-purple flowers give way to oblong violet-blue fruits. *O. j.* 'Vittatus' ('Variegatus') has white-striped foliage. It needs a sheltered, shady spot in humus-rich soil to thrive. *O. planiscapus* (*O. japonicus wallichianus*) eventually forms loose mats composed of tufts of low arching dark-green leaves. The white to lilac flowers and pea-sized deep-blue fruits are not usually freely produced. *O. p.* 'Nigrescens' (*O. arabicus* of gardens) has purplish-black leaves and darker purple-tinted fruits. Although rarely above 15 cm tall it makes a unique subject for the front of a sheltered border or bed.

Origanum

Although this genus of 15-20 species is generally thought of as providing plants for the herb or rock garden, there are a few taller and reasonably hardy sorts that can be used to good effect in the perennial garden. They are generally erect, slender plants with small opposite leaves and tubular, two-lipped flowers in small compact spikes which in turn are often borne in leafy panicles. In some cases the spikes are surrounded by broad bracts which create a hop-like flowerhead. Well-drained soil and sun are essential and planting is best in spring. Propagation is by careful division at planting time, or by seeds or basal cuttings in spring. *O. hybridum* (*O. sipyleum*) (Turkey) grows to 30 cm or more in height with smooth oval leaves and a profusion of pink hop-like flower spikes in late summer. *O. laevigatum* (Syria, Turkey) can eventually form wide clumps of wiry, much-branched stems to 45 cm tall bearing tiny blue-grey leaves and an abundance of red-purple flowers in autumn. An unusual plant with the appeal of a gypsophila and reliably hardy in Britain. *O. vulgare* (Europe) is the common marjoram, a clump-forming species about 60 cm tall with clustered white, pink or red-purple flowers but hardly worth growing in the flower border. *O. v.* 'Aureum' has the young leaves golden yellow and can be quite showy in spring and early summer.

Orchis – see under *Dactylorrhiza*.

Orobus – see under *Lathyrus*.

Osmunda (Flowering Ferns) (*Osmundaceae*)

Although only one species in this genus is well known – the royal fern – there are at least ten species of almost world-wide distribution. Unlike many ferns, the spore cases (sporangia) are carried on reduced, rolled-up pinnules (leaflets) which may form separate fronds or be inserted in the middle or tip of a frond, and then resemble a cluster of small flower buds. The osmundas need moist, preferably humus-rich soil and partial shade, though *O. regalis* will grow in sun if the soil is wet. Planting is best in spring and propagation is by division or spores at the same time. *O. cinnamomea*, fiddle heads, cinnamon fern (N. and S. America, E. Asia) is clump-forming, to 90 cm tall when happily established. The spore-bearing fronds are separate, bright green at first, maturing lustrous cinnamon-brown. *O. claytoniana*, interrupted fern (N. America) forms clumps to about 1 m tall, the fertile fronds sometimes even larger and with the middle part bearing the dark-brown sporing leaflets, giving them an interrupted appearance. *O. regalis*, royal fern (Europe, W. Asia, India, S. Africa, N. and S. America) eventually develops massive clumps which can reach 1.5-3 m in height, depending on the richness and wetness of th soil. It best merits the name flowering fern, as the fertile fronds terminate in long panicle-like clusters of beaded, bud-like pinnules that ripen light rusty-brown.

Ourisia (*Scrophulariaceae*)

The 24 species of ourisia are generally thought of as suitable only for the rock garden, peat bed or alpine house. The following however, are robust enough to grace the front of a herbaceous bed or border, adding interest and a touch of distinction to the sites they occupy. A humus-rich, moisture-retentive but well-drained soil in sun or partial shade is required. Spring is the best planting time or just after flowering, with propagation by division at the same time. *O. macrocarpa* (New Zealand) is known as mountain foxglove in its homeland. It forms mats of thick-textured pleasing foliage above which rise stems 30-50 cm tall bearing whorls of pure white, 2.3 cm-wide mimulus-like flowers in summer. Also from New Zealand and much like it in general appearance is *O. macrophylla*, but the flowers are smaller — 1.5-2 cm — and more profusely borne.

Paeonia (Peony) (*Paeoniaceae*)

Although not all of the 33 known species qualify, taken as a whole this genus is surely queen of the hardy perennials. It is in fact the equivalent of the rose in the shrub world, giving us large and sumptuous blooms in a delightful range of colours and shades, with good foliage on long-lived plants. What a pity the plant breeder has not yet been able to give us remontant peonies! A further attraction of some of the species is the large three-lobed seed pods which split open to disclose red interiors and a mixture of crimson sterile, and black or bluish glossy pea-sized fertile, seeds. Especially effective in this respect are *P. mlokosewitschii* and *P. wittmanniana*. They require humus-rich soil that is well drained but moisture retentive and a sunny site, though some shade is tolerated. Planting can take place from autumn to early spring, preferably early autumn. Propagation is by careful division at planting time or by seeds when ripe. Dried seeds should be sown immediately and usually take a year or more to germinate. Cultivars do not come true to type, seedlings take three to four years to reach flowering size. For the *P. albiflora* of catalogues see *P. lactiflora* and for *P. arietina* see under *P. mascula*. *P. cambessedesii* is a gem from the Balearic Islands with handsome, beetroot-purple backed foliage and stems to 45 cm, topped by deep rose-pink flowers in late spring. Regrettably it is not fully hardy and needs the foot of a sheltered wall. *P. emodii* (Kashmir) is one of the tallest species attaining 90 cm or more, with pleasing bright foliage and pure-white flowers with yellow stamens, in late spring. It seems to thrive best with some shade and looks well in a mixed border among shrubs. *P. lactiflora* (*P. albiflora*) Chinese peony (Tibet, Siberia, China) is similar and allied to *P. emodii*, usually 60-90 cm tall with fragrant white, pink or red flowers in summer. It is represented in gardens under the names 'Whitleyi Major' and 'The Bride' (white flowered) and is a major parent of the single and double cultivars now available. Many cultivars are available from specialist nurserymen and the choice is largely a personal matter. The following however can be recommended: 'Balliol' (single, maroon-red), 'Bowl of Beauty' (single mallow-purple filled with a large boss of pale yellow staminodes), 'Duchesse de Nemours' (double, pure white), 'Felix Crousse' (double rose-red), 'Festiva Maxima' double, white-flecked, red-purple in the centre), 'Lady Alexandra Duff' (large double, pale pink, ageing white), 'Monsieur Jules Elie' (double, silvery lilac-pink), 'Sarah Bernhardt' (double, rose-purple, edged pink), 'Solange' (double, waxy-white, flushed buff-salmon to yellow in the centre), 'The Moor' (single, deep maroon-crimson). For *P. lobata* – see under *P. peregrina. P. mascula (P. corallina)* (S. and E. Europe) is 60 cm or more tall with deeply cut leaves and rose-red flowers in early summer. *P. m. arietina* (SE Europe, Turkey) has the leaves downy beneath. *P. mlokosewit-schii* (Caucasus) is one of the most distinctive species with grey-green leaves, reddish-tinted when young and lemon-yellow flowers in spring. White and pink-tinted forms occur, probably hybrids with *P. wittman-niana* and other species. *P. obovata* (China, Japan, Sakhalin) grows 45-50 cm tall, with obovate grey-green leaf segments that are coppery-tinted when young and with rose-purple or white ('Alba') flowers in late spring. *P. officinalis* (France to Albania) in its double forms is the common cottage peony, forming sturdy 60 cm-tall clumps of glossy leaves and 8-13 cm-wide red flowers in early summer. *P o.* 'Alba Plena' is double white; 'Anemoniflora Rosea' has deep-pink single blooms filled with crimson and yellow petaloids; 'China Rose' appears to be a hybrid, probably with *P. peregrina* and has single salmon-red flowers with orange-yellow stamens, while 'Rubra Plena' is the popular double deep red. *P. peregrina (P. decora, P. lobata,* 'Fire King') (Italy, Balkan peninsula, Romania) is like a more refined *P. officinalis* with beautifully rounded, cup-shaped, rich-red flowers with yellow stamens, in early summer. The cultivar 'Sunshine' has salmon-red petals with an orange patina. *P. "sinensis"* is a name used by some nurserymen for the hybrid cultivars of *P. lactiflora* (q.v.). *P. tenuifolia* (SE Europe to the Caucasus) has the most distinctive and elegant foliage of all the peonies, each leaf being finely cut into almost grassy segments and creating a frothy-ferny effect which makes a perfect background for the deep crimson, almost globular flowers. At only 30-40 cm tall it makes a splendid talking point for the front of a sunny border. *P. veitchii* (SW China) is also dwarf, 30-40 cm tall, but with fingered glossy leaves and nodding rose-purple flowers that open out flat in early summer. It thrives best in partial shade. *P. v. woodwardii* is a desirable pure-pink form but difficult to obtain. *P. wittmanniana* (Caucasus) is akin to *P. mlokosewitschii* but a little taller and with glossy foliage and white flowers.

Papaver (Poppy) (*Papaveraceae*)

Botanists seem rather at odds over the exact number of poppy species, the numbers ranging from 50-100. Only a few of these are hardy perennials but they can provide bright patches of colour to the garden as few other perennials can. They grow in ordinary well-drained soil and need a sunny site. Planting can be done from autumn to spring. Propagate by careful division at planting time, by root cuttings in late winter or by sowing seeds in spring. *P. atlanticum* (Morocco) resembles *P. rupifragum* but is a little taller, silky-hairy throughout and with pale-orange flowers. It can self-sow annoyingly, seedlings appearing over several years. *P. nudicaule* (Arctic regions) is the familiar Iceland poppy and is only a short-lived perennial. It has pale-green, deeply divided leaves in dense tufts and 5-6.5 cm-wide fragrant flowers in shades of orange, yellow, red and white from summer to autumn. Several seed strains and cultivars are available, some with larger and double blooms which flower the first year from seed, but are not so long lived as perennials. *P. orientale* (SW Asia) is the oriental poppy, a robust clump-former with roughly hairy, coarse, fern-like foliage and large flowers 10 cm or more wide on 1 m-tall stems in early summer. Several cultivars are available and the following can be recommended: 'Marcus Perry' (very large orange-scarlet blooms); 'Mrs Perry' (clear pink), 'Perry's White' (chalk white), 'Salmon Glow' (double, salmon pink). 'King George' is particularly noteworthy in having its black-blotched, rich-red petals deeply fringed. *P. rupifragum* (S. Spain) has most of its almost hairless, pinnately lobed leaves in basal tufts. Above these, brick-red flowers sway on slender stems to 50 cm high in summer.

Paradisea liliastrum (St Bruno's Lily) (*Liliaceae*)

The only one cultivated in this genus of two species, the St Bruno's lily is closely allied to *Anthericum* and can be likened to a superior version of *A. liliago* but with larger flowers like small, pure-white lilies. A modest but charming plant worthy of planting more often. Culture is as for *Anthericum*.

Peltiphyllum peltatum (Umbrella Plant) (*Saxifragaceae*)

This splendid foliage plant is the only member of its genus. Formerly *Saxifraga peltata*, it is native to streamsides in the mountain evergreen forests of California and Oregon. It is rhizomatous and eventually forms wide colonies of lobed, peltate leaves to almost 30 cm wide carried on robust stalks 1-1.5 m in height. Rich lustrous green all the summer, the foliage takes on shades of bright red in the autumn before dying away for the winter. In spring, before the leaves, starry pink flowers in dense rounded heads slowly rise up on pinkish, hairy stems to 60 cm or more. Moist fertile soil is required and ideally, partial shade sheltered from strong winds. Planting is best just after flowering or early autumn; propagation is by division at planting time.

Pennisetum (*Gramineae*)

This genus is credited with 130-150 species of annual and perennial grasses, many of which are decidedly attractive but not hardy enough for our purposes. Those mentioned here are reasonably winter-hardy clump-formers with charming, soft, bottle-brush-like flower spikes. They need ordinary well-drained soil and a sheltered sunny site. Planting should take place in spring with propagation by division at the same time or by seeds under glass. *P. alopecuroides* (E. Asia to E. Australia) can reach 1 m or more in height, with very narrow arching leaves and bottle-brushes up to 20 cm long, bluish-purple in the best forms, but also yellowish or greenish in autumn. *P. orientale* (SW to C. Asia and NW India) is similar to the previous species but seldom above 40-50 cm in height with shorter bottle-brushes, lightly tinted pink or purple, in late summer. *P. villosum*, feather top (mountains of NE tropical Africa) is cast in the mould of the above species but has much fatter, feathery brushes of tawny-white, from late summer onwards.

Penstemon (*Scrophulariaceae*)

All but one of the estimated 250 species of penstemons are found in the northern part of the Americas. Most species are sub-shrubs and are too small for the perennial garden, but the following are decidedly garden worthy with their tubular, five-lobed flowers in spire-like panicles. Well-drained fertile soil and a sunny site are required. Planting is best in early autumn or spring. Propagation is by careful division, or by sowing seeds in spring or by basal cuttings in late summer. *P. barbatus* (Utah to Mexico) grows to 1 m in height, with narrow leaves and 2.5 cm-long scarlet flowers with yellow beards; a pink form is known. *P. campanulatus* (*P. pulchellus*) (Mexico and Guatemala) achieves 40-60 cm in height with narrow lance-shaped, sharply toothed leaves and pink, purple or violet flowers to 3 cm long. It is usually represented in gardens by hybrid cultivars, e.g. 'Evelyn' (pink) and 'Garnet' (wine-red). For *P. confertus* – see under *P. procerus*. *P. gentianoides* (Mexico, Guatemala) is a short-lived plant 1-1.5 m tall with 3 cm-long blue-purple flowers. It is however, rare in cultivation being confused with *P. hartwegii* (q.v.). *P. gloxinioides* is a name of no botanical standing for variants of *P. hartwegii* and its hybrids with the white to pale purple *P. cobaea*. Several cultivars are available, most of them somewhat tender. Among the hardiest are: 'Schoenholzeri' ('Firebird', 'Ruby') bright red, 'Gentianoides' ('Lady

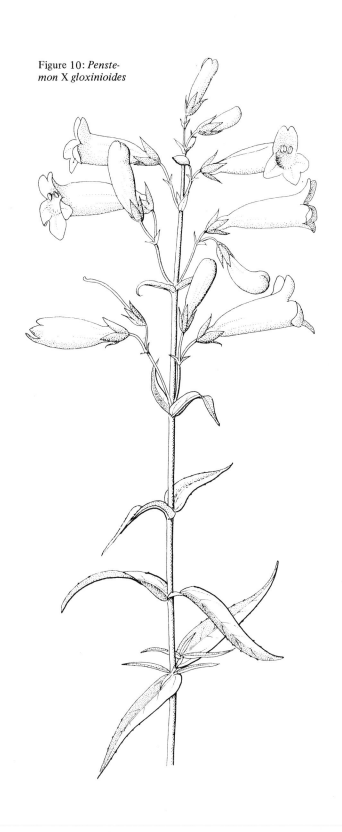

Figure 10: *Penste-mon* X *gloxinioides*

Alice Hindley' and not to be confused with the species of the same name) and 'White Bedder'. *P. hartwegii* (Mexico) has 5 cm-long scarlet flowers on stems to 1 m more or less, from summer to autumn and is a fine thing for a sheltered site. The name *gentianoides* has also been used for this species but by priority belongs to the plant described under that heading above. *P. heterophyllus* (California) is sub-shrubby but is best cut back each spring. It is bushy, with narrow, greyish, smooth leaves clothing stems to 60 cm tall and blue-purple flowers; 'Blue Gem' and 'California Blue Bedder' are good blue-flowered selections. *P. isophyllus* (Mexico) is also sub-shrubby but best cut back in spring. Despite its reputation it is hardy in Britain in all but hard winters. The best forms have a certain elegance, with slim stems to 1 m and a long succession of narrow, crimson-scarlet flowers until the first frosts. *P. ovatus* (British Columbia to Oregon) grows 75-90 cm tall with toothed, oval or lance-shaped leaves and deep purple-blue flowers in summer. *P. procerus* (*P. micranthus*) (Alaska and Yukon to Colorado) has lance-shaped leaves and blue-purple flowers on 45 cm-tall stems. The closely allied *P. confertus* (from Alberta and Montana to Oregon) has pale sulphur-yellow to cream flowers; both bloom in summer.

Perovskia (*Perowskia*) (*Labiatae*)

The seven species in this genus are technically sub-shrubs or shrubs, but the two described below perform best in the garden if treated as herbaceous perennials, being cut back close to ground level in early spring. Well-drained ordinary soil and a sunny site are required. Planting is best in autumn or spring and propagation by basal cuttings in early summer. *P. abrotanoides* (S. USSR, Iran) produces slim woody stems to 1.2 m tall, much branched above to form a long panicle of small, tubular violet-blue flowers in late summer. The deeply lobed leaves are aromatic and thinly covered with grey-white hairs. It is not commonly grown and sometimes confused with forms of the following species. *P. atriplicifolia* (W. Himalayas, Afghanistan) resembles the previous species but is more conspicuously white-hairy, has more shallowly lobed or merely toothed leaves, and lavender flowers. The cultivars 'Blue Haze' and 'Blue Spire' are superior garden plants and are probably hybrids.

Petasites (Butterbur) (*Compositae*)

Although several of the 15 species of butterbur are attractive in either flower or leaf, those generally available are invasive and should only be planted in the wildest corners of large gardens. Ordinary moist soil and partial shade or sun are basic requirements. Planting can take place from autumn to spring with propagation by division at the same time. *P. fragrans*, winter heliotrope (W. Mediterranean) has rounded, somewhat lustrous evergreen leaves to 20 cm wide, and 20-30 cm tall large, groundsel-like lilac-purple, vanilla-scented flowers in winter; very invasive. *P. japonicus giganteus* (Korea, China, Rykyu) is the giant of the genus with leaves up to 90 cm wide or more on stalks 1.5-2 m high when grown in wet, rich soil. The flowering shoots are surrounded by large lime-green bracts and when young, resemble small cabbage hearts. A colony can provide a quite remarkable sight in late winter or early spring. Later, the bracts spread out and white flowerheads emerge on stems which eventually grow to about 30 cm. It is very invasive in wet soils but much less so in ordinary garden soil. The northern Asian *P. hybridus* produces equally fine large leaves but lacks the floral interest and if anything, is even more invasive.

Phalaris arundinacea (*Gramineae*)

This is the only perennial member of a 15-species genus of annual and perennial grasses considered worthy of garden room. Native to the north temperate zone and known in Britain as reed canary or ribbon grass it is a rhizomatous plant forming wide colonies of reed-like stems to 1 m or more, with pale to almost whitish green ribbon-like leaves. The pale-green or purplish-tinted flowering spikelets form dense, narrow panicles in summer. *P. a.* 'Picta' ('Variegata') is the well-known gardener's garters, a somewhat smaller plant with white-striped leaves. Ordinary soil and a sunny site are satisfactory though partial shade is tolerated. In rich damp soil this grass can be invasive. Planting and propagation by division is in spring.

Phlomis (*Labiatae*)

Very few of the 100 species in this genus are cultivated and the best known are the shrubby members. The following clump-forming members are well worthy of garden room, being trouble-free and long-lived and intriguingly handsome when sporting their whorled clusters of tubular, hooded flowers. Well-drained fertile soil in sun or light shade are the basic requirements. Planting is best done in autumn or spring and propagation by division or seeds in spring. *P. russeliana* (*P. viscosa* of gardens, not the true shrubby species of this name) is a sturdy clump-former 90-120 cm tall with finely wrinkled, sage-green leaves 15-30 cm long and whorled spikes of yellow flowers in summer. *P. samia* (Greece, S. Yugoslavia) forms clumps to 1 m in height with white-downy leaves, particularly beneath, and purple flowers.

Phlox (*Polemoniaceae*)

This very garden-worthy genus of 60 species is as indispensable to the rock and alpine gardener as to the hardy-perennial enthusiast. The species described here require well-drained but moisture-retentive, preferably humus-enriched soil and partial shade. They will grow in full sun but only where the soil stays moist. Planting can take place from autumn to spring with propagation by division at the same time. *P.* X *arendsii* (*P. divaricata* X *P. paniculata*) basically resembles the familiar *P. paniculata* but inherits the dwarf stature and lavender-violet hues of *divaricata*. It is represented by the following cultivars: 'Lisbeth' (lavender-blue) 'Anja' (red-purple), 'Hilda' (lavender) and 'Susanne' (white with a red eye). *P.* X 'Chattahoochee' is a fine 30 cm-tall hybrid between *P. divaricata laphamii* and *P. pilosa* with a long succession of luminous lavender-blue flowers with crimson eyes, starting in early summer. It makes an eye-catching front of the border subject. For the *P. decussata* of catalogues – see under *P. paniculata*. *P. divaricata* (EN America) forms loose mats of leafy, prostrate, rooting shoots above which arise the slender flowering stems to 30 cm or more. The 3-4 cm-wide flowers have notched, lavender to pale-violet petals that open in late spring. *P. d. laphamii* (*P. canadensis laphamii*) has blue-violet, un-notched petals. Best in humus-rich soil in shade. *P. maculata* (E. Central USA) is known as wild sweet William in its homeland. In its main essentials it resembles *P. paniculata*, but has more graceful, longer and narrower panicles of fragrant flowers in shades of purple to red-violet borne on purple-spotted stems. 'Alpha' has pink flowers; 'Omega' is white with a lilac eye and has plain stems. *P. paniculata* (*P. decussata*) (E. USA) is the common, delightfully showy border phlox with fragrant rose-purple flowers in broadly pyramidal panicles during late summer and autumn. It is represented in gardens by dozens of cultivars, some of which are probably hybrids with *P. maculata*. Some reliable ones are: 'Balmoral', rosy lavender, 1 m; 'Brigadier', bright orange-red, vigorous, 1.2-1.4 m; 'Dodo Hanbury Forbes', clear pink, weather resistant, 90 cm; 'Fairy's Petticoat', palest mauve with darker eye, vigorous, 90 cm; 'Harlequin', boldly white-variegated leaves and violet-purple flowers, 90 cm; 'Marlborough', rich violet-purple, compact habit, 75-90 cm; 'Mother of Pearl', ivory white, flushed pink, 90 cm; 'Prince of Orange', orange-red, 60 cm; 'Starfire', bright crimson, 80 cm; 'Vintage Wine', claret-red; 'White Admiral', the best pure white, 90 cm.

Phormium (New Zealand flax) (*Agavaceae*)

Two imposing evergreen perennials from New Zealand comprise this genus. They are not totally hardy but survive all but the most severe winters in Britain, though the variegated sorts which are now in vogue are generally less hardy. Even with the green-leaved forms much depends on the provenance of the parent material and plants should be obtained from reliable sources. They thrive best in fertile, moisture-retentive soils in sun or light shade; in cold areas they need the shelter of a wall or hedge. Planting is best in spring; propagation is by division or seeds at the same time. *P. cookianum* (*P. colensoi*) is called mountain flax, though forms of it come down to near sea level in the wild. It is much like the more familiar *tenax* but often smaller, with leaves that arch or droop more freely when mature and seed pods which are pendulous, cylindrical and spirally twisted. Several attractive clones are now available but have not yet been fully tested for hardiness and vigour in Britain. Names to look out for are 'Dazzler', 'Cream Delight', 'Aurora'. The long-cultivated 'Purpureum' with somewhat lustrous, dark-purple leaves is certainly not fully hardy. *P. tenax* is invariably robust, with stiff leaves 1.5-3 m tall, that arch at the tips with age; more so in windy sites. The leaves are often greyish beneath and invariably edged with an orange or reddish line. The candelabra-like inflorescences can reach 3-5 m in height, with tubular, reddish flowers followed by erect seed capsules that are almost triangular in cross-section. Several cultivars are available and the same comments under *cookianum* apply here. A fair percentage of the cultivars are hybrids with *cookianum* which shows in the smaller stature, more flaccid leaves and seed capsules that are halfway between that of the species. Names to look out for are: 'Bronze Baby', 'Purpureum', 'Radiance', 'Rainbow', 'Rubrum', 'Sundowner', 'Variegatum', 'Veitchii'. The variegated forms can be especially appealing with the leaves striped cream or white suffused red, orange or pink.

Phuopsis stylosa (*Rubiaceae*)

Also known as *Crucianella stylosa* and a native of the Caucasus, E. Turkey and NW Iran, this ally of the bed-straws is the only member of its genus. It is rhizomatous, forming thick, pungently smelling mats of frothy, light-green foliage to 30 cm tall. The slenderly pink, four-lobed flowers are carried in abundance during the summer and autumn. A spendid plant for between shrubs or in the mixed border, but apt to be invasive, especially in light soils. Well-drained soil is essential and a site in sun or light shade. Planting can take place from autumn to spring with propagation by division at the same time.

Phygelius (Cape Figwort) (*Scrophulariaceae*)

The two species in this South African genus are technically sub-shrubs but in Britain the top growth is regularly killed back in winter and plants behave as herbaceous perennials. They require ordinary, well-drained but not dry soil and a site in sun. Planting is best in spring; propagation is by careful division in spring, by cuttings of non-flowering shoots under glass in summer or by seeds in warmth in spring. *P. aequalis* generally attains 1 m in height, with four-angled stems, opposite pairs of narrow leaves and terminal panicles bearing well-spaced, tubular flowers. The latter are almost straight-sided, 3-4.5 cm long, soft coral-red with a yellow throat and dark lower lobes, opening during the summer and autumn. *P capensis*, Cape fuchsia or figwort is much like the preceding one, but the bright-red flowers are strongly curved.

Phyllitis scolopendrium – see under *Asplenium*.

Physalis (Chinese Lanterns) (*Solanaceae*)

The 80-100 species in this genus which covers annuals and peren-nials, some of them food plants, are typified by a lantern-shaped calyx which enlarges after flowering to enclose the berry. The hardy perennial mentioned here has red calyces and is very ornamental, but it is also invasive and is not recommended for the main beds and borders. Ordinary soil and sun or partial shade are all that is needed. Planting should be carried out from autumn to spring with propaga-tion by division at the same time. *P. alkekengii* (*P. bunyardii, P. franchetii*) is also known as bladder, winter or ground cherry and produces colonies of erect, unbranched stems 40-60 cm tall with almost triangularly oval leaves and potato-like white flowers solitary in the upper axils. The fruiting calyces are coral-red, up to 5 cm long and enclose red, edible berries.

Physostegia virginiana (*Scrophulariaceae*)

This is the only member of a 15-species genus from N. America to be cultivated in Britain. It is a rhizomatous perennial forming colonies of erect, simple or branched stems 90-120 cm tall, bearing opposite pairs of toothed, narrow leaves and terminal spikes of rose-purple flowers. The latter are narrowly funnel-shaped and some-what two-lipped. If gently pushed sideways each flower will stay where it is put, hence the vernacular name of obedient plant. Late summer to autumn is the flowering season. *P. v. speciosa* is rather more robust and with larger, more coarsely toothed leaves. It is represented in gardens by 'Rose Bouquet' (soft pink) and the dwarf (45 cm) 'Vivid', bearing rich-pink blooms. Other cultivars are the 75 cm-tall 'Summer Snow' (pure white) and 'Summer Spire' (rose pink). Ordinary soil that does not dry out and sun or partial shade are minimum require-ments. Planting is best in autumn or spring with propagation by division in spring. Several other *Physostegia* species would seem to have garden potential and *P. formosior* in particular should be looked out for.

Phyteuma (Horned Rampion) (*Campanulaceae*)

About 40 species form this genus, some of the most attractive being small mountain plants. Quite unlike their near ally campanula, the flowers of the rampions are small and slender with petal tips that remain joined. They are aggregated into spikes and heads however and can then be quite showy. Well-drained ordinary soil and sun are required though partial shade is tolerated. Planting is best in autumn or spring, and propagation by division or seeds in spring. *P. nigrum* (Belgium to Austria) has very distinctive, though hardly showy flowers of blackish-violet in ovoid to cylindrical spikes on 40-60 cm-tall stems in summer. Blue and white (*P. n. album*) forms are known. *P. scheuchzeri* (S. Alps, N. Apennines) varies from 25-40 cm in height and forms small clumps of long-stalked broadly lance-shaped toothed leaves and deep-blue flowers in globose heads about 3 cm in early summer; an interesting front of the border subject. *P. spicatum*, spiked rampion (Europe), is more interesting than beautiful with clumps of erect stems 60-80 cm tall bearing dense, tapered spikes of cream to pale yellow-green — rarely blue — in late summer.

Phytolacca (Pokeweed, Pokeberry) (*Phytolaccaceae*)

Trees, shrubs and perennials can be found among the 25 species in this genus. The perennials are stalwart plants with large leaves, tiny whitish or pinkish flowers and later, spikes of purple-black glossy berries. They thrive best in fertile, mosisture-retentive soil in sun or partial shade and are best planted in autumn or spring. Propagation is by division in spring or ideally by seeds when ripe. *P. acinosa* (*P. esculenta*) (China, naturalised elsewhere) grows 1-1.5 tall with elliptic, edible leaves to 25 cm long. The flowers are whitish and the fruits are borne in erect spikes in autumn. *P. americana* (*P. decandra*) Virginian pokeweed, (E. USA to Mexico) is similar to the previous species but the flowers are pink-tinted and the fruiting spikes nod when ripe. *P. clavigera* (China) eventually forms massive clumps 1.5-2 m or more in height with rose-purple flowers and erect fruiting spikes. In autumn the stems turn bright red.

Plantago major (Greater Plantain) (*Plantaginaceae*)

This common weed of garden, field edge and roadside is one of 250 species of world-wide distribution. It is easily identified by its rosettes of long-stalked, very boldly ribbed oval leaves which may reach 15 cm in length. It has produced several mutants which have long been cultivated as curiosities: 'Rosularis', green rose plantain, has the flower spike reduced to a dense cluster of green, petal-like bracts; 'Rosularis Rubrifolia' is the same but suffused red-purple; 'Atropurpurea' is a normal plant with the leaves shaded bronze-purple. All grow well in ordinary soil and have the best colour in sun. Plant at any time and propagate by division in spring; 'Atropurpurea' comes at least partially true from seeds.

Platycodon grandiflorum (Balloon Flower) (*Campanulaceae*)

The only species in its genus and a native of E. Asia, the balloon flower resembles a choice bellflower. It is clump-forming to 60 cm tall with oval to lance-shaped leaves that are glaucous beneath, and balloon-like flower buds that expand in to 7.5 cm-wide purple-blue flowers in summer. *P. g.* 'Album' is white; 'Apoyama' ('Apoyensis') is very dwarf, seldom above 23 cm in height; 'Mariesii' grows to 45 cm with almost blue flowers; 'Mariesii Album' is the white version; 'Mother of Pearl' is soft lilac-pink; 'Roseum Plenum' is semi-double pink and 'Snowflake' is a white replica. Ordinary fertile soil and sun are the basic requirements. Planting is best in autumn or spring; propagation is by division, cuttings of basal shoots or seeds in spring.

Podophyllum (*Podophyllaceae*)

Depending on the botanical authority, there are five to ten species in this genus. Allied to the barberries and formerly included in their family (*Berberidaceae*) they are nevertheless true clump-forming herbaceous perennials. Each stem bears a pair of broad, handsome leaves and a solitary, nodding flower which, though pleasing, is rather hidden and somewhat fleeting. The flowers are followed by comparatively large edible berries. A humus-rich soil in partial shade gives the best results. Planting can be carried out from autumn to spring. Propagation is by seeds when ripe or careful division in early spring. *P. hexandrum* (*P. emodii*) (Himalayas) at full height attains 45 cm but is usually somewhat less at flowering time in spring. Each flower is white or pinkish and is followed by a 5 cm-long ellipsoid, glossy red berry. The mature leaves are deeply three to five lobed and often attractively marbled purple-brown. *P. h.* 'Majus' is a good large form and *P. h. chinense* has pink flowers. *P. peltatum*, May apple, American mandrake (E. North America) grows 30-45 cm tall, with five to nine lobed leaves that can span 30 cm when mature. The white flowers are neatly bowl shaped and are followed by reddish or yellowish berries.

Polemonium (Jacob's Ladder) (*Polemoniaceae*)

Depending on the botanical authority there are 20-50 different sorts of Jacob's ladder. Among their ranks are garden-worthy species for both rock garden and herbaceous border. They thrive in ordinary well-drained soil in sun or partial shade. Planting can take place from autumn to spring, and propagation by division at planting time or by sowing seeds in spring. *P. caeruleum*, common Jacob's ladder (northern hemisphere) forms clumps to 60 cm in height with long, pinnate, ladder-like leaves and terminal clusters of 2.5 cm-wide blue flowers in summer. 'Album' has white flowers; 'Cashmirianum' is somewhat larger, paler and brighter blue; 'Richardsonii' is compact and richly coloured, a hybrid with *P. reptans* it should be correctly known as *P.* X *jacobaea* 'Richardsonii'. *P. carneum* (*P. luteum*) (Washington State to California) forms large mounds to 45 cm in height clad with bright-green pinnate leaves and bearing a succession of widely bell-shaped pink, purple or yellow flowers in summer. The yellow phase was formerly known as *P. luteum*. *P. foliosissimum* (*P. archibaldae*, *P. filicinum*) (Rocky Mountains to Arizona) much resembles a robust *P. caeruleum* to 80 cm or more tall with larger flowers of deep violet to purple-blue. White, cream and blue forms are known. The plant listed as *P. archibaldae* is a compact version to 45 cm. If dead-headed it will flower well into autumn.

Polygonatum (Solomon's Seal) (*Liliaceae*)

About 300 species form this familiar genus though comparatively few are grown and some are too small for our purposes. They form knobbly, horizontal, fleshy rhizomes from which emerge erect, un-branched stems that bear either alternate leaves in two ranks or much narrower leaves in regular whorls. The pendent tubular flowers are followed by red or black berries. Ordinary, preferably humus-rich soil and partial shade are required. Planting is best from late summer to late autumn with propagation by division at the same time. Seeds may be sown when ripe but take several years to flower. *P. commut-atum*, great Solomon's seal (E. North America) is sometimes known as *P. giganteum* and can attain 1.5 m or more in height, the arching stems with alternate oval leaves often up to 18 cm long. The yellow-green to greenish-white flowers open in early summer. *P. falcatum* (Japan, Korea) grows 50-80 cm tall with alternate lanceolate leaves and 2 cm-long greenish-white flowers. A dwarf plant sometimes listed under this name is probably *P. pumilum*. *P.* X *hybridum* (*P. multiflorum* X *P. odoratum*) is the common Solomon's seal of British gardens and often parades under the first parent's name. It grows to 90 cm tall, the ridged stems bearing alternate elliptic leaves and whitish-green flowers that are somewhat constricted in the middle. *P.* X *h.* 'Variegatum' has the leaves white striped. For the *P. japoni-cum* of gardens – see under *P. odoratum thunbergii*. *P. multiflorum* (Europe to Japan) is usually about 60 cm tall, rather like a less robust *P.* X *hybridum* with smooth stems and flowers that are definitely con-stricted in the middle and carried in clusters of two to five. Blue-black berries regularly follow. Most plants grown in gardens under this name are in fact *P.* X *hybridum* which is largely sterile. *P. odora-tum* (Europe to Japan) rarely exceeds 45 cm and is often less, with slender, ridged or angled stems and alternate leaves. The flowers are solitary or in pairs and noticeably fragrant, opening in summer. *P. o. thunbergii* (*P. japonicum*, *P. thunbergii*) is more robust, usually

60-90 cm tall with longer, white and green flowers. *P. o. t.* 'Variegatum' has each leaf cream-tipped and lightly striped. *P. verticillatum*, whorled Solomon's seal (Europe, Caucasus, Himalayas) is the most distinct of the species described above, having totally erect stems — not arching at the top — with whorls of slender leaves, small greenish-white flowers in summer and red berries. Other species with whorled leaves are sometimes encountered; *P. roseum* (pink-tinted flowers), *P. sibiricum* (cream flowers and tendril-tipped leaves) and *P. stuartianum* (pinkish flowers and mottled fruits turning red).

Polygonum (Knotweed) (*Polygonaceae*)

There are at least 150 species in this varied genus and according to some authorities twice this number. Sub-shrubs, annuals and perennials are included, some of them invasive weeds. The following are garden worthy, thriving in ordinary soil in sun or part shade. Planting can be carried out from autumn to spring and propagation by division at planting time. *P. affine* (Himalayas) barely meets our height requirement but makes such a good front-of-the-border subject it must be included. It is a mat-former with erect, narrow leaves that turn bronze in late autumn and persist all the winter. The flowers are rosy-red in cylindrical spikes and appear during the summer and early autumn. *P. a.* 'Darjeeling Red' has crimson flowers; 'Donald Lowndes' is pink with rusty-brown winter foliage. *P. amplexicaule* (*P. oxyphyllum*) (Himalayas) forms wide, bushy clumps 1-1.5 m tall set with numerous erect, tail-like spikes of red flowers during the summer and autumn. The plant often labelled *P. oxyphyllum* has white or faintly pink-tinted flowers. *P. a.* 'Atrosanguineum' ('Speciosum') has darker flowers; 'Firetail' has larger spikes of brighter red flowers. *P. bistorta* 'Superbum' is a robust form of the wild, common bistort or Easter ledges, forming wide colonies of paddle-shaped basal leaves and sending up stems to 75 cm with bottle-brush-like pink flower spikes from early summer to autumn. *P. campanulatum* (Himalayas) forms spreading colonies of branched stems to 90 cm clad wih elliptic, hairy, prominently veined leaves and large terminal clusters of small pale-pink bells in summer and autumn. *P. cuspidatum* (*Reynoutria japonica*), Japanese knotweed, Mexican bamboo (Japan) is mentioned only as a warning. Its thick woody rhizomes spread rapidly in all directions and are difficult to remove. The bamboo-like stems, large leaves and white flowers are handsome, but best enjoyed by the roadside where it is not infrequently naturalised. A less invasive yellow variegated form 'Spectabile' ('Sieboldii') is sometimes seen but should be planted with caution. More compact is *P. c. compactum* 90-120 cm tall. It is less invasive and more clump-forming. *P. c. c.* 'Pink Cloud' has fine pink flowers; 'Variegatum' has the leaves splashed with creamy-yellow and pink. *P. filiforme* (*P.*

virginianum filiforme, Tovara v. f.) (Japan) is a rhizomatous plant to 80 cm tall with ample oblong leaves sometimes with dark *V* markings or blotches. Spikes of small, pink or white flowers emerge from the upper leaf axils in late summer. *P. f.* 'Variegata' has the leaves splashed creamy-yellow; 'Painters' Palette' adds a touch of pink to the yellow, overlaying a brown zone or pattern. *P. macrophyllum* (*P. sphaerostachyum*) (China, Himalayas) is akin to *P. bistorta* with larger wavy-edged leaves and deep rose-red flower spikes. *P. milletii* (China, Himalayas) is also much like bistort, but is a stiffer plant, about 45 cm tall with narrower leaves and spikes of deep crimson flowers. It has been known also as *P. sphaerostachyum* and must not be confused with *P. macrophyllum* (q.v.). *P. molle* (*P. rude, P. paniculatum*) (N. India to W. China) forms a bushy plant to 1.5 m tall clad with lance-shaped leaves that are silky hairy beneath. The white flowers appear in large terminal panicles during summer. *P. polystachyum* (Himalayas) somewhat resembles and can be confused with *P. molle*, but it rapidly spreads underground to form wide colonies and flowers in autumn. An attractive plant for the wild garden or where there is abundant room. Not a border plant. For *P. sphaerostachyum* of catalogues — see under *P. macrophyllum*. For *P. virginianum* — see under *P. filiforme*.

Polystichum (Shield Ferns) (*Aspidiaceae*)

At least 120 species of clump-forming ferns of cosmopolitan distribution form this genus. Some species have simply pinnate fronds, others have bipinnate ones. The hardy members of both sorts described here are evergreen and worthy of being cultivated more often. They grow in ordinary, preferably humus-enriched soil in partial or full shade. Planting can take place from autumn to spring. Propagation is by division at planting time or spores in spring. *P. acrostichoides*, Christmas fern (E. North America) is a handsome species 60-90 cm tall with simply pinnate, lustrous fronds which taper to a point, hence the vernacular name sword fern in its homeland. Each pinna or leaflet is lance shaped with a small ear-like lobe from the upper side of the base. Although hardy, it appreciates a sheltered spot and thrives best in a rich, limy soil. *P. aculeatum* (*P. lobatum*) hard or prickly shield fern (Europe, Asia, S. America) has somewhat lustrous, leathery-textured bipinnate fronds firmly held in a neat clump. It is confused with the more widely grown *P. setiferum*, but the individual pinnules or leaflets have bristle-tipped teeth. *P. lonchitis*, mountain holly fern (Arctic and north temperate zone) has simply pinnate fronds 30-45 cm long with somewhat lustrous, hard-textured bristle-toothed pinnae. Although hardy it needs a cool, humid climate to thrive. *P. munitum*, Christmas fern (W. North America) is like a superior *P. acrostichoides* and for some curious reason it is seldom commercially available. It is well worth the trouble to find a source of supply. *P. setiferum* (*P. angulare*) soft shield fern (temperate climates of northern and southern hemispheres) is related to *P. aculeatum* but the fronds are softer textured, arching out at a low angle from the clump and the pinnule teeth have soft hair points. It is largely represented in gardens by several cultivars with more intricately and often beautifully dissected fronds. *P. s.* 'Acutilobum' ('Proliferum') forms dense clumps of almost mossy, drooping fronds which when fully mature produce tiny plantlets along the midrib. If a frond is pegged down to the soil or removed and pinned to a box of compost in a cool propagating case the plantlets can be grown on and afford an easy means of increase. *P. s.* 'Divisilobum Densum' has densely plumose fronds of great elegance. Several other similar cultivars are sometimes available.

Potentilla (Cinquefoil) (*Rosaceae*)

Among the 500 species in this genus are shrubs, annuals and perennials, some weedy, others of great garden merit. The best of the taller perennials are described here. They thrive in any moderately fertile soil, preferably in sun though light shade is tolerated. They can be planted from autumn to spring with propagation by division at the same time. Seeds of the true species may be sown in spring. *P. argyrophylla* (Himalayas) forms clumps 45 cm tall composed of strawberry-like foliage which is white-hairy beneath. The 2-3 cm-wide flowers are yellow, carried in loose clusters from summer to autumn. *P. atrosanguinea* (Himalayas) was formerly considered a variety of *P. argyrophylla* and resembles that species but for its deep velvety red flowers. Hybridised with *P. argyrophylla* and probably also *P. nepalensis* it has given rise to the popular large, often semi- or fully double-flowered cutlivars, e.g. 'Gibson's Scarlet' and 'Flamenco' both scarlet; 'Gloire de Nancy', coral red and orange-brown, semi-double; 'Monsieur Rouillard', mahogany-crimson; 'William Rollison', orange-red and yellow; 'Yellow Queen', bright yellow with a red eye. *P. nepalensis* (Himalayas) has a tufted habit to 45 cm in height with hairy leaves divided into five coarsely toothed leaflets. Rose-red, 2.5 cm-wide flowers open in summer, often continuing into autumn. *P. n.* 'Miss Willmott' is shorter, with flowers of a more crimson shade, while 'Roxana' is salmon-orange with a red eye. *P. recta* (Europe) forms tufted clumps up to 60 cm tall. The hand-like leaves are composed of five to seven oblong leaflets which are boldly toothed or lobed and densely downy. The yellow flowers are freely borne in summer. The best garden form is 'Warrenii' (sometimes misspelt *warrensii* or used as a species name), with larger (3 cm-wide) bright-yellow flowers. It appears to be the same as *P. recta macrantha*. There is also 'Sulphurea' with pale-yellow flowers but it is difficult to obtain. *P. rupestris*, rock cinquefoil (Europe to C. Asia) rises to about 45 cm or more from good tufts of hairy basal leaves composed of five to nine oval, doubly toothed leaflets. The flowers are pure white, 2-3 cm wide in large leafy clusters in early summer. Not a top flight species but pleasing and useful for its early flowers.

Poterium — see under *Sanguisorba*.

Primula (Primrose) (*Primulaceae*)

About 400 species of evergreen and herbaceous perennials form this popular genus. Most species are rock and alpine plants or otherwise too small for our purposes, though it is permissible to plant primroses and polyanthus in frontal positions in our beds and borders. It is nevertheless the latter sorts that make the greatest impact and only the best species for combining with other perennials are described here. They require fertile, moisture-retentive soil and a site in sun or partial shade. Planting is best after flowering or late summer to late autumn. Propagation is by division at planting time, or by seeds sown as soon as ripe or in spring. In the following list the letter (C) denotes that the plant belongs to the *Candelabra* species group which is typified by having the flowers in tiered whorls on tall stems. *P. aurantiaca* (C) (W. China) is one of the smaller candelabra primulas with stems to 30 cm tall bearing two to six whorls of reddish-orange flowers. It can be used very effectively at the front of a border. *P. beesiana* (C) (W. China) forms lush clumps of large primrose-like leaves above which soar 60 cm stems carrying rose-carmine flowers with yellow eyes. *P. bulleyana* (C) (W. China) has the same height and stance as the previous species but with orange-yellow flowers. *P. burmanica* (C) (Upper Burma to China) is another 60 cm candelabra, with red-purple, golden-eyed flowers. *P. chionantha* (W. China) is the easiest member of the generally not too easily pleased *Nivales* group. It has attractive pale-green, narrow leaves coated with yellow farina beneath, and erect stems to 40-60 cm bearing candelabra-like whorls of fragrant, creamy-white flowers in early summer. *P. chungensis* (C) (Bhutan, Assam, W. China) has red and orange flowers on 60 cm-tall stems. It has given rise to a very garden-worthy vigorous hybrid with *P. pulverulenta*, aptly called *P.* X *chunglenta*. *P. denticulata*, drumstick primrose (Himalayas) has gained steadily in popularity since it was first introduced in 1842. Its globular posies of lilac flowers begin to open low down with the unfolding leaves in spring, extending steadily upwards to a final 30 cm or more. There is now available a range of purple, red and violet shades, also white. *P. florindae*, giant cowslip (SE Tibet) can, as its vernacular name implies, be likened to a 1 m or more tall cowslip with 2 cm-wide bright-yellow fragrant flowers in large umbels. Reddish and orange-tinted forms are known. Although essentially a bog plant it will grow very satisfactorily in ordinary moist soil. *P. helodoxa* (C) (W. China) grows to 90 cm with whorls of bright, rich yellow, fragrant flowers; *P. smithiana* (*prolifera*) is very similar but to 60 cm. *P.* X 'Inverewe' ('Ravenglass Vermilion') is a vigorous hybrid between probably *P. cockburniana* and *pulverulenta*, about 60 cm tall with bright brick-red flowers. *P. japonica* (C) (Japan) is perhaps the best known candelabra species forming lush clumps of large primrose leaves and stems to 60 cm bearing red-purple blooms; several colour forms are available, e.g. 'Etna', 'Glowing Embers', 'Millars Crimson' and 'Postford White'. *P. pulverulenta* (C) (W. China) is almost as well known as *P. japonica* and distinguished from it by its red flowers and whitened stems, usually 75 cm or more tall. The 'Bartley' strain has the flowers in shades of pink. It has given rise to several hybrids with *P. bulleyana* and other species, e.g. 'Inverewe'. *P. secundiflora* (W. China) is not unlike a smaller version of *P. florindae* with stems to 60 cm tall and crimson-rose to purple-red flowers; robust plants can produce stems with two tiers of flowers. *P. sikkimensis* (*P. microdonta*) (Himalayas) is closely allied to *secundiflora* and about the same height with larger yellow flowers in early summer. *P. s. hopeana* has creamy-white flowers on more slender stems; *pudibunda* is a small alpine form. *P. waltonii* (W. China) is best likened to a *P. sikkimensis* with pink to wine-purple flowers.

Prunella grandiflora (Self Heal) (*Labiatae*)

Of the seven species in this genus this is by far the most decorative and is a fine plant for a frontal position. It forms low, wide clumps of rich-green oval leaves and stems to about 30 cm, bearing short dense spikes of tubular, prominently hooded deep-violet flowers in summer and autumn. *P. g. pyrenaica* (*P. hastifolia*) has shorter leaves with pointed basal lobes. *P. g. webbiana* (*P. webbiana* of gardens) covers several cultivars derived from crossing *P. grandiflora* with *P. g. pyrenaica*. Of this origin are: 'Loveliness', pale-violet; 'Pink Loveliness', clear bright pink; 'White Loveliness', pure white, large flowers. Ordinary soil and sun or partial shade are basic requirements. Planting can be done from autumn to spring with propagation by division at the same time. Seeds may also be sown in spring but the cultivars cannot be relied upon to come true to type.

Pulmonaria (Lungwort) (*Boraginaceae*)

About ten species form this genus of European plants. All are rhizomatous and form slowly spreading clumps of ample leaves which make good ground cover. The flowers are tubular with five spreading lobes and have a somewhat primula-like appearance. The winter to spring flowering sorts are particularly valuable for front-of-the-border interest at that time of the year. They grow in ordinary soil, preferably enriched, in partial shade, though full sun is tolerated if the soil is moist. Planting can take place from autumn to spring with propagation at the same time. Seeds may be sown, ideally when ripe, or in spring. *P. angustifolia* (*P. azurea*) blue cowslip, has oblong to lance-shaped unspotted leaves which can exceed 30 cm when full grown. The bright-blue flowers open on 20-30 cm-tall stems in spring. *P. azurea*, 'Mawsons' and 'Munstead' are all similar with intense blue flowers. *P. longifolia* has narrow lance-shaped, white-spotted leaves to 50 cm long, and 30 cm-tall stems carrying pink buds that open violet or pink-violet in late spring and early summer. Unspotted-leaved forms sometimes occur and can be confused with *P. angustifolia*. *P. officinalis* (*P. maculata*) is the commonly grown Jerusalem cowslip with white spotted, bristly-hairy, oval leaves to 60 cm long and reddish to bluish-violet flowers in spring. *P. rubra* has oblong to oval softly hairy leaves to 15 cm long; usually they are plain green but in autumn a very faint spotting can often be detected. The brick-red flowers open in winter and spring. *P. r.* 'Bowles Red' is light red. *P. saccharata* can be confused with *P. officinalis*, but it has larger elliptic leaves to 27 cm long and flowers that open reddish, become violet and change to blue. *P. s.* 'Argentea' has the leaves almost entirely silvery white (possibly of hybrid origin). *P. s.* 'Cambridge Blue' has pink and blue flowers; 'Pink Dawn' is entirely pink and 'White Wings' and 'Alba' are white.

Pulsatilla (Pasque Flower) (*Ranunculaceae*)

There are twelve species of pasque flower, some of them very closely allied and difficult to identify. All are worthy of garden room, some more so than others with their clumps of ferny dissected leaves and handsome cup-shaped flowers. The plumy seed heads come as a decorative bonus. Well-drained soil and sun are the basic requirements. Planting is best carried out in autumn or spring. Propagation is primarily by seeds sown when ripe, though careful division can be attempted. *P. albana* (*P. caucasica* and *P. vulgaris caucasica* of gardens) (Caucasus, Iran) is similar to *P. pratensis* but the leaves are more coarsely dissected and the flowers a clear pale yellow. *P. alpina*, alpine anemone (mountains of C. and S. Europe) has bipinnate downy leaves and purplish-budded white flowers on stems to 30 cm or more tall. It is not always easy to please and rarely commercially available. *P. a. apiifolia* (*Anemone sulphurea*) has sulphur-yellow flowers and is more amenable to cultivation. *P. halleri* (Alps to Balkan peninsula) resembles *P. vulgaris* but has simply pinnate, densely woolly leaves with each leaflet deeply cut. The flowers are deep violet. *P. pratensis* (C. and E. Europe to N. Yugoslavia and Scandinavia) has silky-downy, thrice-cut leaves, each leaflet being sharply lobed. There is a wide colour range in the nodding, bell-shaped flowers, from greenish-yellow to pale violet, but the cultivated plants are usually a deep bright purple. *P. vulgaris* (Europe eastwards to the Ukraine) is the common pasque flower and a variable plant in the wild and cultivation. It has pinnate leaves, the leaflets of which are bi- or tri-pinnatisect and silky-hairy when young. The usual colour of the flowers is pale to deep purple; 'Alba' is white and *P. v. rubra* comes in shades of red. *P. v. grandis* is the best sort for the border, a robust plant to 30 cm or more with large purple-violet flowers.

Pyrethrum roseum — see under *Chrysanthemum coccineum*.

Ranunculus (Buttercup) (*Ranunculaceae*)

No less than 400 species of annual and perennial buttercups have been listed from the temperate regions of both hemispheres. Most of the horticulturally desirable species are rock or alpine plants but the following make useful additions to the perennial garden. They thrive in ordinary, moderately moist soil and are best in sun. Planting can be done from autumn to spring with propagation by division at the same time. True species may be raised from seeds sown when ripe, or in spring. *R. aconitifolius*, fair maids of France (C. Spain to C. Yugoslavia) forms clumps of cleft and toothed, somewhat aconitum-like leaves and branched stems to 60 cm or so bearing pure-white buttercups in early summer. *R. a.* 'Flore Pleno', white bachelors' buttons, has fully double blooms. *R. acris* 'Flore Pleno', bachelors' buttons, is the neatly and fully double, bright-yellow form of the meadow buttercup of Europe and Asia. A non-invasive clump-former 80-90 cm tall with deeply cleft palmate leaves, it deserves to be grown more often. There is also a pretty double form of the creeping buttercup — *R. repens* but it is very invasive and should be avoided at all costs. *R. bulbosus* 'Pleniflorus' is a double form of the European bulbous buttercup, a modestly attractive plant which grows to about 40 cm tall. The plant listed as *R. b.* 'Speciosus Plenus' has handsome foliage, usually pale to greyish flecked and the double flowers are about 5 cm wide, opening in late spring. *R. gramineus* (S. Europe) forms clumps of very narrow, almost grassy grey-green leaves of very un-buttercup-like appearance and worth while in themselves. In late spring and early summer slim grey stems arise to 45 cm or more and bear several shapely, bright-yellow flowers. There are inferior forms of this species and plants should be obtained from a specialist nurseryman. *R. insignis* and *R. lyallii* are both New Zealanders and the most splendid buttercups of all. They have handsome, large, rounded leaves, stems 60-100 cm tall and 5 cm-wide cup-shaped flowers of yellow and white respectively. Regrettably they thrive only in the cool moist climate of NW England and Scotland.

Reineckia carnea (*Liliaceae*)

This East Asian plant is the only member of its genus and closely allied to *Liriope* in which genus it was once classified. It forms wide clumps or colonies of narrow lance-shaped leaves to 40 cm long and shorter spikes of pale-pink, bell-shaped, fragrant flowers in summer. Regrettably, in Britain it tends to be shy flowering so the red berries that follow flowering are seldom seen. A variegated form is known. A useful plant for sheltered, shady corners. Culture is as for *Liriope*.

Reynoutria – see under *Polygonum*.

Rhazya orientalis (*Apocynaceae*)

Of the two species described for this genus only *R. orientalis* is generally cultivated. It is a woody-based clump-former to 45 cm tall, each erect, unbranched stem bearing pairs of narrow leaves and topped by a head of blue to violet flowers in summer. In general appearance it resembles a superior *Amsonia tabernaemontana* and requires the same cultural treatment.

Rheum (Rhubarb) (*Polygonaceae*)

About 25 species of rhubarb are recorded, most of them statuesque in appearance. They are best used as specimen plants where both the large basal leaves and the imposing floral stems can be enjoyed. Humus-rich moisture-retentive soil provides the best growing conditions with a site in partial shade or sun. Planting can take place from autumn to spring, and propagation by division or by sowing seeds in spring. *R. alexandrae* (Himalayas) is often offered as young plants or seeds, but the plants need a cool, moist climate to thrive. When they do, the result is quite spectacular; clumps of oval, dark-green, prominently ribbed leaves above which climb steeples of large, creamy-white bracts to about 1 m in height. *R. nobile* is similar, the bracts being pale straw-coloured and often pink tinted, but it is even more difficult to please. *R. officinale* (W. China, Tibet) is a medicinal rhubarb with big green leaves to 90 cm wide and white floral plumes on 1.5-2 m stems in early summer. *R. palmatum* (NE Asia) can reach 2 m or more in height with large, deeply and sharply lobed basal leaves and plumes of red flowers in early summer. The best forms are 'Atrosanguineum' and 'Bowles Variety' or 'Bowles Crimson' all very similar with leaves that are totally red when young and retain this colour beneath when mature. This is an imposing plant that makes a splendid specimen and tolerates shade. *R. p. tanguticum* is less effective, with broader inflorescences of white, pink or crimson flowers and less deeply lobed, often purple-flushed, leaves.

Rodgersia (*Saxifragaceae*)

All six members of this genus have bold, handsome foliage and effective astilbe-like plumes of tiny flowers in summer. They require moisture-retentive, humus-rich soil and partial shade, though full sun is tolerated if the soil is perpetually moist. They make splendid subjects for the bog garden or for planting by water. Planting can take place from autumn to spring, with propagation by division at the same time. *R. aesculifolia* (China) has basal leaves very like those of the horse chestnut (*Aesculus hippocastanum*), generally bronze tinted and with long hairy stalks. The creamy-white or pink-tinted flowers are carried in large, tiered, conical panicles to 1.2 m or more in height. *R. pinnata* (China) has leaflets similar to those of the previous species but they are arranged in pinnate fashion. The panicles of red and white flowers are more rounded than those of *aesculifolia*, rising to 1 m or so. *R. p.* 'Superba' has more strongly bronze-tinted leaves and bright-pink flowers. *R. podophylla* (China, Japan) forms wide colonies in time, composed of large digitate leaves after the fashion of *aesculifolia*, but with broader leaflet tips, bearing pointed lobes. The young foliage is suffused reddish-bronze gradually turning green, then becoming reddish again in late summer; some forms are permanently bronzed. The creamy-white flowers are borne in tall panicles with arching branches on stems 1 m or more in height. *R. purdomii* of gardens is similar and may well be only a form of *podophylla*. *R. sambucifolia* (China) has relatively long pinnate leaves, each pair of leaflets being well spaced, not closely crowded as in *R. pinnata*. It bears white flowers in comparatively small, flattish topped panicles. *R. tabularis* (China) is quite different from all the other rodgersias with its long-stalked orbicular, shallowly lobed leaves which can be as much as 90 cm wide when growing in rich soil. It is well worth a place in the garden for its leaves alone and is even more superb when the 90 cm-tall, white plumy panicles are held aloft.

Romneya (California Tree Poppy) (*Papaveraceae*)

Depending on the lumping or splitting propensity of the classifying botanist, there are one or two species in this Californian genus. Common sense now generally decides upon one, *R. coulteri*, a 1.5-2 m-tall coloniser with dissected grey leaves and magnificent white poppy flowers. The latter are fragrant, 10-15 cm wide and open in late summer from smooth grey, beaked buds. *R. c. trichocalyx* (*R. trichocalyx*) differs in the following small ways: stems more slender, tending to branch lower down, leaves smaller (to 10 cm as against the 15 cm of *coulteri*) and rounded flower buds with bristly hairs. Most of the plants grown in Britain are hybrids between these two entities and in which the above characteristics are blurred. In general the hybrids thrive more satisfactorily, the best clone being 'White Cloud' with more shapely flowers and a sturdy habit. Ordinary soil and a sheltered sunny site are required. Planting is best in spring. Propagation is by root cuttings, seeds or careful division in spring. Young plants are often slow in getting established but then grow vigorously.

Roscoea (*Zingiberaceae*)

The 15 species that form this member of the ginger family are remarkably orchid like. Fleshy or tuberous rooted, they have narrow leaves and short spikes of long-tubed flowers. The latter have three-petal lobes, the upper one erect or hooded, and a broad petal-like staminode equivalent to the lip or labellum of an orchid. The species described are hardy and do not appear above ground until early summer when they grow rapidly and soon flower. Humus-rich, moisture-retentive soil in partial shade or sun provides the best conditions. Planting should be carried out in autumn or spring, with propagation by division in late spring just as the shoots begin to grow, or by seeds when ripe. *R. capitata* (Himalayas) can achieve 30 cm in height when well established, with blue-purple flowers. *R. cautleoides* (China) is the most elegant and desirable of those species in cultivation, with slender stems to 30 cm or more, lance-shaped leaves and clear primrose flowers. *R. humeana* (China) is the most robust species but flowers with very young leaves at about 20 cm. The violet-purple flowers are long-tubed, the petals to 5 cm in length. *R. purpurea* (Himalayas) can best be described as a taller, slenderer version of *R. humeana*, flowering somewhat later. *R. p. procera* has purple and white flowers and an eye-catching appeal.

Rudbeckia (Coneflower) (*Compositae*)

Several of the 25 species in this genus of cheerful N. American daisies can be numbered among the indispensables of the hardy planter's stock in trade. They thrive in any moderately fertile soil in sun or partial shade. Planting can take place from autumn to spring, with propagation by division at the same time. *R. fulgida* is a rhizomatous plant, forming wide clumps to 60 cm tall with lance-shaped hairy leaves and a long succession of bright-yellow flowerheads with short conical brown-purple discs. *R. f. deamii* (*R. deamii*) differs only in its more ample ovate to elliptic leaves which clothe the base of the plant and the stems. *R. f. speciosa* (*R. newmanii* and *R. speciosa* of gardens) has the stem leaves either coarsely toothed, or with tooth-like lobes. *R. f. sullivantii* (*R. speciosa sullivantii*) is like *R. f. deamii* but the stem leaves are successively reduced in size, the uppermost ones small and bract-like; 'Goldsturm' is a selection of it with somewhat larger flowers. *R. hirta*, black-eyed Susan, is at the most a short-lived perennial but a useful filler and easily raised from seeds. It is a bristly-hairy plant, 60-90 cm tall with 10 cm-wide flowers having orange-yellow rays and a conical purple-brown disc. *R. h. pulcherrima* (*R. bicolor*, *R. serotina*) has somewhat larger flowers with yellow and maroon rays. It has given rise to the tetraploid 'Gloriosa' daisies, with even larger flowers in shades of yellow, orange and maroon, some bi-coloured, in singles and doubles, but they are little more than biennials at the most. *R. laciniata* is perhaps the most familiar tall species, a clump-former, 2-3 m in height with pinnate or deeply lobed leaves and large, bright-yellow flowers with conical olive-green discs in late summer and autumn. *R. l.* 'Hortensia' ('Golden Glow') has double flowers; 'Soleil d'Or' is single but with broader ray florets. See also *R. nitida* for 'Goldquelle'. *R. maxima* has large, erect elliptic leaves to 30 cm or more long that have a grey patina. The stems reach 1.2-2 m in height and carry golden-yellow flowerheads centred with greenish-black cylindrical-conical discs in summer. *R. nitida* is similar to *R. laciniata* but rarely grows above 1.2 m with simple, oval leaves. 'Goldquelle' is a somewhat harshly yellow double form.

Salvia (Sage) (*Labiatae*)

There are no less than 700 species in this world-wide genus. Many are shrubby, others annuals and biennials, and often are rather tender. The hardier species described here include some first-rate, indispens-able border perennials. All salvias are typified by their square sectioned stems, opposite pairs of generally boldly veined leaves and spikes of tubular two-lipped, hooded flowers. Ordinary well-drained fertile soil and a sunny site are required, preferably sheltered from strong cold winds. Planting is best in autumn or spring with propaga-tion by division or by seeds in spring. *S. argentea* (S. Europe) has delightful silky woolly leaves up to 20 cm long and is well worth growing for them alone. In summer erect, branched stems 75-90 cm tall arise, bearing white or pink-tinted flowers to 5 cm long. A first-rate plant and much hardier than it is usually given credit for. *S. haematodes* (Greece) is one of the most prolific flowerers in the genus, producing 90 cm-tall, narrow flame-shaped clusters of lavender-blue flowers. The big basal leaves are handsomely corrugated. It seems incredible that this showy plant was only brought into cultiva-tion in 1938 — by that doyen of plant collectors, Edward K. Balls. *S. jurisicii* (Yugoslavia) is very distinct among the sages, having deerly lobed leaves. It grows to about 45 cm and produces spikes of deep-lilac flowers in early summer. A strange quirk of this plant is to bear its flowers upside down (resupinate). For the *S. nemorosa* of cata-logues — see under *S.* X *superba*. *S. nutans* (E. Europe) has a certain quiet charm, forming substantial clumps of dark, veiny leaves and nodding, 1 m-tall spikes of smallish, light mauve-blue flowers. *S.*

patens (Mexico) grows 60-80 cm tall and has the most glorious 5 cm-long rich gentian-blue flowers in late summer and autumn. It has a dahlia-like tuberous root which is not fully hardy, but survives most winters in well-drained soil, especially if protected with a mound of peat, sand or pulverised bark. *S. pratensis* (meadow clary) (Europe) is a poor man's version of *S. haematodes*, though it looks pretty enough when seen gracing our roadsides. Worth seeking out however are the pink *S. p.* 'Rosea', the deep-violet 'Baumgartenii' and the blue-violet *S. p. tenorii*. *S.* X *superba* is probably a triple hybrid combining *S. nemorosa, pratensis* and *villicaulis*. Like all the best hybrids it is superior to its parents as a garden plant, being more vigorous and free-flowering. It forms clumps of erect branched stems to 90 cm in height, clad with finely wrinkled oblong leaves. In summer, terminal spikes of violet-purple flowers surrounded by red-purple bracts stay attractive for a long period. Several cultivars have arisen: 'Lubeca' and 'East Friesland' are similar, compact of growth and seldom above 45 cm. 'May Night' ('Mainacht') is 60 cm tall with dark-violet flowers. 'Lye End' is a chance seedling that arose in the Lye End Nursery, Surrey, owned by that saviour and former chairman of the Hardy Plant Society, Miss R. B. Pole. It favours *pratensis*, but has great vigour, reaching 1.5 m in good soil, having lavender-blue flowers in purplish calyces. *S. uliginosa* (S. Brazil, Argentina) is so nearly hardy and such a lovely thing for autumn colour that it must get an honourable mention. Rising to 1.5 m or more in height, it has strong but slender branched stems and dense spikes of sky-blue flowers. It needs moist but not wet soil and well repays a sheltered site. *S. verticillata* is a collector's plant but has a certain quiet appeal with its 1.2 m-tall leafy stems and curving spikes of small purple flowers in late summer.

Sanguisorba (*Poterium*) (Burnet) (*Rosaceae*)

Depending on the botanical authority there are 3-30 species in this genus. They are clump-forming perennials with long-stalked pinnate foliage and globular to cylindrical bottle-brush-like flower spikes. Ordinary soil that does not dry out is required and preferably a sunny site, though some shade is tolerated. Planting can take place from autumn to spring with propagation by division at the same time. *S. canadensis* (E. North America) grows to 1.5 m or more with arching, white bottle-brushes in late summer. *S. obtusa* (*Poterium obtusum* and *P. obtusatum* of gardens) (Japan) achieves 1.2 m in height with rose-purple flower spikes in summer. *S. officinalis*, great burnet (Europe, Asia) is similar in general appearance to *S. canadensis* but has smaller, deep reddish to purplish flower spikes. Better known in the herb garden, its leaves can be used to flavour salads. *S. sitchensis* (NW North America) has been classified as a sub-species of *canadensis* and much resembles it. In general, the stems are less leafy and the sometimes pink-tinted flower spikes more erect. *S. tenuifolia* (Asia) is the most graceful species, being a more slender version of *S. obtusa* with pink or red flowers.

Saponaria officinalis (Soapwort) (*Caryophyllaceae*)

Of the 30 species recognised in this genus, the common soapwort or bouncing Bet is the only hardy perennial tall and attractive enough to be allowed into the herbaceous garden. Even so, it must be planted with caution, for it ramps underground in fertile soils. It should certainly not be put into a traditional bed or border. A native of Asia and Europe and often seen naturalised by roadsides in Britain, it is an erect plant to about 90 cm with oval to lance-shaped leaves in pairs and terminal clusters of campion-like pink or white flowers in summer. The double flowered forms give best value, i.e. 'Alba Plena' (white) 'Roseo Plena' (pink) and 'Rubro-Plena' (purple-crimson). Any soil will do and a sunny site is preferred. Planting is from autumn to spring with propagation by division at the same time.

Satureja — see under *Calamintha*.

Saxifraga fortunei (*Saxifragaceae*)

Most of the 350 different species of saxifrage are small mountain plants and a standby of the rock gardener. Even *S. fortunei* only qualifies for inclusion here on a height basis when in bloom. However it is such a fine plant in both foliage and flower and so useful for the shady border, it must be included. A native of China it forms clumps of long-stalked, somewhat maple-shaped leaves to 15 cm wide, lustrous rich green above and purplish beneath. In October it suddenly sends up wiry stems to 40 cm or so carrying airy panicles of pure-white blossom. Individual flowers are about 1 cm wide with one or two pendulous, much longer petals. *S. f.* 'Wada's Form' has the leaves flushed deep wine-purple; 'Rubrifolia' is similar but more compact and redder tinted.

Scabiosa (Scabious) (*Dipsacaceae*)

An estimated 80-100 species form this genus. Although few are hardy perennials, the best of them, *S. caucasica* is another of the hardy planter's indispensables. The species described here thrive in ordinary well-drained, fertile, preferably alkaline, soil in sun. Planting is best in autumn or spring; propagation is by division or by sowing seeds in spring. *S. caucasica* (N. Iran, Caucasus, C. and N. Russia) forms clumps of lance-shaped basal leaves and branched wiry stems bearing dissected leaves. The typical scabious flowers

Figure 11: *Schizo-stylis coccinea* 'Major'

are 6 cm or more wide in shades of lavender-blue from early to late summer. Several cultivars are available, e.g. 'Bressingham White', an improvement on 'Loddon White' though both have good white flowers; 'Clive Greaves' is still a reliable lavender-blue though raised in 1929; 'Moorheim Blue' is deep lavender-blue. *S. columbaria* (Europe) is the small scabious of chalk and limestone country in Britain; it resembles a small-flowered *S. caucasica* and rather lacks the impact of that species. In the garden it usually grows taller — up to 70 cm or so — and the flowers then look out of proportion. Nevertheless it is a pretty thing for poor, dryish limy soil. Pink forms occur and *S. ochroleuca* is an exact replica in pale yellow. *S. graminifolia* (S. Europe) barely reaches 30 cm in height and makes a nice front-of-the-border feature with its silvery grassy leaves and mauve flowers; *S. g.* 'Pinkushion' is clear pink and arose at Alan Bloom's Bressingham Gardens.

Schizostylis (Kaffir Lily) (*Iridaceae*)

Two species of evergreen perennials from S. Africa form this genus but only *S. coccinea* is cultivated. It has slender iris-like leaves in tufts, and wand-like spikes of crocus-shaped crimson flowers from autumn to early winter. *S. c.* 'Gigantea' ('Grandiflora') and 'Major' have larger flowers; 'Mrs Hegarty' is clear pink, 'Rosalie' is salmon pink; 'November Cheer' is a large pink sort — a sport from 'Major'. Humus-rich, moisture-retentive soil, in a sheltered sunny site gives the best results. In cold areas it is best protected in winter with straw, bracken or a cloche. Planting and propagation by division should be in spring.

Scopolia carniolica (*Solanaceae*)

The six species that form this genus are mostly rather sombre though intriguing plants that flower in spring on young shoots. Later the leaves get large and tend to occupy too much space. *S. carniolica hladnikiana* is the best of the bunch, with nodding yellow bells about 2.5 cm long from the axils of young, bright-green leaves. It starts to flower at about 15 cm, extending to 45 cm or more. Ordinary soil and sun or shade are suitable. Planting can take place from autumn to spring with propagation by division at the same time.

Scrophularia (Figwort) (*Scrophulariaceae*)

About 200 species of sub-shrubs, biennials and perennials are spread around the northern hemisphere but only one is commonly grown in Britain. This is *S. auriculata* 'Variegata' formerly known as *S. aquatica* and wrongly identified in its variegated form as *S. nodosa*. It forms robust clumps of square-sectioned stems 60-90 cm in height clad with pairs of oval 6-12 cm-long leaves that are boldly cream-margined. The tiny bladder-shaped purple-brown flowers are no more than interesting. Moisture-retentive, fertile soil gives the best results, in either sun or part shade. Planting can take place from autumn to spring with propagation by division at the same time.

Sedum (Stonecrop) (*Crassulaceae*)

Botanists seem undecided as to the exact number of stonecrops and 500-600 are generally stated. Most of the garden-worthy species are rock plants but there are a few tall kinds which are indispensable for beds and borders. Ordinary well-drained soil and sun are all they require. Planting can be done between autumn and spring with propagation by division at the same time. *S. aizoon* (China, Japan, Siberia) forms clumps of erect stems 35-45 cm tall with narrow, coarsely toothed leaves and compact, flattened clusters of yellow flowers in summer. *S. a.* 'Aurantiacum' has reddish stems and orange-yellow flowers. *S.* X 'Autumn Joy' is probably *S. telephium* X *S. spectabile* and comes midway between them, with stems 50 cm or more tall, prominently toothed, pale, fleshy leaves and deep-pink flowers that age dusky crimson, turning to a coppery hue. For the *S. maximum* of catalogues — see under *S. telephium. S. rosea* (*S. rhodiola, Rhodiola rosea*), rose root (circumpolar and mountains farther south) has an almost woody crown and a dense sheaf of erect stems clad with more or less oval, bright glaucous leaves. The flowers are a bright greenish-yellow and open in late spring. The dried roots are fragrant. *S. spectabile* (China, Korea) is rather confusingly known as ice plant in Britain. Very familiar, the beauty of its blue-white surfaced, fleshy obovate leaves and large flat heads of pink flowers is often overlooked; a good example of the undeserved contempt of over-familiarity. It is a splendid plant for attracting the butterflies of late summer. *S. s.* 'Brilliant' is deep rose-pink, 'Iceberg' is white and 'September Ruby' is darkest of all. See also under 'Autumn Joy'. *S. telephium*, live-long, orpine (Europe, Asia, represented in America by the almost identical *S. telephioides*) forms clumps to 60 cm tall clad with dark sometimes greyish-green irregularly toothed leaves and topped by flattish heads of purple-red flowers in late summer. It is a variable plant in the wild and in gardens: *S. t. maximum* (*S. maximum*) is more robust, to 80 cm tall but with greenish- to yellowish-white flowers and hardly worthy of garden room. *S. t. maximum* 'Atropurpureum' is quite another matter, a fine red-purple-leaved plant with pinkish flowers. *S. t.* 'Munstead Red' has rich brownish-red flowers and purple-tinted leaves; 'Variegatum' has the leaves marked creamy white, while 'Roseo-variegatum' has pinkish shoots in spring, later turning green.

Figure 12: *Sedum spectabile*

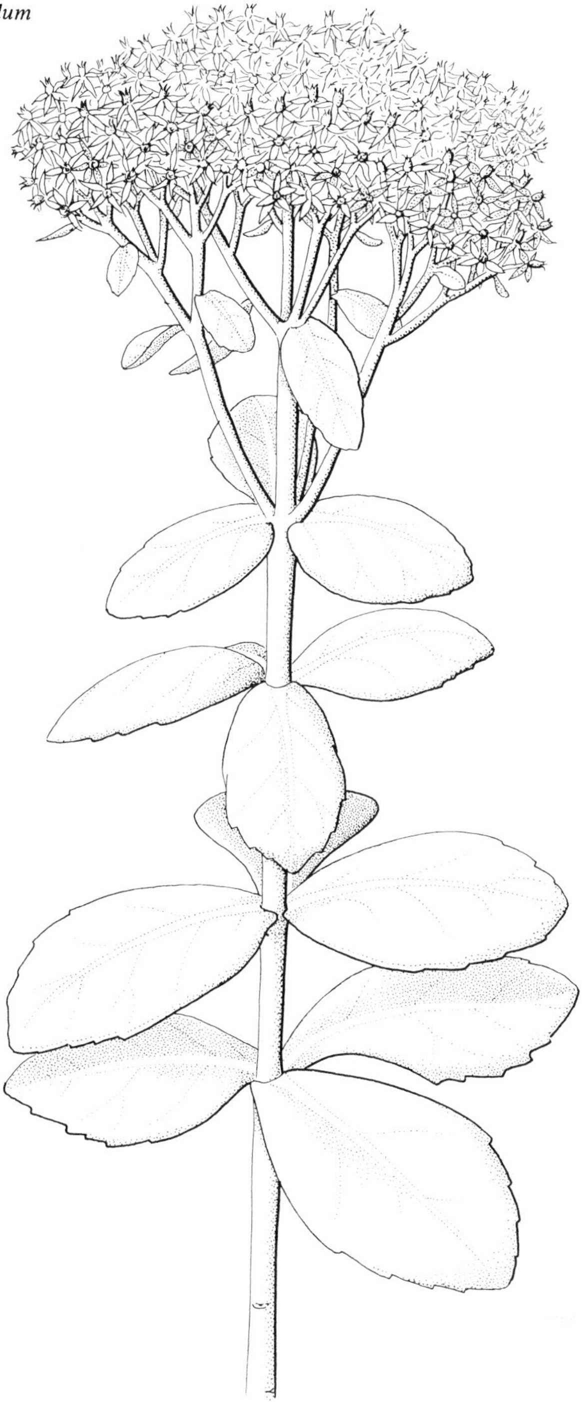

Senecio (Ragwort) (*Compositae*)

This is the largest genus of flowering plants with perhaps as many as 3,000 species of trees, shrubs, annuals and perennials, including many succulents. Only one hardy herbaceous perennial seems to be available commercially, *S. tanguticus* from China. It is a rhizomatous plant to 1.5 m or more tall with deeply lobed leaves and large terminal plumes of small, yellow daisy flowers in early autumn. The fluffy seed heads too are attractive. In the moisture-retentive soil it likes best it can be invasive and should be planted with caution. Ordinary soil is suitable in sun or partial shade. Planting can take place autumn to spring, and propagation by division at planting time.

Sidalcea malviflora (*Malvaceae*)

Of the 22-25 species in this W. North American genus only *malviflora* is generally cultivated and it is a plant of real garden merit. Clump-forming, it has erect stems 90-120 cm in height and substantial, rich-green, rounded basal leaves. The stem leaves are smaller and lobed, and above them develop wand-like spikes of mallow-shaped flowers. It is represented in British gardens by several cultivars, e.g. 'Croftway Red. (1 m tall), 'Sussex Beauty' (clearest pink, 1.2 m), 'William Smith' (salmon pink, 1 m) and Alan Bloom's 'Oberon' and 'Puck', also in shades of pink to about 90 cm tall and sturdily self-supporting. *Sidalcea* thrives best in fertile, moisture-retentive soil in sun. It can be planted from autumn to spring with propagation by division at the same time. Seeds may also be sown in spring but cannot be expected to come entirely true to type.

Silene dioica (Red Campion) (*Caryophyllaceae*)

Most of the few members of this 500 species genus in cultivation are rock or alpine plants or annuals. Even the red campion is seldom grown, attractive though it is, being too often seen gracing our roadsides. *S. d.* 'Flore Pleno' is a very different thing however, with fully double rose-red blossoms somewhat reminiscent of a pink. It is clump-forming, about 50-60 cm in height and apt to be short lived if not regularly divided, ideally every second or third spring. Ordinary fertile soil and sun or partial shade are required. Planting can take place from autumn to spring.

Silphium (Compass Plant) (*Compositae*)

About 20 species of resinous plants form this E. North American genus, none of which are very distinguished. *S. laciniatum* is the only one generally available. It can make an imposing plant, often exceeding 2 m in height, with large pinnately lobed, north-south aligned basal leaves and 12 cm-wide yellow daisies from late summer onwards. It must be admitted however that it has a certain coarseness that does not appeal to all. *S. perfoliatum* has a similar impact but with leaf pairs that unite around the stem to form cups. Worth looking out for is *S. terebinthaceum*, no better in flower than the others but with huge dock-like basal leaves up to 90 cm long which are rather handsome. Ordinary but not dry soil and a site in sun are all that is required. Plant from autumn to spring with propagation by division at the same time.

Sisyrinchium striatum (*Iridaceae*)

Most of the 75 species in this genus are too small or too tender for the hardy planter. *S. striatum* from S. Chile is the exception. Easily mistaken for an iris when not in bloom, it has grey-green leaves in upstanding clumps and in summer clusters of six-petalled pale-yellow flowers with a dark veining. Unlike those of the small blue-eyed-grass members of the genus, these flower clusters are arranged one above the other to form a long spike. Particularly attractive is *S. s.* 'Variegatum' ('Aunt May') with greyer, cream-striped leaves. It is apt to be short lived unless divided every other year. Well-drained, moderately fertile soil and a sunny, ideally sheltered site are required. Planting should take place in autumn or spring. Propagation by division is best in late summer, or by seeds in spring. The type plant regularly self-sows.

Smilacina (False Solomon's Seal) (*Liliaceae*)

About 25 rhizomatous perennials comprise this Asian and N. American genus but few are regularly cultivated. They are much like Solomon's seal (*Polygonatum*) in foliage, but have very small, starry flowers in terminal racemes or panicles above the leaves; culture is as for *Polygonatum*. *S. racemosa* (N. America) is sometimes known as false spikenard and is by far the showiest member. It forms dense, wide clumps 60-90 cm tall with slender-pointed oval, lustrous leaves and pale-cream plume-like flower clusters in late spring. The berry fruits are red, sometimes purple-spotted. *S. stellata* (W. North America) makes much less of an impact in the garden, having narrower leaves, small racemes of white flowers and a somewhat invasive growth habit.

Solidago (Golden Rod) (*Compositae*)

Depending on the botanical authority, there are 100-130 different kinds of golden rod. Very few are cultivated, the genus being largely represented in gardens by hybrid cultivars derived from a mere handful of species. They thrive in ordinary but not dry soil and are sturdiest in sun, though tolerating partial shade. Planting can take place from autumn to spring; propagation is by division at planting time. For *S. brachystachys* — see under *S. virgaurea*. *S. caesia* (N. America) is very different from the usual concept of a golden rod. It has dark, wiry, arching, branching stems 60-90 cm tall set with very slender willow-shaped foliage. In autumn, bobbles of bright-yellow flowers spangle the upper leaf axils. *S. canadensis* (N. America, east of the Rocky Mountains) forms wide clumps to 1.5 m tall with crowded, narrow, downy leaves and broadly pyramidal clusters of yellow flowers from late summer to autumn. It is a primary parent of the garden cultivars described below and is naturalised in Britain. *S. virgaurea* (Europe, Asia, N. Africa) is a variable plant 30-75 cm tall with narrow leaves and rather open leafy panicles of yellow flowers from summer to autumn. It is largely represented in gardens by *S. v.* 'Brachystachys', a neat, compact form barely 30 cm in height. Hybrid cultivars: the crossing together of *S. canadensis*, *S. virgaurea* and a few other species has resulted in the race of popular cultivars we grow today, e.g. 'Cloth of Gold', 45 cm, vigorous, deep yellow; 'Crown of Rays', 60 cm, wide-spreading panicles, bright yellow; 'Golden Thumb' ('Tom Thumb', 'Queenie') 30 cm, bushy, yellow-tinted foliage and medium-yellow flowers; 'Goldenmosa', 75 cm, bright-yellow mimosa-like panicles; 'Lemore', 75 cm, wide panicles of comparatively large lemon to primrose-yellow florets (evidence suggests that this cultivar should be placed in the following genus).

X Solidaster luteus (*Compositae*)

Also known as *Aster hybridus luteus* this plant is reputedly derived from crossing *Aster ptarmicoides* (a white-flowered, linear-leaved species) with a golden rod, perhaps *S. canadensis*. It much resembles a 60-75 cm-tall golden rod with rather broad topped, summer-borne panicles of yellow flowers that age to a creamy tint. Culture as for *Solidago*.

Spartina pectinata (Prairie Cord Grass) (*Gramineae*)

This genus of 16 species is perhaps best known by its salt marsh building members (*S. maritima*, *S. alterniflora* and their hybrid *S. X townsendii*) none of which is especially decorative. *S. pectinata*, particularly its yellow-striped leaf mutant 'Aureo Marginata', has elegant arching leaves and stems that can reach 2 m by late summer. The rather stiff, erect flowering spikes are greenish, but for a short period in autumn are transformed by numerous dangling purple stamens. This is a grass of swamps and wet prairies in N. America and needs moist soil and sun to do best. Planting should take place in spring with propagation by division at the same time.

Stachys (Woundwort) (*Labiatae*)

This widespread genus of about 300 species contains annuals, sub-shrubs and perennials, many of them rather coarse or weedy. The species described all have garden worthiness and all hardy-plant nurserymen stock some of them. They require ordinary well-drained soil and sun though some shade is tolerated. Planting can take place from autumn to spring; propagation is best by division in autumn or spring. Seeds can be sown in spring. *S. byzantina* (*S. lanata*, *S. olympica*), bunny's ears, lamb's ears, lamb's lugs, lamb's tongue (SW Asia to European Turkey) is the best-known species, a mat-former with thickly silvery-woolly leaves and spikes of not very special small purple flowers in summer. A useful ground cover, particularly if its non-flowering clone 'Silver Carpet' is used. *S. grandiflora* (*S. macrantha*, *Betonica macrantha*) (Caucasus) without doubt is the finest flowering species and also stands the most shade. It is clump-forming to 60 cm in height with rich green, oval, round-toothed leaves and spikes of 3-4 cm-long, mauve-purple flowers in summer. *S. g.* 'Robusta' with richer-toned flowers and more vigorous growth should be chosen. *S. officinalis* (*S. betonica*, *Betonica officinalis*) betony (Europe to Caucasus) is about 45 cm tall with smaller leaves and darker flowers than *S. grandiflora*. *S. o.* 'Alba' is white and 'Rosea' clear pink.

Statice — see *Limonium*.

Stipa (Feather Grass) (*Gramineae*)

Depending upon the classifying botanist, there are 150-300 species in this genus of elegant grasses. They need ordinary well-drained soil and a sunny site. Planting should be done in spring; propagation is by division or by sowing seeds in spring. *S. arundinacea* (New Zealand) forms dense clumps of arching evergreen leaves which take on overtones of purple-brown when mature. The very slender flowering stems attain 90-150 cm and bear drooping panicles of lustrous purple-brown spikelets in summer. A quietly lovely grass that is best in a sheltered but not dry site. For *S. barbata* — see under *S. pennata*. *S. calamagrostis* (*S. lasiagrostis*, *Lasiagrostis calamagrostis*) (S. Europe) eventually forms wide clumps 90-120 cm in height, composed of arching leaves and airy, plumy flowering panicles. The spikelets are often violet tinted ageing to creamy-fawn, and persist into winter. *S. gigantea* (Spain, Portugal, Morocco) is aptly named, the dense clumps rising to 2 m when well established. Its large airy panicles or purplish spikelets are its *pièce de resistance*, each spike with an awn 15-20 cm long, ageing to cornfield yellow. *S. pennata*, common feather grass (C. to SE Europe) grows 50-75 cm tall with clumps of very slender, rolled leaves and panicles of whitish spikelets with feathery awns 18-30 cm in length. The plant offered as *S. barbata* is similar with shorter, less plumy awns. *S. splendens* (C. Asia to Siberia) is much like a giant form of *S. calamagrostis*, to 2.5 m in height. At least one nurseryman offers *S. calamagrostis* under this name.

Stokesia laevis (*Compositae*)

Also listed as *S. cyanea* and known as Stokes aster, this is the only member of its genus. A native of SE USA, it is allied to *Chrysanthemum* and *Achillea* but the flowers more nearly suggest a knapweed (*Centaurea*). It forms clumps of 10-20 cm-long spoon-shaped leaves, above which rise stems to 45 cm or more bearing solitary or small clusters of 6-10 cm-wide lavender-blue blooms from summer to autumn. Forms with white, creamy-yellow, purple, pink and deeper blue flowers are known. Fertile, well-drained but not dry soil in sun is required. Planting can take place from autumn to spring, propagation is by division or by seeds in spring.

Strobilanthus atropurpureus (*Acanthaceae*)

This is the only hardy species available in a predominantly tropical genus. It is well branched and clump-forming, 1-1.5 m tall with somewhat nettle-like leaves and tubular autumn-borne flowers which open bluish-violet each morning, ageing to purple by about midday. Ordinary soil and sun are required, ideally in a sheltered site. Plant and propagate by division in spring.

Stylophorum diphyllum (*Papaveraceae*)

Aptly, but not commonly known as the celandine poppy this is the only one of a three-species genus to be cultivated in Britain. A native of E. North America it has a tufted habit, long-stalked, pinnately lobed, fresh green leaves and deep-yellow poppy-like flowers carried on 30-45 cm-tall stems from late spring onwards. It thrives in humus-rich soil in partial shade and is best planted in autumn or spring. Propagation is by division in spring or by seeds when ripe.

Symphyandra (*Campanulaceae*)

There are eight to ten species in this campanula-like genus, those described here being rather short lived but usually self-sowing or easily raised from seeds. Culture as for campanula, but division is difficult if not impossible. *S. armena* (Caucasus) tends to sprawl to about 30 cm tall, with oval-cordate leaves and in summer, velvety-downy blue or white flowers which are held erect. *S. hofmannii* (Yugoslavia) is 30-60 cm tall from an over-wintering rosette of coarsely toothed lance-shaped leaves. The nodding, cream bell flowers are 3 cm long and carried in leafy panicles in summer. It often behaves as a biennial. *S. pendula* (Caucasus) can reach 60 cm in height, with oval, toothed leaves and pendent cream bells. *S. wanneri* (Bulgaria, Romania, Yugoslavia) is up to 45 cm tall with narrow leaves and nodding violet bells in summer. It thrives in partial shade.

Symphytum (Comfrey) (*Boraginaceae*)

There are 25 species of comfrey but only those described here are cultivated to any extent. The larger ones are rather coarse, but all have ground-covering foliage and nodding clusters of tubular bell flowers. Ordinary soil and sun or partial shade are their modest requirements. Planting can take place from autumn to spring and propagation is by division at planting time. *S. caucasicum* (Caucasus) is a softly hairy plant to 60 cm with oval to lance-shaped leaves up to 20 cm long. The late spring-borne flowers open red-purple and age to sky-blue. *S. grandiflorum* (Caucasus) rarely achieves 30 cm in height but is a good, neat ground coverer with its rich-green elliptic leaves to 10 cm in length. The cream flowers open from spring to summer. It will survive even in moderately dry shade once established. There are colour forms of hybrid origin offered as 'Hidcote Blue', 'Hidcote Pink' and 'Lilacina'. *S. officinale*, common comfrey (Europe to W. Siberia and Turkey) has tuberous roots and grows to 60 cm or more, with narrow oval leaves and white, cream, purple or pink flowers in early summer. *S.* X *rubrum* (of gardens) is possibly a hybrid between a red-flowered *S. officinale* and *S. grandiflorum* and is roughly midway between these species, attaining 45 cm, and with crimson flowers. *S.* X *uplandicum* (*S. asperum* X *S. officinale*), Russian comfrey, is sometimes listed as *S. peregrinum* and is a varied but invariably vigorous hybrid 90-120 cm tall. In overall appearance it favours *officinale*, but combines also the hooked-bristle and blue-flower characteristics of *asperum*. The flowers open in summer and are usually in shades of blue and purple. *S.* X. *u.* 'Variegatum' is a handsome foliage plant, each large leaf having a greyish cast and a bold cream border.

Tanacetum vulgare (Tansy) (*Compositae*)

T

About 50 species form this genus which is closely allied to *Chrysanthemum*. Only the common tansy is tall enough and hardy enough for our purposes. A native of Europe to Siberia and Turkey, it is clump forming, 70-100 cm in height with rich-green ferny leaves and flattened clusters of button-shaped yellow flowers in late summer and autumn. The whole plant is pleasantly aromatic and was formerly much used as a medical and pot herb. It requires ordinary soil and sun but will stand some shade. Plant from autumn to spring with propagation by division at the same time.

Telekia — see under *Buphthalmum*

Tellima grandiflora (Fringecup) (*Saxifragaceae*)

A native of W. North America from California to Alaska the fringe-cup is the only member of its genus. It is essentially a foliage plant forming dense hummocks of long-stalked hairy maple-like leaves which make appealing ground cover. In early summer the stems rise to above 60 cm bearing racemes of small greenish-white flowers with delightfully fringed petals. *T. g.* 'Purpurea' is superior as a garden plant with red-purple flushed leaves especially in winter, and pink-flushed flowers. Ordinary soil and partial shade are suitable and it thrives beneath trees if not too dry. Planting can take place from autumn to spring, and propagation by division at planting time or by seeds in spring.

Teucrium (*Labiatae*)

Comparatively few of the 300 species in this genus are grown, and even fewer are suitable for the perennial border. They need well-drained soil and sun though partial shade is tolerated. Planting can take place from autumn to spring, propagation is by division, or by seeds in spring or cuttings in late summer. *T. scorodonia*, wood sage (SW to C. Europe) is strictly a sub-shrub but behaves as an evergreen perennial. The wild plant with its oval to triangular, finely wrinkled, somewhat sage-like leaves and small, pale yellow-green flowers in late summer, is rarely grown. Much more garden worthy are: *T. s.* 'Crispum' with the leaf margins waved and crested and purple-tinted in winter and 'Crispum Marginatum' also having the leaf margins whitish and pink flushed. Some nurserymen erroneously list *T. scorodonia* under *T. scordium*. The latter is the water germander and totally distinct, with oblong leaves and purple flowers.

Thalictrum (Meadow Rue) (*Ranunculaceae*)

Among the 100-150 species in this genus are several indispensable border perennials. All the species mentioned here have dissected, often fern-like foliage. Some have frothy masses of multi-stamened flowers, others have more airy clusters of individual, larger flowers with four to five petal-like sepals. They require fertile, well-drained but not dry soil, and sun or partial shade. Planting is best in autumn or spring, and propagation is by division at planting time, or by seeds when ripe or in spring. For the *T. adiantifolium* of gardens — see under *T. minus*. *T. aquilegifolium* (E. Europe to N. Asia) is clump forming to about 90 cm with bright-green foliage and large panicles of flowers with small white sepals and lilac, pink, purple or white stamens. Cultivars to try are: 'Album', 'Purpureum', 'Purple Cloud' and 'Thunder Cloud'. *T. chelidonii* (Himalayas) is a stately plant much like the better known *T. delavayi*. It needs rich, peaty soil and a cool climate to do really well. *T. delavayi* (W. China) grows to 1.5 m and presents a lovely sight in summer when producing its clouds of mauve to lilac-sepalled flowers with their yellow stamens. *T. d.* 'Hewitt's Double' lasts longer, but the fully double flowers lose some of their single charm. It is frequently listed as a cultivar of *T. diptero-carpum*, a plant of almost identical appearance but to botanists, distinct by reason of its winged fruits (seeds). *T. flavum*, common meadow rue (Europe, Asia) grows 1-1.5 m tall with leaflets that are deep green above and pale beneath, and frothy yellow flower clusters in late summer. *T. f. glaucum* (*T. f. speciosum*, *T. glaucum*, *T. specio-sissimum*) is a superior variety being more robust, with glaucous foliage and larger clusters of lemon-yellow flowers. *T. minus*, lesser meadow rue (Europe, N. Asia) is purely a foliage plant, the flowers being greenish or purple tinted. It is very variable, some forms being under 30 cm, others exceeding 1 m; all can be invasive. One of the best forms for the border is *T. m.* 'Adiantifolium' ('Majus' or 'Foetidum' of gardens) growing to about 60 cm. *T. rochebrunianum* (wrongly *rocquebrunianum* in some catalogues) is cast in the mould of *T. delavayi* with pale-purple flowers opening a little later.

Thermopsis montana (*Leguminosae*)

This is the only member of its 20-30-strong genus likely to be obtainable. The name *Thermopsis* means lupin-like and is most apt. *T. montana* comes from NW USA and forms colonies of erect stems 60-90 cm tall bearing trifoliate leaves with a pair of leaf-like basal stipules and golden-yellow flowers in summer. It can be invasive in fertile soils. Other somewhat similar species are occasionally offered, notably *T. caroliniana*, *mollis* and *lupinoides* (*lanceolata*). The latter is clump-forming and worth acquiring. Culture is as for lupin.

Tiarella (Foamflower) *(Saxifragaceae)*

All six species in this genus thrive well in shade and some make first-rate evergreen ground cover. The flowers are tiny but when borne in profusion aptly suggest the vernacular name. Ordinary, preferably humus-rich soil in partial shade provides ideal conditions. Planting can take place from autumn to spring with propagation by division at the same time. *T. cordifolia* (SE USA) forms wide mats spreading by rhizomes and stolons with maple-like leaves that are sometimes flecked deep maroon and flush reddish-bronze in winter. The white or pink-tinted flowers open in spring on slender stems 20-30 cm tall. For *T. c. collina* — see under *T. wherryi*. *T. polyphylla* (Himalayas to Japan, Taiwan) is clump forming, the rounded leaves shallowly three to five-lobed and toothed. The nodding white flowers are carried on stems 30-40 cm high. *T. trifoliata* (NW North America) has hairy trifoliate leaves and cylindrical panicles of nodding, pinkish-budded white flowers. *T. wherryi* (*T. collina*, *T. cordifolia wherryi*) as grown in Britain is a clump-forming version of *T. cordifolia* with more regularly flecked leaves. It is apparently a variable plant in the wild and more robust forms are known. The plant currently available under the *T. collina* name is very vigorous, densely clump forming, with longer stalked plain green leaves and flowers from late spring to autumn; a fine plant.

Tolmiea (Pickaback Plant) (*Saxifragaceae*)

Also known as youth on age, this is the only species in its genus. It has affinities with *Tellima* and *Tiarella* and favours the former in general appearance. Each mature leaf, however, develops a plantlet at the junction between leaf-blade and stalk, rendering it very distinct and intriguing. The little flowers are greenish-purple and make no impact from a distance but are very rewarding under a hand-lens with their thread-like chocolate-coloured petals. Culture is as for *Tellima*, but it stands full shade and makes a good companion for ferns.

Tovara virginiana — see under *Polygonum*.

Trachystemon orientalis (*Boraginaceae*)

One of two E. Mediterranean species, this is a rather coarse borage-like plant but with mainly basal leaves, often 30 cm or more long and a slowly colonising habit. The bluish-purple flowers with their semi-reflexed petals open in spring often quite early. It makes handsome ground cover but can be invasive. Culture is as for *Symphytum*.

Tradescantia (Spiderwort) (*Commelinaceae*)

Depending on the botanical authority there are 20-60 species of spiderwort, most of them from the warmer parts of the Americas. A few hardy species and their hybrids are indispensable for the border, flowering over a long season. They form clumps of broad, somewhat fleshy, arching, grassy leaves. The branched erect stems tipped by spathes produce a succession of wide-open three-petalled flowers. Ordinary fertile soil in sun provides ideal conditions. Planting can be done from autumn to spring with propagation by division at the same time. *T.* X *andersoniana* (*T. virginiana* of gardens) covers cultivars derived from crossing *T. ohiensis*, *T. subaspera* and the true *T. virginiana*. They grow to 60 cm in height with velvety flowers up to 3.5 cm wide in summer and autumn. 'J. C. Weguelin' is azure blue; 'Osprey' white with blue-bearded stamens; 'Purple Dome' rich purple and 'Rubra' is deep rose-red; at least 15 other cultivars are available, all variations on a theme, a few are double.

Figure 13:
Tradescantia X
andersoniana

Tricyrtis (Toad Lily) (*Liliaceae*)

About half of the species in this genus are in cultivation but only three or four are commercially available. This is a pity as the toad lilies are intriguing plants and if not showy always provide a talking point. They form clumps or colonies of erect to arching stems topped by clusters of six-petalled, usually heavily spotted flowers. These may be funnel-shaped and nodding or erect and flared. Bulbous nectaries are always present at the base of each flower and the prominent stamens and styles together form a central crown. Humus-rich, moist but not wet soil and sun or partial shade sheltered from strong winds provide ideal conditions. Planting is best in autumn or spring with propagation by division at the same time. For the *T. bakeri* of gardens – see under *T. latifolia*. *T. formosana* (Taiwan) is clump-forming to about 90 cm, with glossy, deep-green leaves and panicle-like clusters of erect flowers in autumn. Each blossom is basically white but so heavily spotted as to appear red-purple from a distance. *T. f. stolonifera* (*T. stolonifera*) has wide-spreading stolons and narrower leaves. *T. hirta* (Japan) forms clumps to 75 cm or more with hairy, oval leaves and erect white flowers with lilac spots, in autumn. *T. h.* 'Alba' has off-white flowers. *T. latifolia* (*T. bakeri* of gardens) (Japan) is 75-90 cm tall with oval, bright-green leaves and erect yellow flowers which are finely but closely purple-dotted and open in late summer. *T. macrantha* (Japan) has erect, coarsely brown-hairy stems to 60 cm tall, oval to lance-shaped leaves and pendulous yellow flowers with purple-brown spots and more elongated spurs. *T. macropoda* (Japan) rises to 90 cm and bears in autumn erect, creamy or greenish-white flowers thickly spotted purple to mauve.

Trillium (Wood Lily) *Trilliaceae* (*Liliaceae*)

Also aptly known as wake-robin, the 30 species in this genus are mainly N. American and all the most garden-worthy sorts come from there. They are very distinct plants in having all their parts in threes: each stem is topped by a whorl of three leaves in the centre of which is borne a solitary stalked or stalkless flower composed of three sepals and three petals. The fruit is a three-lobed berry. Although their period of attraction is fairly short and at least six months are spent underground, trilliums have an undeniable appeal. However, they are difficult to place in beds and borders with traditional perennials and only the larger, vigorous sorts are described below. They need humus-rich, moisture-retentive but not wet soil and partial shade sheltered from strong winds. Planting is best from late summer to late autumn but can extend to late winter. Propagation is by careful division at planting time, or by seeds when ripe. Seeds may take one-and-a-half to two-and-a-half years to germinate and several more

Figure 14:
Tricyrtis formosana

to flower. *T. cernuum* (E. North America) grows 30-45 cm tall with leaves to 15 cm long and stalked white or pink flowers that nod bashfully half beneath them. *T. chloropetalum* (California to Washington State) is robust and when established can reach 60 cm, with large oval leaves that are often pleasingly mottled. The stalkless flowers vary from greenish-white to pure white or purple. *T. erectum*, birthroot (E. North America) is usually under 30 cm in height but can exceed this, with stalked crimson to purple-brown flowers. *T. e.* 'Album' is white, while 'Flavum' (*T. e. luteum*, *T. flavum* of gardens) is yellow. *T. grandiflorum*, common wood lily (E. North America) is without doubt the most generally garden-worthy species. It forms substantial clumps of rich green leaves and bears large white flowers that age to pink. There are many forms, as it is very prone to mutation and some of them are available now and then. Among the several doubles, 'Plenum' is the most shapely; 'Variegatum' has green striped petals — no improvement as far as beauty is concerned. *T. sessile*, toadshade (E. North America) is the eastern expression of *T. chloropetalum* but generally a shorter plant with smaller leaves. It can form substantial clumps when happy. *T. s.* 'Rubrum' with red-purple flowers, is the commonest in gardens, but other shades occur. *T. viride luteum* is almost identical in the plant but has yellow flowers.

Trollius (Globe Flower) (*Ranunculaceae*)

At least a few of the 20-25 species in this genus are among the hardy planter's indispensables for early summer. They are clump forming with deeply fingered and toothed leaves which make a pleasing foil for the big buttercup-like flowers. Moist, fertile soil and sun is preferred though partial shade is tolerated. They make fine bog subjects. Plant from autumn to early spring, and propagate by division at planting time or by seeds when ripe. Dry seeds can take up to two years to germinate. *T.* X *cultorum* (*T.* X *hybridus* of catalogues) combines the characters of *T. chinensis*, *T. asiaticus* and *T. europaeus* and basically resembles the latter but with larger flowers. Several cultivars are available, e.g. 'Alabaster', pale primrose; 'Canary Bird', lemon-yellow; 'Commander in Chief', very large, deep orange; 'Earliest of All', lemon-yellow, late spring; 'Golden Queen', (*T. ledebourii* 'Golden Queen'), golden-orange with prominent petaloids; 'Orange Princess', orange-yellow and 'Salamander', deep orange. *T. europaeus* (Canada to the Caucasus) grows 45-60 cm tall with fresh green, three to five lobed leaves and 3 cm-wide pale-yellow flowers in late spring. For the *T. ledebourii* of catalogues (not the distinct true species) — see under *T.* X *cultorum*. *T. yunnanensis* (W. China) grows to 60 cm in height and is markedly different in having blooms which open out flat and are centred with a prominent crown of staminodes.

Tropaeolum (*Tropaeolaceae*)

Depending on the botanical authority there are 50-90 species in this genus, the best-known member being the annual nasturtium (*T. majus*). A few members have tuberous or semi-tuberous roots and are just hardy enough to include here. Cultural conditions are mentioned with each species. *T. polyphyllum* (Chile) graces dry mountain screes in its homeland and must have sharply drained but moderately fertile soil and a warm sunny site to thrive. It can, if happily situated, make wide mats of trailing stems set with small, brightly glaucous leaves which are divided and folded. In early summer the stem tips bear leafy racemes of spurred yellow flowers with notched and waved petals. Orange-yellow forms and those with crimson veins occur in the wild and were introduced in 1972 by the Beckett, Cheese and Watson Expedition. *T. speciosum*, flame nasturtium (Chile) garlands the forests of high rainfall areas and needs humus-rich, moist but well-drained soil in partial shade. It is a climber to 3 m or more with fingered leaves and wide-open vermilion-scarlet flowers in late summer. The blue seeds that follow are a delightful bonus. This is a plant for the mixed border where it can scramble through an evergreen shrub. *T. tuberosum* (Bolivia, Peru) is strictly half-hardy. If however the autumn-produced tubers are buried more deeply, covered with at least 10 cm of soil they will survive all but the severest winters. Ordinary well-drained soil or partial shade are required; the climbing stems need support, which can be provided by tall pea sticks or a shrub. It has rounded, lobed, somewhat glaucous leaves and spurred, cup-shaped flowers of orange yellow and scarlet. The early-flowered form 'Ken Aslet' must be obtained. This blooms from late June to autumn, whereas the original introduction comes out so late in autumn that it often gets cut by frost first. All the above species can be propagated by seeds in spring, and *T. polyphyllum* and *T. speciosum* by very careful division in spring or basal cuttings in early summer. All are best planted in spring.

Uvularia (*Liliaceae*)

This genus of four to five species from E. North America has the delightfully appropriate name of merrybells. They are rhizomatous plants forming colonies of erect, wiry stems and bright green oblong-oval to lance-shaped leaves. The shoots appear fairly late but grow with great rapidity and as they unfold the nodding tips produce six-petalled, yellow bell-flowers. They need humus-rich soil and partial shade sheltered from strong winds. Planting can take place from late summer to early spring with propagation by division at planting time. *U. grandiflora* produces branched stems 40-60 cm tall but begins to produce its 5 cm-long lemon-yellow flowers when half this height in early summer. *U. perfoliata* is much like and often confused with *U. grandiflora* but is less robust and has smaller, paler flowers.

Valeriana (Valerian) (*Valerianaceae*)

Very few of the 200 species contained in this world-wide genus are cultivated and even fewer are suitable for the hardy perennial garden. The species thrive in ordinary moistish soil in sun or partial shade. Planting can take place from autumn to spring, with propagation by division at the same time. *V. officinalis*, common or cats' valerian (Europe, Asia) is an overlooked native plant of quiet attraction. A clump-former to 1 m or more it has pinnate leaves and terminal panicles of small, tubular, pink flowers in summer. *V. phu* (Caucasus) is a clumper to 90 cm with oblong elliptic leaves and whitish flowers. It is entirely represented in cultivation by *V. p.* 'Aurea' which has the young leaves bright yellow.

Vancouveria hexandra (*Berberidaceae*)

This is one of a three-species genus which is N. America's version of *Epimedium*. *V. hexandra* is deciduous and forms wide colonies of dissected leaves above which rise wiry stems carrying delicate panicles of white flowers with prominent stamens and reflexed petals. The allied *V. chrysantha* has yellow flowers. Culture is as for *Epimedium*.

Veratrum (False Helleborine or Hellebore) (*Liliaceae*)

The most garden worthy of this 25 species genus are statuesque foliage and flowering plants with sheaves of large, elliptic, heavily pleated leaves and tall, dense panicles of six-petalled starry flowers. They need moist, humus-rich soil and are best in partial shade but will stand full sun. Planting can take place from autumn to spring, and propagation by careful division in late winter, or by seeds in spring. Seedlings take several years to flower. *V. album*, white false hellebore (Europe to Asia) reaches 2 m in height with 30 cm long basal leaves and palest green flowers in late summer. *V. nigrum*, black false hellebore (Europe to N. Asia) is similar to *V. album* but with maroon flowers. *V. viride* (Indian poke, American white hellebore (E. North America) is 1.2-2 m tall with leaves 20-30 cm long and yellow-green flowers in summer.

Verbascum (Mullein) (*Scrophulariaceae*)

This familiar genus contains, depending on the botanical authority, 250-360 species of sub-shrubs, biennials and perennials of widely differing sizes and habits. Comparatively few are reliable perennials suitable for our purposes. Those described thrive in ordinary well-drained soil and sun. Planting is best in autumn or spring, with propagation by careful division or seeds in spring. *V. chaixii* (Europe) grows to 90 cm in height with grey-hairy basal leaves to 30 cm, sometimes slightly lobed. The yellow flowers have purple woolly stamens and are carried in slim spires in summer. *V. c.* 'Album' is white — see also *V. vernale*. *V. olympicum* of gardens (reputedly from Greece) can behave as a biennial or short-lived perennial. It is a statuesque plant to 2 m or more with large white-woolly leaves and bright rich-yellow flowers in summer. *V. phoeniceum*, purple mullein (C. Europe to Asia), unlike most other species forms real clumps and has oval, dark-green leaves. It usually attains 1 m or more, with flowers in shades of purple in early summer. Several cultivars, some of hybrid origin, are available; 'Bridal Bouquet' is white; 'Cotswold Beauty' has biscuit-coloured petals and woolly lilac stamens; 'Cotswold Queen' is terracotta; 'Gainsborough' is primrose yellow and can reach 1.4 m in height, while 'Hartleyi' has biscuit-yellow petals suffused plum-purple. *V. vernale* of gardens has been equated with *V. chaixii* and occasionally with *V. nigrum* and *V. pyramidatum*, but is a distinct entity with grey basal leaves to 30 cm or more long and freely branching stems to 2 m bearing innumerable vivid-yellow flowers in summer.

Verbena (*Verbenaceae*)

Most of the 250 species of verbena are too tender for the hardy planter. There are several N. American sorts of undisputed hardiness but only the two mentioned here are sometimes available. They need ordinary well-drained soil and sun. Planting is best in spring, propagation is by division when possible, or basal cuttings or seeds in spring. *V. canadensis* (*V. aubletia*) (E. North America to Mexico) is known in its homeland as rose verbena. It grows to about 45 cm in height, with often reclining stems, pinnately lobed leaves and flowers in shades of red-purple, lilac, pink and white in summer and autumn. *V. hastata* (N. America) forms erect clumps to 1 m or more with stiff, candelabra-shaped panicles composed of small purple flowers and bracts in summer. The familiar bedding plants *V. bonariensis* (1-1.5 m) and *V. rigida* (*V. venosa*) (45-50 cm) are potentially perennials and survive in warm sheltered sites.

Veronica (Speedwell) (*Scrophulariaceae*)

This varied and often very decorative genus comprises about 300 species, most from the northern hemisphere. The perennial sorts are mainly clump-forming with lance-shaped to oval leaves in opposite pairs and terminal spikes of small wide-open flowers, often in shades of blue. They grow in ordinary soil and sun and can be planted from autumn to spring. Propagation is by division at planting time or by sowing seeds in spring. *V. austriaca* (*V. latifolia*) (Europe) is a very variable plant both in height and degree of leaf lobing. The best sort

for the border is the sub-species *V. a. teucrium* (*V. teucrium*), generally 30-45 cm tall with deeply to rounded toothed leaves. Ideal for
the front of the border is *V. a. t.* 'Crater Lake Blue', 30 cm tall,
producing spikes of deep-blue flowers in summer; 'Trehane' is only
about 20 cm tall but has the added attraction of golden-green foliage;
tallest is the pink 'Pavane' at almost 60 cm. *V. derwentiana* (*V.
derwentia*) (SE Australia) forms dense clumps to 1 m or more tall,
the erect stems bearing stalkless, thick-textured, lustrous deep-green
leaves to 10 cm long. From the upper leaf axils 15 cm-long paired
spikes of pure-white flowers open in summer. Considering its country
of origin this is a surprisingly but not totally hardy species that deserves to be grown more often. It is unique among the herbaceous
veronicas in being evergreen. After flowering, the stems sprawl and
continue growing at their tips, making passable and pleasing winter
ground cover. For *V. exaltata* – see under *V. longifolia*. *V. gentianoides* (Crimea, Caucasus) forms mats of lance-shaped to oval, glossy
leaves, above which rise elegant, 40 cm-tall spires of palest blue
flowers with darker veins, in early summer. *V. g.* 'Variegata' is the
most commonly seen, its basal leaves zoned with white. For *V.
incana* – see under *V. spicata*. *V. longifolia* (Europe) is a clump-
former to 1m or more having lance-shaped, slender pointed leaves to
12 cm and long spires of lilac or blue flowers in summer. *V. l. subses-
silis* (*V. hendersonii*) from Japan is a better garden plant averaging
about 60 cm in height with bright deep-blue flowers; 'Foerster's
Blue' is probably a selection of it. *V. l. exaltata* (Siberia) is superior
in elegance, rising to 1.2 m tall with more deeply toothed leaves and
flowers of clear pale blue. *V. spicata*, spiked speedwell (Europe-
Asia) forms neat clumps of erect stems 30-60 cm in height topped by
slim spires in shades of blue. *V. s. incana* is almost identical but has
silvery-white hairy leaves and tends to be shy flowering. It has been
crossed with true *V. spicata* at Bressingham, to give rise to 'Barcarolle'
(30 cm, deep rose-pink) and 'Minuet' (35-45 cm, clear pink) both with
grey-green leaves. Cultivars of straight *V. spicata* include: 'Blue Fox',
40 cm, bright lavender-blue; 'Heidikind', 25 cm, pink; 'Red Fox', cerise-
red and 'Snowhite', pure white. *V. virginica* (*Veronicastrum virgini-
cum*), Culver's root, blackroot (E. USA) forms dense clumps 1.4-
1.8 m in height. Each stem bears whorls of about five lance-shaped,
slender pointed leaves to 15 cm long and is topped by very long,
spikes of tiny flowers in shades of palest lilac-pink in late summer
and autumn. Palest blue forms are known and *V. v.* 'Alba' with
entirely white flowers is commonly grown.

Viola (Violet, Pansy) (*Violaceae*)

Although there are no less than 500 species of world-wide distribution in this genus, very few of the hardy ones are tall enough for our

purposes. The following need fertile, well-drained but not dry soil and a wind sheltered site in sun or partial shade. Planting can take place from autumn to spring, and propagation by division at planting time or by sowing seeds in spring. *V. cornuta* (Pyrenees) when well established can grow to 30 cm tall, the densely bushy plants bearing 2-3 cm-wide, long-spurred violets in shades of purple to lilac; *V. c.* 'Alba' is pure white; an excellent front-of-the-border species blooming from early summer to late autumn. *V. elatior* (Europe, W. Asia) forms small clumps of slender, erect stems 35 cm or more in height, with narrow leaves and pale-blue flowers in early summer. *V. rugulosa* (N. America) usually well exceeds 30 cm in height, with leaves to 10 cm long and bluish-tinted white flowers in summer. It spreads underground and can form sizeable colonies. *V. canadensis* is almost identical but does not wander.

Viscaria vulgaris – see under *Lychnis viscaria*.

Yucca (Adam's Needle) (*Agavaceae* (*Liliaceae*))

Although all the 40 species in this genus are classified as shrubs, several species have stemless rosettes and are essentially evergreen perennials. A few of these are reasonably hardy and make fine contrast plants with their sword-shaped leaves and waxy bell-flowers. They thrive in ordinary well-drained soil in sunny sheltered sites. Planting is best in spring, with propagation by detaching offsets at the same time. *Y. filamentosa* (SE USA) forms clumps of rosettes, the slightly glaucous 40-70 cm-long leaves margined with horny, curly threads. Panicles of white flowers thrust up to 2 m, in late summer. It is confused with the next species and *Y. smalliana*, in gardens. *Y. flaccida* (SE USA) has less rigid and more tapered leaves than *Y. filamentosa*, with straight marginal threads. *Y. glauca* (S. Dakota to N. Mexico) is clump-forming, with very narrow leaves, to 60 cm long by 1-1.5 cm wide. The panicles are about 1 m tall bearing greenish-cream, often red-brown tinted blooms in summer. *Y. smalliana* is much like *Y. filamentosa* but with narrower, sharp-pointed leaves and taller flower stems.

Zauschneria (California Fuchsia) (*Onagraceae*)

Although the four species in this genus are not fully hardy they survive most winters in Britain if well established in sheltered sites. Well-drained fertile soil and sun are essential. Planting should be done in spring. Propagation is by cuttings of non-flowering side shoots in late summer, or careful division in spring. *Z. californica* (*Z. mexicana*) (California to Mexico) is a woody-based plant with a bushy habit, 30 cm or more in height. The narrow leaves are grey-downy, and the slender, tubular, somewhat fuchsia-like scarlet flowers are carried in panicles. Flowering is from late summer to autumn. *Z. c. latifolia* (*Z. c. canescens*) has broader leaves and is more truly herbaceous. *Z. c.* 'Glasnevin' is most distinctive in having dark-green leaves and richer scarlet flowers; it is sometimes erroneously offered as 'Dublin Variety'. *Z. cana* (*Z. microphylla*) (California) is much like *Z. californica*, but the extra grey downy leaves seldom exceed 2 mm in width (those of *californica* are 2-6 mm).

Hardy Perennials — Lists for Special Purposes

Actaea	Disporum	Milium effusum	Plants suitable for shade
Ajuga	Eomecon	Myrrhis	
Alchemilla mollis	Epimedium	Peltiphyllum	
Anemone	Euphorbia robbiae	Phlox	
Aquilegia	Galax	Physostegia	
Aruncus	Gillenia	Podophyllum	
Astilbe	Glaucidium	Polygonatum	
Astrantia	Helleborus	Pulmonaria	
Baptisia	Heuchera	Saxifraga fortunei	
Bergenia	Hosta	Smilacina	
Brunnera	Kirengeshoma	Tellima	
Cardamine	Lamiastrum	Tiarella	
Cimicifuga	Lamium	Tolmiea	
Corydalis	Liriope	Trillium	
Deinanthe	Luzula	Uvularia	
Dentaria	Meconopsis	Vancouveria	
Dicentra	Melica	Veratrum	
Digitalis		ferns	

Aciphylla	Blechnum	Glaucidium	Best in Acid Soils
Asclepias	Deinanthe	Galax	

Aconitum	Astrantia	Cimicifuga	Suitable for Moist Soils (w = wet)
Acorus w	Buphthalmum	Eupatorium	
Ajuga	Caltha w	Euphorbia palustris	
Aruncus	Cardamine	Filipendula (not	
Arundo donax	Carex	F. vulgaris) w	
Asclepias	Cautleya	Gentiana	
Astilbe	Chelone	Glyceria w	

Gunnera *w*   Ligularia *w*   Peltiphyllum *w*
Hemerocallis   Lobelia *w*   Petasites *w*
Heracleum mantegaz-   Lysichiton *w*   Phormium
   zianum   Lysimachia   Primula *w* (candelabra)
Hosta   Lythrum *w*   Rodgersia
Houttuynia *w*   Matteuccia   Scrophularia auri-
Inula   Mimulus *w*   culata *w*
Iris   Myrrhis   Symphytum
Kirengeshoma   Osmunda *w*   Trollius *w*

Drought Resistant

Acanthus   Crepis incana   I. germanica
Adonis   Dianthus   Lamiastrum
Alstroemeria   Dictamnus   Lavatera
Althaea   Echinops   Limonium
Anaphalis   Elymus   Linaria
Anemone   Eremurus   Linum
Armeria   Eryngium   Malva
Artemisia   Euphorbia characias   Nepeta
Asphodeline   E. robbiae   Origanum
Asphodelus   Festuca   Papaver
Ballota   Filipendula vulgaris   Perowskia
Berkheya   Foeniculum   Phuopsis
Brunnera   Gaillardia   Pulsatilla
Campanula   Gypsophila   Romneya
Catananche   Helictotrichon   Sedum
Centranthus   Helleborus   Valeriana
Cheiranthus   Hieracium   Yucca
Cortaderia   Iris pallida   Zauschneria
Corydalis

Suitable for Ground Cover

Ajuga   Heuchera   Prunella
Alchemilla   Hosta   Pulmonaria
Bergenia   Lamiastrum   Rodgersia
Brunnera   Lamium   Tellima
Epimedium   Liriope   Tiarella
Euphorbia robbiae   Peltiphyllum   Tolmiea
Galax   Petasites   Vancouveria
Geranium   Phuopsis

Fine Specimen Plants

Acanthus   Cynara   Heracleum mantegaz-
Buphthalmum   Eremurus   zianum
Cortaderia   Gunnera   Hosta

Macleaya
Meconopsis napaul-
  ensis/superba
Miscanthus
Paeonia

Peltiphyllum
Phormium
Phytolacca
Rheum
Rodgersia

Silphium
Stipa gigantea
Veratrum
Veronica virginica
Yucca

Good Foliage Plants

Acanthus
Alchemilla mollis
Bergenia
Brunnera
Cortaderia
Cynara
Echinops
Elymus
Epimedium
Euphorbia characias
Filipendula
Foeniculum
Galax
Geranium
Glyceria
Gunnera
Heracleum man-

  tegazzianum
Heuchera
Hieracium
Hosta
Iris
Kirengeshoma
Kniphofia
Lamium
Ligularia
Lysichiton
Macleaya
Meconopsis
Miscanthus
Myrrhis
Paeonia
Peltiphyllum
Phormium

Podophyllum
Polygonatum
Rheum
Rodgersia
Romneya
Salvia argentea
Sanguisorba
Sisyrinchium
  striatum
Spartina pectinata
Tellima
Thalictrum
Tiarella
Tolmiea
Vancouveria
Veratrum
Verbascum

Variegated Foliage

Acorus
Astrantia
Brunnera
Glyceria
Hakonechloa
Hosta
Iris

Luzula
Milium
Miscanthus
Molinia
Phalaris
Phormium

Polygonatum
Polygonum
Pulmonaria
Scrophularia
Sisyrinchium
Symphytum

Coloured Foliage

(coppery, purple,
  reddish)
Ajuga
Astilbe
Bergenia
Clematis recta

Galax
Heuchera
Ligularia dentata
Oenothera tetragona
Phormium
Rheum

Rodgersia
Saxifraga fortunei
Sedum telephium
Tellima
Tiarella cordifolia

Grey or Silvery Foliage

Achillea
Anaphalis

Anthericum
Artemisia

Arundo
Athyrium goerin-

gianum
Crambe
Cynara
Dianthus
Dicentra
Elymus
Eryngium mari-
    timum
Festuca
Helictotrichon
Hieracium

Hosta sieboldiana
H. tokudama
Kniphofia caulescens
K. northiae
Lychnis coronaria
L. flos-jovis
Lysimachia ephe-
    merum
Meconopsis
Perowskia
Romneya

Rudbeckia maxima
Salvia argentea
Sedum rosea
S. spectabile
Sisyrinchium
    striatum
Thalictrum flavum
Verbascum
Veronica spicata
    incana
Yucca

Glossary

A bristle-like organ that projects from the spikelets of certain grasses, the tips of sepals (e.g. *Geranium*) and seeds (e.g. *Pulsatilla*).	**Awn**
Cleft into two lobes or parts.	**Bifid**
Twice pinnate q.v.	**Bipinnate**
A modified leaf often associated with the inflorescence. Flower buds often arise in the axils of bracts. Sometimes bracts are coloured and function as petals, e.g. *Astrantia, Euphorbia*.	**Bract**
The whorl of leaf or bract-like organs known as sepals which enclose and protect a flower bud. They may also be fused into a tube, e.g. primrose, *Silene*. In some plants the sepals may function as petals, e.g. *Anemone, Helleborus*.	**Calyx**
A group of plants all raised from one individual by vegetative means (division, cuttings, grafting).	**Clone**
Used for plant parts that are multiple, e.g. pinnate leaves and such floral clusters as panicles.	**Compound**
Short for cultivated variety and used of plants that are distinct variants of species or hybrids maintained in cultivation. Cultivars may be purposefully bred by man or arise spontaneously as a mutation in gardens or the wild, e.g. plants with variegated foliage or double flowers. Although there are exceptions, generally such plants are sterile or do not come true from seeds and are propagated vegetatively. See also clone.	**Cultivar**
A type of flower cluster formed by repeated lateral branching. In the monochasial cyme each inflorescence stem terminates in a flower bud and a branch and so on. *Symphytum* and *Cynoglossum* are examples. In the dichasial cyme, each stem terminates in a flower bud and two opposite facing branches and so on, e.g. *Lychnis, Silene*.	**Cyme**
A compound leaf with all the leaflets radiating out from the tip of the leaf stalk, e.g. *Rodgersia podophylla*.	**Digitate**
A category of plant classification in which are grouped all species (q.v.) with characters in common.	**Genus**

Glossary

Glaucous	Blue-green or bright grey-green.
Hispid	Bristly-hairy.
Inflorescence	That part of the plant which bears the flowers. Often loosely used for any flower cluster. See also cyme, panicle, raceme, spadix, spike.
Lanceolate	Shaped like the head of a lance and used of leaves, bracts and petals. In the strict sense it should be no more than three to six times as long as wide.
Linear	Used of very narrow leaves and bracts etc., with parallel sides.
Monocarpic	A term for plants which take two or more seasons to reach maturity then flower, seed and die. Biennials also come into this category.
Nectary	A small gland which secretes nectar, usually located at the base of a flower. In *Helleborus* they are found within specially modified petals called floral leaves.
Oblanceolate	A lanceolate leaf or bract which is broadest beyond the middle.
Oblong	In a botanical sense used of leaves, bracts etc., that have the sides parallel for at least part of their length.
Ovate	Leaves, bracts, petals which are egg-shaped in outline, the stalk being at the broadest end.
Palmate	Like an outstretched hand, generally used of rounded leaves that have finger-like lobes.
Panicle	An inflorescence made up of several racemes or cymes, e.g. *Linum*.
Peltate	A rounded or broadly oval leaf with the stalk appearing to be attached to a more or less central point beneath, e.g. *Peltiphyllum peltatum*.
Pinnate	A compound leaf divided into two parallel ranks of small leaflets arising from a central stalk or midrib.
Pinnatifid	Basically like pinnate, but with the leaflets fused together at their bases and appearing as deep lobes.
Pseudobulb	A swollen stem of one to several joints typical of tree-dwelling orchids but sometimes found underground, as in *Bletilla*.
Raceme	An inflorescence formed of a single, usually erect, stem bearing stalked flowers at intervals, e.g. *Campanula persicifolia*, delphinium.
Rhizome	Underground or partially above ground stem; usually much thickened and acting as a food store, e.g. *Iris*, *Polygonatum*, but equally applicable for the wiry underground stems of grasses, e.g. *Phalaris*.
Sepal	See comments under calyx.
Sessile	Without a stalk or appearing so.
Sorus	Group of sporangia, sometimes covered with a membrane of characteristic shape found on the undersides of fertile fern fronds. Plural, sori.
Spadix	A generally fleshy flower spike with the flowers carried flush to the surface or in little pits. Typical of the members of the arum family, e.g. *Lysichiton*.
Spathe	A green or coloured bract surrounding an inflorescence, as in *Lysichiton*, or a single flower, e.g. *Iris*.
Spathulate	Spoon-shaped in outline.

178

A group of individuals which breed together and have the same constant and distinctive characters though minor differences may occur, e.g. degrees of hairiness, flower size and colour.	**Species**
As in raceme, but with sessile flowers. In a loose gardening sense spike is often used for racemes and other erect inflorescences.	**Spike**
A small or secondary spike. Also used for the 'flower' of a grass which is formed of several bract-like structures, two plumy stigmas and three large stamens.	**Spikelet**
Plural of sporangium. Used of the tiny spore-containing capsules (spore cases) borne by ferns. See also sorus.	**Sporangia**
A minute sexual reproductive body of one or a few cells together, which in ferns grows into a tiny leaf-like organ (prothallus) which bears the sex cells.	**Spore**
The male organ of a flower, composed of a stalk or filament, and two joined anther lobes which contain the male sex cells or pollen.	**Stamen**
A sterile stamen often more or less petal-like.	**Staminode**
The tip of the ovary (immature seed pod) which is receptive to the pollen grains. It is usually sticky, but can be feathery and even decorative as in some grasses.	**Stigma**
Overground stems which root when they touch the soil.	**Stolon**
The equivalent of a cultivar (q.v.) but always raised from seeds collected from carefully selected parents.	**Strain**
The stalk – when present – that joins the stigma (q.v.) to the ovary.	**Style**
A plant that is halfway between a perennial and a shrub, having persistent woody basal stems and seasonal flowering shoots that die back to them each autumn.	**Sub-shrub**
A distinct true-breeding variant of a species, usually isolated geographically from the main species.	**Sub-species**
A petal-like sepal, particularly when petals and sepals occur together and look alike.	**Tepal**
Used of plants that have double the usual number of chromosomes in their cells. Each species of plant (and animal) has a set number of chromosomes in each cell, the chromosomes themselves containing units of inheritance, called genes.	**Tetraploid**
Underground stems and roots swollen with food-storage material. For example, some of the sunflowers have stem tubers and *Roscoea* has root tubers.	**Tuber**
An inflorescence of stalked flowers, all of which arise from the same point, usually a stem tip, e.g. *Myrrhis*.	**Umbel**
A botanical unit of variation within a species. It is often indistinguishable from a sub-species (q.v.) but is usually found growing mixed with the main species. Flower size and colour are the most obvious variations.	**Variety**

Index of Common Names

Index of Common Names